HUMAN RIGHTS
AND
ISLAM

HUMAN RIGHTS
AND
ISLAM

by
Nayyar Shamsi

Reference Press
4831/24, Ansari Road
Darya Ganj
New Delhi - 110 002
Phone: 23260807
Fax: 23274173
E-mail: essess@del3.vsnl.net.in

First Published 2003

ISBN: 81-88583-15-4

Price Rs.750/-

Published by
Reference Press
4831/24,Ansari Road
Darya Ganj
New Delhi - 110 002
Phone: 23260807
Fax: 23274173
E-mail: essess@del3.vsnl.net.in

Printed in India by:
Printline, New Delhi.

Contents

Preface

Human Rights, relatively a new phenomenon for the world, has always been preached and practised by Islam. Interestingly, the West woke up centuries later and began championing the same cause, while followers of Islam had consistently been doing so for over a millennium.

The Human rights idea is universal now, It has virtually been accepted by all Nations, States and Societies, around the world. Over the years, the concept of Human Rights has assumed importance globally. In fact, the respect for Human Rights only, makes freedom meaningful and really effective. Islam teaches the same. Islam, as a progressive religion was the first among faiths to uphold the dignity of the individual and protection of one's personal and as well as social rights. It stood for the basic and fundamental rights of each and every human being.

In Islam the protection of Human Rights is a constant fight and every individual gets involved in it. The polity and society is not to be impartial, but it has to essentially be a party, supporting the struggle going on in all parts of the world, in general and the Muslim world, in particular. Each and every follower of Islam has his or her responsibility towards this noble cause and intellectuals and academics owe much to contribute and do a lot in this direction, by way of showing solidarity with the Human Rights activists in letter and spirit.

This study is the result of a painstaking research and toilsome efforts for several years on the part of the undersigned, who took the accomplishment of this book as a mission. This comprehensive, authentic and exhaustive book, is a valuable addition to the 'not so rich' treasure of works on the subject. It fills a vacuum on the basis of its merits in totality.

Hence, this modest effort. If it succeeds in clearing the air against Islam and in creating an awareness among the ignorant critics of Islam, the author would feel honoured and encouraged to continue his academic pursuit and his endeavours, in projecting Islam, as the standard bearer of Human Rights, now and for the times to come.

Author

ONE

Introduction

By his vary nature, the man is sociable. His herd instinct urges him on to live together with fellow beings. Right from his birth until death he stands severely in need of the attention, aid and support of innumerable individuals. Not only to meet the needs of his upbringing, food, clothing, lodging and education and training, but also for the development and blossoming of his natural capabilities and their practical demonstration, he is compelled to lead, and participate in collective life. This corporate life binds up a vast fabric of relationships around him, the small and big spheres of relationships of the family, brotherhood, locality, town, country and humanity as a whole, determine his rights and obligations. He has certain obligations in the various capacities of mother, father, son, pupil, teacher, the employer, employee, trader, customer, citizen and the ruler, and as against all these obligations, he is entitled to certain definite rights.

Among these rights some are of a moral nature, for instance, the right of respect for the elders, the right of affection and consideration for the youngsters, the right of help for the needy, the right of the guest to be entertained, and so on. And some have a legal protection and support, for example, the right of ownership, the right of wages (for work done), the right of obtaining dower (mahr), and the right of compensation and the like. These are the rights of a nature related to some interests, and the law of the land recognizing such interests makes them realizable through the judiciary. These rights are known as Legal Rights or Positive Rights.

There is yet another sphere of the rights of the individual concerning his relations with the state. In this sphere the rights given to an individual in relation to a state with vast powers and resources, are called Fundamental Rights. They are also sometimes termed Basic Human Rights and Birth Rights of man. These rights are guaranteed to him under the highest law of the land, the "Constitution" instead of the ordinary laws obtaining in a country. They are called "Fundamental Rights" because none of the various arms of the state, executive or legislature can violate them. These rights are enjoyed by the individual not as the citizen of a state but as a member of the universal brotherhood of mankind. They transcend all distinctions of colour, race, territory, language and the rest, and man is entitled to them as human being. They have not been conferred on him as a result of legislation by any state legislature, or as the outcome of a covenant, but naturally enjoyed by him and forming an integral part of his existence. In case of a state failing to recognize or enforce them, it is considered guilty of usurping the rights of man conferred on him by nature, since they are inalienable and irrevocable. The state has no power even to amend, abridge or hold them in abeyance temporarily on some pretext, not to speak of revoking them, save in case of the sovereign or the people all having conferred those powers on it with definite limits and conditions expressly mentioned in the constitution. And even this scope has been provided in the western constitutions. The Islamic constitution does not allow any individual, institution or even the Muslim Ummah as a whole to revoke, abridge or suspend the fundamental rights in any form whatsoever.

It was only three or three centuries and a half ago that this term fundamental rights came to be introduced in Europe. In fact it is just another name for the "Natural Rights" first used by the Greek thinker, Zeno, and later explained in legal and constitutional language by the Roman legislator, Cicero. W.Friedman thus:

But the conception of a society based on definite rights of the individual citizen is a relatively modern one, developed in reaction, first against the medieval order of society and secondly, against the absolutist government of the modern state, in the seventeenth and eighteenth centuries. It finds expression in the legal philosophy of Locke, the French Declaration of the Rights of Man, and the American Constitution.

Gaines Ezejiofor defines fundamental rights thus:

Human or fundamental rights is the modern name for what have been traditionally known as natural rights, and these may be defined as moral rights which every human being, everywhere, at all times, ought to have simply because of the fact that, in contradistinction with other beings, he is rational and moral. No man may be deprived of these rights without grave affront to justice.

Elucidating the nature of Fundamental Rights Justice Jackson says:

One's right to life, liberty, and property, to free speech and a free press, freedom of worship and assembly, and other fundamental rights may not be submitted to vote; they depend on the outcome of no elections.

Two Aspects

The concept of fundamental rights has two aspects. One of them is moral, according to which man must occupy a respectable and dignified position in the society. Man as such is worthy of respect, and like other members of the society this respect for him must come from the rulers as well. Those who happen to deal with them in authority, should not forget that they themselves are men (like all other men) and as regards human dignity and honour, the fact of their holding any office of authority does not bring to them any superiority or supremacy. The other aspect of the fundamental rights is their legal aspect, according to which these rights must be recognized legally and must be given protection by the highest law of the land. From the angle of practical enforcement this aspect comprises three factors:

(1) Fundamental Rights get human dignity recognized and furnish guiding principles for legal and administrative procedures.

(2) These rights provide a person protection against tyranny and oppression. The limits prescribed by them, which cannot be violated, safeguard him against the discriminatory treatment of the law, and officers of the

executive and the judiciary, since well defined sections are provided for the law relating to these rights.

(3) Fundamental rights bring into existence an institution which guarantees the enforcement of these rights against all other individuals and the rulers. This institution is the Judiciary.

Inclusion of the Fundamental Rights in the constitution of a country aims at demarcating the sphere of legislative powers of the state, and also limits its activities through the judiciary within the limits and protections provided by the constitution, so that the rulers may not usurp the fundamental rights of the people and take to the dictatorial pattern of rule. The real motive behind the recognition of these rights is to offer protection to man's honour and greatness and his dignity and respect against the high-handedness of dictatorship or cruel collectivism, to furnish it with guarantee of leading a respectable life, and provide him opportunities to develop his personal capabilities and to be benefited by the prints of these capabilities, and to maintain a certain sphere of the freedom of thought and action which may be immune from the interference of other individuals of the society. The term fundamental rights has emerged in the peculiar historical background of Europe. A civil war extending over a thousand years, the despotism of the monarchs, the exploitation of the feudal order, the unbearably tight hold of the Church on the individual, the blood-shed due to the differences of the creed, nationalism and the hunger for expansionism created by it, and taking over countries by the sword, and the way, it injured the self-respect of man, and ruthlessly trampled his life, property and honour and dignity, and rendered him powerless and totally helpless against the tyrannical state. This roused the conscience of those left with any feeling for humanity and compelled them to ponder over the measures to protect man against degradation and debasement and to restore the respect and honour due to him, and to show the despots and dictators the way humanity should be respected. It was under these conditions that the theory of natural rights during the course of its attaining the state of practical application, was transformed into Fundamental Rights, and the movement for definite rights for the individual and constitutional safeguards, started gathering momentum. When the entire globe got converted into a smouldering hell due to the tyranny of the days of colonialism and the use of fire arms and atom bomb in the two world wars and its flames engulfed the entire human race, the din made by the echoes of "Fundamental Rights" in Europe became a world-wide demand, as a result of which the charter of the United Nations, and the charter of Human Rights came into existence. In this way the technical term which had emerged in an atmosphere of tyranny and oppression, reached every nook and corner of the world.

Since the Islamic concept of rights does not have the background which gave birth to the European concept of basic rights, it is totally different from it. We shall deal with it at length later on.

History

Before taking up the Islamic concept of man's fundamental rights and their determination and protection, it will be in the fitness of things to take stock of the history of human rights, the various theories of the Westerners regarding the source and origin of these rights as also the protective measure provided by them for their preservation. Let us see how far is man, in the west and in the rest of the world, following them is the recipient of the bounties of the protection of the life and property, establishment of an order of justice and equity, safety of his honour and dignity, freedom of action, and independence of thought; how far are his fundamental rights inalienable, and what have been his chances of leading a life of peace and safety, and honour and dignity as a result of the continuous struggle during the past three or four centuries for the determination and acquisition of these rights.

The Westerners commence the evolutionary history of the concept of the Fundamental Human Rights, from Greece of the Fifth century B.C., and then linking their political thought with the degenerate Roman Empire of the Fifth century A.D., they take a big leap into the eleventh century, thus leaving a wide gap of five hundred years from the sixth to the tenth century A.D., in the history put together by them. And, pray, why is it so? Most probably for the reason that this is the Islamic period (to which the Christian West has ever been most allergic- Tr.).

Undoubtedly the Greek philosophers have laid great stress on the rule of law and (meting out) justice and equity, and have written books on its need and importance with great erudity. But the concept of human equality is conspicuous by its absence there. They divide men into different classes very much like the water tight compartments into which Brahmins (the ruling class and religious leaders), Kshatriyas (reserved for military services), Vaisya (the traders and the cultivators) and the Shudras (performing menial services for the other three classes, and their slaves), were placed in ancient India, and where they are very much there even today. Exactly like that of Manu-Shastra they (the ancient Greeks,) too had these four classes. Plato, in his book *The Republic* grants the right to rule only to the philosophers, and divides the remaining population into soldiers (fighting men), cultivators and slaves. He says:

Citizens, you are brothers, yet God has framed you differently. Some of you have the power of command, and these he has composed of gold: others of silver, to be auxiliaries: others again who are to be farmers and craftsmen he has made of brass and iron.

And here is Plato's concept of justice:

> I proclaim justice is nothing else than the interest of the stronger. Everywhere there is one principle of justice, which is the interest of the stronger.

And let us see what he has to say in his further elucidation of Justice:

> Justice is the art which gives good to friends and evil to enemies.

According to Plato, the greatest weakness of democracy is that it grants equal status to all citizens.

> Democracy is a charming form of government, full of

> disorder and dispensing a sort of equality to equals and unequals alike.

Elucidating the objective of law, Plato says:

> The object of laws is to make those who use them happy. Plato does not believe in equality in the matter of dispensing justice. He is in favour of separate laws for every class. About slaves he writes in his book *Laws*:

Slaves ought to be punished as they deserve, and not admonished as if they were freemen, which will make them only conceited.

He is tolerant of equality between man and woman. He says:

> Women's nature is inferior to that of men in capacity of virtue.

Like his teacher, Plato, Aristotle too stands for a society divided into various strata or classes. He too is embarrassed at the idea of equality. In his book *The State* pointing out democracy as the worst form of government he says:

> A democracy is a government in the hands of men of low birth, poverty, and vulgar employments.
>
> The last and worst form is that which gives a share to every citizen.

Aristotle's concept of justice, too, is near about the same as that of his teacher, Plato. He says:

Now justice is the virtue by which each has his own as the law prescribes.

Here, introducing the condition of position he strikes at the very roots of justice. His views about slavery are very well defined:

> It is clear that some are free by nature, and others are slaves, and that in the case of the latter the lot of slavery is both advantageous and just.

He grants the free and "noble" men the right to divide this large number of slaves among themselves, put them to work the worst type of drudgery Tr.) and look after their food and clothing. It is in his *The State* that he writes:

> It is worthy of a sensible and generous nobility to divide the poor amongst them, and to induce them to work by supplying them with what is necessary.

The nobility does not enjoy this privilege in the case of the male slaves alone. It extends to their wives and children too who are just as well their property. Aristotle says:

> The poor were in a state of bondage to the rich, both themselves, their wives, and their children.

Aristotle does not allow the slaves the rights of citizenship. According to his definition of citizenship residence alone does not confer on any one the rights of citizenship. If this principle (residence as the basis of citizenship) is accepted, the slaves and free men would come to enjoy equal status. Citizen is only one who partakes in executive and judicial affairs. And this is the (exclusive) right of free men and even among them of only those who can boast of nobility both on the paternal and the maternal side.

> For common use, men define a citizen to be one who is sprung from citizens on both sides, not on the father's or the mother's only.

These concepts of Plato and Aristotle regarding man and justice, give us an idea of the fate of fundamental rights in Greece, the fountain-head of guidance for Europe. Robert E. Dewy commenting on these thoughts and views of the Greeks has written:

> In a city of some 300,000 slaves and 90,000 so-called free men, Plato sat down and praised freedom in exquisitely elegant phrases.

In Greece the slaves enjoyed no better fate than animals capable of speech:

> For them natural law was universal in that it applied not only to citizens of certain states but rather to every body every where in the cosmopolis. It was superior to any

> positive law and embodied those elementary principles of justice which were apparent to the "eye of reason." The natural rights conferred by it were not the particular privileges of citizens of certain states, but something to which every human being, everywhere, was entitled in virtue of the simple fact of being human and rational.

The Stoics theory of Natural Rights profoundly influenced the Roman thinkers, and legislators and they very strongly stressed "Freedom" and equality in their philosophy of law and politics. The Western people attribute it to the Stoics influence alone. But the reality is just the opposite. This was the result of the consciousness endowed by religion and its teachings. Cicero, the renowned Roman jurist who was a Christian, elaborating the concept of natural laws writes:

> It is of universal application, unchanging and everlasting It is a sin to try to alter this law, nor is it allowable to attempt to repeal any part of it, and it is impossible to abolish it entirely. We cannot be freed from its obligation by Senate or People. And there will not be different laws at Rome and at Athens or different laws now and in the future, but one eternal and unchangeable law will be valid for all nations and for all times.

Pointing to the real fountain-head of his thought he says:

All nations (gentes), at all times, will be bound by the one eternal and immutable law: there will be one God who is common to all men and, as it were, their master and ruler (imperator); and He it is who devises, debates, and enacts this law, the which if a man disobeys he will be a runaway from himself, and rejection thereby the nature of man he will pay the utmost penalty by that very act of rejection, even if he escapes other punishments which men believe he will incur.

Cicero and his contemporary jurists have provided special guarantees to the right of individual ownership in the laws framed by them. This helped, on the one hand, in the recognition of the individual's importance and, on the other, a basis was furnished for defining the fundamental rights The striving and struggle in real earnest began in the eleventh century of the Christian era in England, where in 1037 A.D., King Conrad II through a Charter of rights issued by him defined the powers of the parliament. After the award of this charter, the parliament started a campaign for the enhancement of its powers. In 1188 the principal of Habeas corpus was recognized by King Alphonso IX under compelling circumstances. On 15th June, 1215, "Magna Carta" was issued which was declared by Voltair as the Charter of freedoom Undoubtedly Magna Carta is the most important document of fundamental rights that has made history in England. But it interpreted as much later. At the time of its issuance it was sort of a covenant between the barons and king John of England, in which the rights of the feudal lords had been provided protection. The rights of the common people had no place in it. Henry Marsh says:

> And if Magna Carta had done no more it would have been a charter for the great land owners' and nothing else.

In 1355 the British Parliament while approving and accrediting the Magna Carta passed the bill of Due process of law, under which no person could be evicted from his land or imprisoned without proper legal action against him in a court of law, nor could he be sentenced to death without trial.

Machiavellian Theories

From the fourteenth to the sixteenth century Europe was swayed by the Machiavellian theories which encouraged and strengthened dictatorship and the hand of monarchs and made the acquisition of authority the sole objective of life. In the seventeenth century the theory of natural rights came up once again with full force. In 1679 the British Parliament passed the bill of Habeas Corpus and it became a law, and served as a protection against unjustifiable arrests and detentions. In 1684 the revolutionary army denned the limits of the powers of the British parliament. In 1689 the Parliament passed the most important document, the Bill of Rights. In words of Lord Action. This is the greatest achievement of the English people. This bill is regarded as the completion of the freedom movement in Britain since through it the fundamental rights were clearly defined. In 1690 John Locke wrote out a book *Treatises on Civil Government*, justifying the revolution of 1688-89, in which he presented the Social Contract theory and discussed the rights of the individual with strong arguments. In 1762, the well known French thinker, Rousseau (Jean Jacques 1712-78) wrote a book under the title *Social Contract* in which he reviewed the Social Contract theory presented by Hobbes and Locke from a new angle. He made an attempt to create a sort of harmony between the Sovereign of Hobbes and the Democracy of Locke. His theories not only paved the way for the French Revolution but had a profound influence on the political thought of Europe, and played an important role in getting the rights of the individual against the state recognized. On 12th June, 1776, "The Charter of Rights" drafted by George Mason of the American state of Virginia was issued in which the freedom of Press, freedom of creed, and the right of legal proceedings in a court of law were guaranteed. On 12th July 1776 the American Declaration of independence was issued. Its draft was prepared by Thomas Jefferson. Most of his principles were based on the views of the British thinkers and those of John Locke in particular. In the preamble of this declaration, with reference to the natural law, it has been said, "All human beings have been created equal and their creator has conferred on them inalienable rights which include protection of life, freedom and pursuit of happiness. In 1789, three years after the enforcement of the constitution, the American Congress passed those ten amendments known as the Law of Rights. In the same year the National Assembly of France passed the Declaration of the Rights of Man. In 1792 Thomas Paine published his famous booklet, *The Rights of Man*, which made a profound impact on the thought of the western people and further promoted the cause of the protector of human rights. During the nineteenth and the twentieth centuries inclusion of fundamental rights in the constitution of governments became a common tradition. In 1868 the fourteenth amendment of the American constitution was passed in which it was said that no state of America shall deprive any body of his life, freedom and property without due legal proceedings against him, nor shall it refuse to provide him with equal legal protection.

After the First World War, Germany and numerous other new European countries incorporated fundamental rights in their constitutions. In 1940, the famous man of letters, H.G. Wells in his book, *New World Order* suggested the issuance of a charter of Human Rights. In January 1941, President Roosevelt appealed to the Congress to offer their support to Four Freedoms. In August, 1941 the Atlantic Charter was signed whose objective, according to Churchil, was the end of war along with the upholding of Human Rights.

After the Second World War, the inclusion of Human Rights in the written constitutions became more prominent. France included in its constitution of 1946, its charter of Human Rights of 1789. In this year; Japan made Human Rights a part of its constitution. In 1947, Italy guaranteed Human Rights in its constitution.

As a result of efforts for the Human rights, at the national and international levels, at last on 10th December 1948, the U N Charter of Human Rights was issued in which all those rights had been incorporated that already existed in the constitutions of various European countries, or could possibly occur to the human mind. At the time of voting in the General Assembly 48 countries voted in favour of the charter and eight abstained, Russia being among the abstainers. To keep a watch over the enforcement of the charter, and safeguarding the rights guaranteed therein and to offer suggestion for the determination of other rights, a permanent commission of Human Rights was set up.

PART—I

The Concept

TWO

Concepts and Theories

In fact, the issue of the fundamental rights of man involves a proper understanding of the position of man in the universe, the purpose of his life, the nature of his relationship with the society and the State and also the reality behind the creation of this universe and its beginning and the end. What the human rights are cannot be understood until it is ascertained what really is the position of man in this universe. The question of rights, so to say, is directly linked to that of the status and position he occupies. Without a realistic knowledge of the position of man or in the absence of a definite idea about it, we cannot determine his rights.

Western View

To solve these basic problems concerning human life, guidance could be had from revealed faiths only, since we have no other reliable source of knowledge in this behalf. But when man overlooked the source of revealed knowledge and tried to seek answers to these vital questions with his wits alone, he started stumbling and falling in the labyrinths of guesses and conjectures and the valleys of ignorance. These facts were beyond the grip of experiences and observations based on senses. Recorded history, which came into existence hundreds of thousands of years after the beginning of human life on this globe had to offer little material from its record to assist him gain access to these facts, in this pitch dark atmosphere totally devoid of the light of revelation when an intellect unaware of the realities tried to solve these intricate problems of life, the first and the greatest difficulty that confronted man was where to begin to tackle this problem. Since human intellect had no established facts on which to base its arguments, it had of necessity to begin with these ideologies and theories (hypotheses) as the basis of talks and discussions. In this way, man's intellect removed its difficulty by discussing serious issues on the basis of unreliable information and based on guesses and conjectures, but failed to offer a satisfactory solution of the problems facing humanity. Then thoughts and theories presented by the intellect being ambiguous, contradictory, disjointed and unbalanced further complicated these problems. And thus humanity got more and more entangled in a whirlpool of ignorance and absurdities. It is to point out this shortcoming of intellect that Quran says:

> "Wert thou (O Mohammad!) to follow the common run of those on earth, they will lead thee astray from the way of God, They follow not but an opinion and they do but guess." ....Al Quran VI:116.
>
> Say: "Have ye any (certain) knowledge? If so, produce it before us. Lo! Ye follow naught but an opinion. Lo! ye do but guess."
>
> *Al Quran VI: 148*

Since the journey of intellect had started in pitch dark therefore its premises have no basis. It proceeds by means of conjectures and in its attempts to solve problems creates more and more complexities. In its attempts to solve the problem of fundamental human rights, it had to lean on hypotheses and theories. The first question that confronted the intellect was whether there was any justification for these rights. On what basis certain rights be recognized for man? And if at all recognized, on what authority? Who has conferred them on man?

After much deliberation the human intellect thought out the answer to the question that since nature has itself conferred certain rights on man, therefore they must be recognized. This theory came to be called the theory of Natural Rights. An objection was levelled against it saying that this form is ambiguous and ill-defined. Nature itself has not so far been defined lucidly in a manner that there could be a consensus on it. How to determine the natural rights then? The greatest objection raised was about the legal position of these rights. The concept of rights in a society is possible only with its sanction. Without social sanction there is no question of rights.

Then in order to provide a legal sanction to these rights and to obtain the sanction of the society for them the theory of Social Contract was put forth. It was suggested that since the very existence of the State depended on it, it must be the fountain-head of the powers of the rulers and the rights of the citizens. In this way a legal justification was provided for the rights of man. But what is the historical importance of this contract? Let us see what J.W. Gough has to say about it.

The whole historical school, from Blackstone and Paley to Maine and his followers, have pointed out, what is now obvious and undeniable, that in actual historical fact states and governments were not deliberately established by contract, but developed naturally from more primitive groupings and loyalties, such as that of the family or the clan.

Professor Ilys says:

> Is the Social Contract theory wholly unhistorical? Is it a. pure fiction? Is it wholly unreal and imaginary? These questions are always answered in the affirmative and no one has yet said 'no' to their answers. The whole thing is more astounding because it has been declared that the Social Contract theory is as old as speculation itself. It has, therefore, its own history without itself being historical in any sense. By historical here we mean that in the whole history of the political development of man we do not find even a single case or instance in which the 'social contract' might have been used in the origin or the making of the state.

The question is that a theory which is so baseless that it enjoys no more respect than a fable and which the western historians have themselves unanimously declared as unhistorical; why was so much importance attached to it, and the entire superstructure of the concept of rights was built on it? Let us see what the westerners themselves have to say about it:

The doctrine made its appearance in the 16th and 17th centuries when political theorists turned to the idea of contract in order to interpret the relationship between the individual and the community.

It means that this contract was invented to provide justification or a legal basis for their theories. J. W. Gough, stating the real worth of this contract, writes:

> For, of deeper importance than this question of terms, or even than that of the truth or falsehood of the contract theory itself, is the principle which contractarians were ultimately striving to uphold.
>
> If the phrase 'social contract' is to be retained, then, it had probably best be interpreted as an abbreviation for the Idea that political obligation involves a relationship analogous to contract.
>
> This, I think, is the maximum that can be conceded to the contract theory.
>
> For, as an historical theory the contract has now long been discredited, and its more recent adherents have wisely confined themselves to the claim that a contract is the philosophical basis of the State. This claim itself has taken various forms. It may be argued, as by Kant, that the contract, though historically a fiction, is valid as an 'idea of reason; and this, we saw, meant that political rights and duties should be ordered as if political obligation were founded on a contract, although really it is not.

These extracts make it very clear why the westerners, in spite of attaching no more importance to Social Contract theory than a tale, are not prepared to reject it. If they were to reject it they would be left with nothing to regularise the "rights and obligations". It was under this compulsion or helplessness that Sir Ernest Barker, supporting the Social Contract theory writes:

> There is still a case to be made for the view that the State as distinct from society, is a legal association which fundamentally rests on the presuppositions of contract.

Through the invention of this contract, justification for the fundamental rights and the powers of the state was certainly furnished, another question confronted its supporters: Who is the sovereign, the State or the people? Considering the rights and the powers, which of them enjoys supremacy?

Attempts to solve this problem were also made with the Social Contract theory as the basis, but each attempt was made keeping in view the demands and particular needs of its period. Hobbes had at heart the legal justification for the despotism of the Stuart Kings. So he drew his own picture of the state of nature prior to the Social Contract to meet the particular needs, and declaring the rulers as sovereigns made them all powerful. And the helpless people, denuded of all power, were left with no option but to unconditionally obey these despotic rulers, without complaining.

When the splendid revolution of 1688'weakened the tight grip of the despotic monarchy, and through the Bill of Rights, the rights of the parliament and the people were strengthened, John Locke felt compelled to offer a new interpretation of the Social Contract for the justification of the newly created situation. So his imagination presented quite a different picture of the State of Nature, in which human life was not "lonely, poverty stricken, worsened, beastly and short-lived, but contrary to the assertion of Hobbes it was a period of peace, good will, of mutual cooperation and protection," in which man was leading a life of great satisfaction based on freedom and equality. Locke with this background, in his new interpretation of Social Contract, divided the sovereignty between the king and the people, giving the people a little higher position, without whose consent no king could acquire the right to rule.

By the time it came to the French thinker Rousseau, since the struggle for rights and powers between the king and the people had covered a long way and had by this time entered a decisive stage, a new interpretation of Social Contract had become inevitable to energise the democratic forces and to give a final blow to the despotic rule of the kings. So we find Rousseau, keeping in view the political and social conditions of his period, presenting a beautiful picture of the state of Nature, and interpreting the Social

Contract in such a way that the crown of sovereignty was taken off the head of the king and placed on the head of the people.

Since the question of Sovereignty is intimately linked with the relationship of the state and the citizens and their rights and obligations, all other political thinkers and legal experts besides Hobbes, Locke and Rousseau, also discussed it in great detail. Among them Grotius, Bodin, Austin, Bentham, Lasky, T.H. Green and Dicey deserve special mention. Commenting on the sum total of their thought Professor Ilyas Ahmad writes:

> Thus Sovereignty in Political Philosophy has been running abegging from door to door-from the one to the few and then to the many, from the individual to the community, from the minority to the majority and from majority to the minority, from the executive to the legislature and even from the legislature to the judiciary and finally from the community to the abstract conception of the state itself.

Through a study of the discussions from the theory of natural rights to that of sovereignty, it becomes evident that the entire thought content of the Western people is based on conjectures and all the theories are based on it alone. Since there is no clear concept regarding the reality about man and his position, great confusion of thought exists regarding all the basic problems of his life. Like other problems that of the determination of the fundamental rights too has been the victim of the same corruption of thought and observation.

Rights in the west do not enjoy a permanent position. They have no eternal source and criteria of a cosmic order. All the sources are either imaginary or like the law of Habeas Corpus, Magna Carta, the Bill of Rights, the French Charter of Human Rights and the ten amendments to the American constitution, are documents of a regional nature and are the product of the peculiar political and social conditions existing in Britain, France and America. There the concept of the fundamental rights has developed along with human consciousness. And these rights have been born one by one out of the agreements during the protracted struggle between the people and the king or other rulers, for the division of powers, the decision of the parliament, charter declarations and the theories put up by the political thinkers. As this struggle advanced, the sphere of rights became wider. That is to say, what are being termed as 'fundamental rights' today were not there till yesterday, and if at all they were, they were no more than mere yearnings which had no sanction at their back. Every one of these rights became a right in the true sense of the word only when the law of the land and the constitution recognizing it conferred validity on it.

Now let us take stock of another aspect of the western concept of rights. So to say, the western people claim upholding of the fundamemental rights for the whole mankind but their attitude is practically against this assertion. Their concept of rights is based on their theory of nationality and racial discrimination. The fundamental right which they want guaranteed for their own nation and the white race, they do not consider other nations and races deserving of those. When the French Charter of Human Rights was incorporated in the constitution of 1791, it was also clarified:

"Although the colonies and the. French possessions in Asia, Africa and America form part of the French Empire, the constitution, aforesaid still does not extend to them."

This makes it evident that the charter which has been termed "The Charter of Human Rights" is in reality the charter of the Rights of the French people. No other nation, rather, the non-French people living in the French possessions, had any right to make and demand for them. And we find the countrymen of Rousseau perpetrating such beastliness and barbarism in Algeria, Vietnam and other possessions, which constitute one of the blackest chapters of modern history.

The same holds good for Britain. The rights enjoyed by the British citizens in its unwritten constitution, were never allowed by the British masters to be incorporated in the laws framed by them in their colonies; their Magna Carta, their law of Habeas corpus and their Bill of Rights were all for them alone. So it would be a mistake and misleading to term them documents of Human

Rights as the rights conferred by these documents were confined to the citizens of Britain alone. If any other nation demanded these rights for themselves from the British rulers, it was branded as an act of rebellion and treason and those making the demand were made the target of tyranny and barbarity. Even today the treatment meted out to the black natives in South Africa and to the subjugated white citizens in Northern Ireland is a proof of the British people's duplicity that speaks for itself.

On 30th November, 1972, when the General Assembly of the UNO passed a resolution to make racial discrimination a cognizable offence, among four dissenters, along with America, South Africa and Portugal, Britain was also one.

America is no different from Britain and France. The white colonizers of America effected the entire race of aborigines of that continent, the so-called Red-Indians. For the building up and development of their "New World" they caught African blacks like animals and enslaving them, transported regular shiploads of them to America. These slaves were regularly sold and purchased. The African coast from which they shipped the freshly caught slaves in Africa, came to be called the Slave coast. The surviving race of descendants of these one-time slaves, has not so far succeeded in attaining equal rights with the white men of America. Whenever it referred to the American constitution and demanded for themselves enforcement of the "Human Rights" mentioned therein, their demand was ruthlessly crushed. Robert Dewey's biting sarcasm on this state of affairs is worthy of note:

> In a colony of 500,000 slaves and thousands of white indentured servants, Thomas Jefferson, a wealthy slaveowner, sat down and wrote the memorable words of the Declaration of Independence.

Apart from this racial discrimination internally, when we take stock of the American role in the world outside, the picture becomes all the more grim. Hiroshima, Nagasaki, Korea, Vietnam, Combodia and the Middle East, do tell the harrowing tales, of the fundamental Human Rights being trampled with impunity.

Now let us take the fourth upholder of Human Rights, communist Russia. This is the cradle of Socialism that had stood up with the banner of liberation of humanity from the American and British imperialism and from every sort of exploitation, and with the promise to bring to mankmd happiness of peace, prosperity and true freedom. But when it, for the first time, had a chance to put up a show of its "Virtues" and "Blessings", its twilight gave way to the ruddy sun from behind a huge mound of seventeen million human corpses. And when its ways illumined the East and the West Hungary, Eastern Germany, Poland, Czechoslovakia, occupied Turkestan and all those other regions where communism had an opportunity to enter, were bathed in blood. The Russian expert of Social Sciences and philosopher. Professor Pitririm Sorokin, giving details of the loss of human lives during the Russian Revolution, says:

> The total number of direct victims of the Red Terror of the Communist Revolution in the year 1918-22, according to a conservative estimate is at least 6,00,000, more than 1,00,000 a year. And this excludes the victims of the civil war, including the White Terror, and all the direct victims of the revolution itself. In one way or another, fifteen to seventeen millions of human lives were thus sacrificed to the ideal of the revolution.

The New Encyclopaedia Britannica writes :

> A far greater number of persons, perhaps 2,000,000, mainly of the educated upper and middle classes, were lost to Russia by emigration to escape Communist rule.

These incidents amply reveal the fact that the concept of rights of the western countries is not that of the rights of the humanity as a whole, but is bedevilled by racial, territorial, national and ideological prejudices. The rights which they consider essential for themselves, they do not believe in granting the same to other nations. They nave with al their might and main tried to withhold the same from others and to keep those exclusively for themselves.

Socialist View

Along with the consideration of the western concept of rights, it will be in the fitness of things to just have a look at the Socialist concept of rights. According to Marx and Lenin, the real fountain-head of the fundamental rights is the dialectical process of history. These rights have not been conferred on man by nature but are the product of this process. Playing their role in the various stages of history they must finally come to an end in the communist classless society. To begin with, these rights helped the bourgeois class in overthrowing the feudal society and establishing the capitalistic society. Later on, the proletariats used them as a weapon in their class struggle against the capitalists. Now under the Socialist order these rights are protecting the interests of the toiling people, and finally for the sake of freedom and equality these will cancel themselves out under communism. According to this philosophy these rights are neither natural nor the essential part of man's person, nor are they inalienable. They have no special significance or importance. They are a part of the general law of the land. Only the ruling party which is the caretaker of the interest of the working people, and the only means of the fulfilment of their aspirations has, the authority to determine the same. Enforcement of the basic rights can be allowed only to the extent to which it is in accord with the interest of the working people. Barring this fundamental principle, the demand for these rights in any other contract is altogether unlawful and unconstitutional. The social interests of the working people is the one principle of determining all the fundamental rights. And this interest is determined by the communist party, since it is the only party comprising the progressive and responsible representatives of the workers and it alone can be expected to keep the interests of the workers in view, to make certain their social welfares, and to frame appropriate laws which include determination of the fundamental rights. Andrei Vishinsky elucidating the Russian philosophy of law, writes;

> Soviet 'Socialist Republic is one of the most important branches of Soviet socialist law, which we have previously defined as the totality of the rules of conduct, established in the form of legislation by the authoritative

> power of the toilers and expressing their will-the application of said rules being guaranteed by the entire coercive force of the socialist state to the end (a) of defending, securing, and developing relationships and orders advantageous and agreeable to the toilers, and (b) of annihilating, completely and finally, capitalism and its survivals in the economy, manner of life, and consciousness of people, with the aim of building communist society.

The expounders of the Russian constitution, Grigorian and Dologoplov present the following definition of the fundamental rights:

> The basic right and duties of Soviet citizens are an expression of the socialist spirit of Soviet state.

It means the state has complete supremacy over the individual which has the authority to determine his rights which in turn are not above the sphere of commn legislation.

This concept of rights is entirely different from the western concept of the fundamental rights rather diametrically opposite to it. In the western countries the real purpose of these rights is to offer protection to the individual against the state. So in the west these rights are given a higher position than the common laws framed by the state. By incorporating them in the constitution the legislative powers 'of the state are limited, and the Judiciary is entrusted with enforcement of the fundamental rights.

As against this, let us turn to C. D. Kering to see what the position of these rights is in Russia and other Socialist countries:

> The Eastern concept on the other hand derives fundamental rights from the objective law imposed and enforced by the State. Any justification on the grounds of natural law is firmly rejected. It is impossible to guarantee the citizen effective protection against the state in this way because the degree of projection is dependent on the normative will of the state.

"Barring Yugoslavia, in all communist countries, ordinary courts provide very limited legal protection. And there is no international institution for the protection of human rights. The protection of civic rights through the public prosecutor is a fraudulent, put up show, since these public prosecutions are not independent, but abjectly follow the directives of the government."

The fundamental rights mentioned in the Russian constitution are the following (1) The right to work (2) The right to rest (3) In old age, sickness or some other disability, the right to the supply of necessities of life. (4) The right of education (5) The right of equality between man and woman (6) Apart from national and racial distinction, the right of equality among all the citizens of Russia (7) Freedom of conscience (8) The right of expression, through speech and written word, assembly, holding meetings, and the right of demonstration. (9) The right to join organisations. (10) The right of non-intervention in the affairs of individuals, families and correspondence and (11) The right to seek asylum.

Alongwith these rights the Russian constitution also prescribes obligations which are as follows:

(1) Honouring the constitution, abiding by the laws, consideration for the organisation of labour, a reasonable attitude in relation to the social obligations and respect for the principles of the Socialist society.

(2) The protection of the Socialist properties and their consolidation,

(3) Compulsory military service and the defence of motherland.

The list of rights in the Russian constitution does not include the right of forming parties. Elucidating this point Andrie Vishinsky says:

> The Soviet State, in granting freedom to citizens, starts from the interests of the toilers and naturally does not include freedom of political parties in the enumeration of these freedoms granted in as much as this freedom, in the conditions prevailing in the USSR, where the toilers

> have complete faith in the Communist Party, is necessary only for agents of fascism and foreign reconnaissance, whose purpose is to take all freedoms away from the toilers of the USSR, and to put the yoke of capitalism upon them once more.

In Russia and other communist countries, the one party system, the control of the ruling party over all the institutions and over the entire resources of the state, the absence of any moral and metaphysical concept of the fundamental rights, the state having all the powers of determining the rights, and the absence of the powers of judiciary to secure these rights or to enforce them, have rendered even those nominal rights, which have been shown in their constitutions totally meaningless. In a communist country, no citizen deprived of the rights conferred on him by the constitutions, can go to a court of law against the State, since neither any courts exist for the redressal of such grievances nor can the state, being the fountainhead of all rights be made the defendant in a case. Whatever it deems right must be accepted as such. And that which it does not recognise as a right or after its recognition cancels, limits or suspends it, it is no more a right that the State may be charged with its denial to anybody. Here right is the other name of the will of the State. Outside the sphere of this will no right has any existence of its own.

This concept of rights, in fact, is based on the concept of man in the socialist philosophy. The concept of life among Socialist thinkers is purely materialistic. To them, like other material objects of this universe, roan is also a material entity and his value is determined by his productive capacity. Just as any part of a machine for the demonstration of its working and productive capacity needs electrical energy, water, lubricating oil and proper care etc; man, also for the development of his productive capacity and its practical demonstration needs support in the matter of food, clothing, education and care. This support can be had only in a system in which all the individuals of the society may be performing their functions as the productive factors, and a central administration be looking after them and meeting their needs of board and lodge, clothing and other material necessities of life.

More than a productive factor, man has no value. Religion, morality, soul, belief, the life hereafter, are all terms coined by the capitalists and their agents for the exploitation of the people. Lenin says:

"We refuse to have any thing to do with morals based on divine injunctions by the capitalists. We reject all such moral values whose basis is above human and class consideration. We say it is a fraud, and the peasants and workers are defrauded to serve the interests of the feudal lords and capitalists. We declare that our moral values follow the class strife of poor. The source of our moral values is the interest of the class strife of the poor. That is why we say that there are no moral values outside the human society."

According to the Socialist concept man is the sum total of a stomach and matter, and economic struggle is its only goal of life. When this position of man in society has been determined what other rights are there to be conferred on him save food and shelter, and clothing and treatment. The communist countries guarantee only these material rights and do not recognize any other right based on moral values, it is the logical outcome of their outlook on life. Unless and until they change their view-point in relation to man, they cannot be expected to extend and expand the sphere of fundamental rights.

Islam and West

People in the West have the habit of attributing every beneficial development in the world to themselves. For example, it is vociferously claimed that the world first derived the concept of basic human rights from the Magna Carta of Britain which was drawn up six hundred years after the advent of Islam. But the truth is that until the seventeenth century no one dreamt of arguing that the Magna Carta contained the principles of ferial by jury, Habeas Corpus and control by Parliament of the right of taxation. If the people who drafted the Magna Carta were living today they would be greatly surprised to be told that their document enshrined these ideals and principles.

To the best of our knowledge, the West had no concept of human and civic rights before the seventeenth century; and it was not until the end of the eighteenth century that the concept took on practical meaning in the constitutions of America and France.

After this, although there appeared references to basic human rights in the constitutions of many countries, more often than not these rights existed only on paper. In the middle of the present century, the United Nations, which may now be more aptly described as the Divided Nations, made a Declaration of Universal Human Rights, and passed a resolution condemning genocide: regulations were framed to prevent it. But there is not a single resolution or regulation of the United Nations which can be enforced if the country concerned wants to prevent it. They are just expressions of pious hopes. They have no sanctions behind them, no force, physical or moral, to enforce them. Despite all the high-sounding resolutions of the United Nations, human rights continue to be violated and trampled upon.

When we speak of human rights in Islam we mean those rights granted by God. Rights granted by kings or legislative assemblies can be withdrawn as easily as they are conferred; but no individual and no institution has the authority to withdraw the rights conferred by God.

The charter and the proclamations and the resolutions of the United Nations cannot be compared with the rights sanctioned by God; the former are not obligatory on anybody, while the latter are an integral part of the Islamic faith. All Muslims and all administrators who claim to be Muslim have to accept, recognize and enforce them. If they fail to enforce them or violate them while paying lip-service to them, the verdict of the Holy Qur'an is unequivocal:

"Those who do not judge by what God has sent down are the disbelievers Kafirun (5:44) The following verse also proclaims:

> "They are the wrong-doers zalimun." (5:45) A third verse in the same chapter says:
>
> "They are the perverse and law-breakers fasiqun." (5:47)

In other words, if temporal authorities regard their own words and decisions as right and those given by God as wrong, they are disbelievers. If, on the other hand, they regard God's commands as right but deliberately reject them in favour of their own decisions, then they are wrong-doers only.

THREE

Islamic Ideology

In this age, anyone who undertakes to speak of 'Islam and Humanity' while, the universal respect for and observance of human rights and fundamental freedoms for all, without distinction as to race, sex, language, or religion, has been highlighted by the Charter of the United Nations (Art. 55), followed by the Declaration of Human Rights of 10th December, 1948 and by the two Covenants that have been subsequently drawn up on social and cultural rights and on civil and political rights, ought to provide the contextual framework of human rights as understood both in the West and in Islam.

In this way, we will throw into better relief those aspects of human rights as conceived by Islam which may be radically different from those normally associated with a modern approach. At the conclusion of the Second World War, when thought was again turned to the orderly functioning and reconstruction of the international community of mankind, the primary purpose which inspired the founding fathers of the United Nations was undoubtedly 'to save succeeding generations from the scourge of war, to maintain international peace and security.'

But the indispensable means for the realisation of that purpose in their thinking could only be the recovery of the individual from the super-incumbent weight that had been imposed on his freedom, initiative and growth by totalitarian regimes. Hence, the emphasis in the United Nations Charter on 'Human Rights and Fundamental Freedoms.'

The full extent of that crisis which had brought about a disruption in the soul-life of the modern man had never been fully appreciated by those publicists who in the mid-twentieth century had set out to make a general survey of the political, economic, social, cultural or humanitarian implications of human rights and fundamental freedoms that had to be guaranteed to the people of United Nations, since, the unhappy predicament of modern man had not as then been fully comprehended.

The forces of modern history have been virtually at war with the harmony of human life. This generation which has been actually involved in the chaos and the crises that have overtaken human civilization is not able to appreciate the extent to which the individual had been made subservient to the authority of totalitarian states that have emerged in the wake of mass society. Ortega de Gessa in The Revolt of the Masses speaks of the characteristics of such societies.

In the welter of contending voices that are even now being heard from the protagonists of the philosophy of enlightenment, and the pioneers of secularist liberalism and Marxist socialism, we have not as yet been able adequately to appreciate the extent of the disruption that has taken place in the contemporary value system.

On the one hand, thanks to the technological and scientific revolution of our times, the social environment of modern man, on a world-wide scale, has become much more integrated, in the sense that the days of isolated civilizations and localised cultures are gone never to return. There was a time when diverse cultures and civilizations could coexist and grow side by side without interaction or interference one with the other. Now, largely due to the application and transport, modern man, no matter where he may be, is involved in the total life of humanity as never before.

On the other hand, although the overall external shell in which the snail of humanity is living has been woven into a more or less homogeneous pattern through the interplay of all those factors which go to define the social and cultural environment of modern man, the springs of modern man's actions are ruled by the most contradictory philosophies of life.

There is, to begin with, the religion of love and universal brotherhood brought to us by the Prophets of universal religions and a great deal of our life, at least in Asia and Africa, is lived as though religious norms even today were the decisive criteria in evaluating the worth of man's activities.

Then .there is the philosophy of life founded upon the secularist approach which, in the name of liberalism, places a high degree of emphasis on the value of the dignity and freedom of the individual and upon the gospel of tolerance, mutual discussion and debate as a means of organising political institutions with a view to securing the development of human personality.

This approach had been countered by the challenge from the Marxist socialists who are prepared to surrender the value of human individuality at the altar of new gods who must be worshipped in the temple of dialectical materialism. Their claim for social justice, security and a planned social order as prime movers of social change in the requisite direction are well known.

The arrogance of race and of power, the worship of the cult of saviours and of heroes who applaud the military virtues of conquest, total discipline and blind obedience, seem to triumph precisely because of the confusion in thinking which is reflected by this western secularistic approach to life. Modern man is so completely caught up in this confusion that he is prepared to sell his soul to anyone who offers him the chance to enjoy what he considers to be the good things of life—the ability to 'eat, drink and be merry.'

Relation with Humanity

There is a fundamental difference in the perspectives from which Islam and the West each view the matter of human rights. The Western perspective may by and large be called anthropocentric in the sense that man is regarded as constituting the measure of everything since he is the starting point of all thinking and action. The perspective of Islam on the other hand is theocentric-God conscious.

Here, the Absolute is paramount and man exists only to serve his Maker, the Supreme Power and presence which alone sustains his moral, mental and spiritual make-up, secures the realisation of his aspirations and makes possible his transcendence. It is this which constitutes the decisive distinction between the two attitudes.

The Western tradition of liberty is evidenced by the most notable of its charters of rights: the Bill of Rights consequent on the English Revolution of 1689, the Bill of Rights promulgated by the State of Virginia in June 1776, the Declaration of Independence issued by the thirteen American States Constitution of 1789. The Declaration of Rights of Men and Citizenship issued by the Constituent Assembly of France in 1789, and later incorporated word by word in the Revolutionary Constitution of 1791 and again more recently in our own time in the Soviet Constitution of 1939, are in the same tradition.

Here, the rights of man are seen in a setting which has no reference to his relationship with God, but are posited as his inalienable birthright. The student of growth of Western civilization and culture notices throughout that the emphasis is on human rights within the framework of an anthropocentric perspective of human destiny. Each time the assertion of human rights is made at, it is done only to secure their recognition from some secular authority such as the state itself or its ruling power.

In marked contrast to this approach the strategy of Islam is to emphasize the supreme importance of our respect for human rights and fundamental freedom as an aspect of the quality of religious consciousness that it claims to foster in the heart, mind and soul of its followers. The perspective is 'theocentric' through and through. Man has first to believe in the cardinal doctrine:

> "There is no God but God and Muhammad is His Prophet."

Before he can hope to do good deeds, the emphasis in the Holy Qur an is on securing the transformation of the quality of man's consciousness. Man is asked to live and work in full awareness that he must show obedience to the Will of God.

Islam in its turn affirms the grand tradition of the development of the institution of universal religions, whose tradition, according to the Holy Qur'an, was consummated in the mission of the last Prophet by means of the revealed word communicated to him by process of divine revelation.

It seems at first sight, that there are no human rights or freedoms admissible to man in the sense in which modern man's thought, belief and practice understand them; in essence, the believer has only obligations or duties to God since he is called upon to obey the Divine Law, and such human rights as he is made to acknowledge stem from his primary duty to obey God.

Yet paradoxically, in these duties lie all the rights and freedoms. Man acknowledges the rights of his fellow men because this is a duty imposed on him by the religious law to obey God and the Prophet and those who are constituted as authority to conduct the affairs of state.

In everything that a believer does his primary nexus is with His Maker, and it is through Him that he acknowledge his relationship with the rest of his fellow men as even with the rest of the creation. In the words of the Qur'an:

"Man has been created only to serve God."

And further he alone is acceptable who has acquired nearness to God.

This distinction between the attitudes of Western man and a Muslim is implicit in the Qur'anic view of life which divides its functions into huqooqullah or obligations to God-and haqooqunnas or haqooqulabad obligations to society. The former category embraces matters like prayers, the need for ritual purity of mind and body, etc., primarily the personal concerns of the individual; the latter category has a social aspect.

In both cases the foundation for 'righteous action' whether on the individual or social plane is no other than the quality of consciousness or niyyat which directs all man's actions to the sole purpose of obeying the will of his maker, in order to please his ever-watchful Lord and Master, who sees even the innermost thoughts and motivations that impel him to act.

He is eventually to return to his Maker and will have to render an account of what he did with the opportunities with which life provided him to do that which was demanded of him by the Divine Law, and his accountability is absolute which constitutes the sanction which Islam provides to secure the believer's obedience to the demands that the Divine Law makes upon him.

The haqooqunnas is obligations to society, in the last resort and come within the scope of the jurisdiction or authority of the state in Islam, and relate largely to what in our own time are treated by Western thinkers as constituting secular affairs and secular dealings or relationships between man and man.

It was in relation to this aspect of enforcing obligations to society that the first four rightly guided Caliphs, in view of the nascent stage through which the Ummat in the early days of Islam had to pass, were forced to keep 'a mild form of patriarchal watch whenever necessary and even interpreted the religious injunctions in their application to new conditions of life in consultation with their companions.' But by doing this they did not claim 'spiritual leadership' of the community.

Indeed haqooqullah and haqooqunnas were as binding on the Caliphs themselves as on any other believer who was a member of the community. The Caliph was himself accountable directly to God no more and'no less than the humblest citizen of the realm, and obedience to the Caliph so long as he conducted the affairs of the community according to the Book of God and the Practice of the Prophet was based on the divine injunction:

> "Obey God, obey the Prophet and those who are acting as constituted authority from amongst you."

This accountability, in the last resort, was owed to the Maker, and the believer knew that even if he erred in disobeying the order of the Caliph and escaped the punishment prescribed for such disobedience, he would eventually be punished on the day of judgment when his accounts would be audited with merciless severity in respect of those aspects of his conduct which injured the rights of others. This is the sense in which though man has no rights within a theocentric perspective, only duties to his Maker, these duties in their turn give rise to all the rights, including those contained within the modern understanding of human rights.

This mode of approach to the problem of human rights has the obvious advantage of dispensing with the need to provide and implement separate procedures for giving effect to human rights since, within the religious context of Islam, no one escapes the penalty for violating the rights of others, and state power is only an earthly agent of the divine power acting by virtue of delegated authority to enforce the Divine Law.

The ruler himself, if he betrays his trust, will also be punished. Since both are bound by the Divine Law, there can, in the strict theory of the Islamic law, be no conflict between the state authority and the individual.

This view is fully reflected in the very first address given by the First Caliph of Islam when elected to his office as Head of the Muslim State which had been founded by the Prophet:

> "My fellow men! I call God to witness, I never had any wish to hold this office; never aspired to possess it. Neither in secret nor in the open did I ever pray for it. I have agreed to bear this burden lest mischief might raise its head. Else, there is no pleasure in leadership. On the other hand, the burden placed on my shoulders in such as I feel I have not the inherent strength to bear, and so cannot fulfil my duties except with Divine help. You have made me your leader, although I am in no way superior to you. Co-operate with me when I go right; correct me when I err; obey me so long as I follow the commandments of God and His Prophet; but turn away from me when I deviate."

Even he who is called upon to handle the affairs of the state is within the grip of Divine Law, and cannot claim any special privileges or prerogatives or immunities.

The affairs of the people are to be run for the benefit of the people as a whole. No Caliph had any special privilege attached to his person. As Abdul Latif points out, he was at best only first amongst equals. When food and clothing had to be rationed in Medina he had but to receive his share just as any other ordinary citizen; every man and every woman had the right to question him on any matter touching the affairs of state; he must appear, as did not Caliphs Umar and Hazarat Ali, before subordinate judges appointed by them, to answer charges against them. The same author goes on to add:

> "The economic system of life formulated by the Qu'ran, laying a special emphasis on the uplifting of the economically depressed, under which a state levy was to be collected from the rich for the relief of the poor, was rigidly enforced by the state. The exchequer of the state was considered to be the treasury of the people; the surplus, if any, accruing at the end of the year came back to the people in the form of annuities distributed on the basis of individual needs."

The Quranic injunctions governing the status of women, as independent economic units functioning in their own individual right, were scrupulously respected and upheld. Similarly, security of life and property and freedom of conscience were guaranteed to non-Muslim minorities who were styled Dhimmis. The Dhimmis were protected by the Prophet of God. The Prophet had proclaimed, 'I shall myself be the complainant against him greater than he can bear or deprive him of anything that belongs to him.' Indeed so mindful was he of their welfare that a few moments before he expired, the thought of the Dhimmi came to him. He is reported to have said:

> "Any Muslim who kills a Dhimmi has not the slightest chance of catching even the faintest smell of Heaven. Protect them; they are my Dhimmi."

In a moment of like remembrance, Caliph Umar, as he lay assassinated, exclaimed, "To him who will be Caliph after me, I commend my wish and testament—Dhimmi are protected by Allah and the Prophet. Respect the Covenants entered into with them, and when necessary, fight for their interests and do not place on them a burden or responsibility which they cannot bear."

Indeed, Islam went further in catering for the welfare of the human race by securing the consent of the believers to certain basic principles guaranteeing its preservation in times of war. These are the principles of justice and moderation laid down by Caliph Abu Bakr for the guidance of the first expedition into Syria:

> "Be just; break not your plighted faith; mutilate none; slay neither children, old men nor women; injure not the date-palm nor burn it with fire, nor cut down any fruit-bearing tree; slay neither flocks nor herds nor camels, except for food; per chance you may come across men who have retired into monasteries, leave them and their works in peace."

The foregoing illustration is typical of the emphasis on what man is not to do, yet the rights of others are implied even when the principles are formulated as prohibitions on the believers.

On the more positive side, the Prophet's last Khutba (congregational address) on the occasion of his final pilgrimage provides the earliest declaration ever made in the history of mankind of what might be called the obligations that were imposed upon believers:

> "Then the apostle continued his pilgrimage and showed the men the rites and taught them the customs of their hajj. He made a speech in which he made things clear. He praised and glorified God, then he said, 'O men, listen to my words, I do not know whether I shall ever meet you in this place again after this year. Your blood and your property are sacrosanct until you meet your Lord, as this day and this month are Holy. You will surely meet your Lord and He will ask you of your works. He who has a pledge let him return it to him who entrusted him with it; all usury is abolished, but you have your capital. Wrong not and you shall not be

wrongged. God has decreed that there is to be no usury and the usury of Abbas b. Abdul Muttalib is abolished, all of it. All bloodshed in the pagan period is to be left unavenged. The first claim on blood I abolish is that of b. Rabia b. al-Harithb. Abdul Muttalib (who was fostered among the b. Layth and whom Hudhay killed). It is the first bloodshed in the pagan period which I deal with. You have rights over your wives and they have rights over you. Your have the right that they should not defile your bed and that they should not behave with open unseemliness. If they do, God allows you to put them in separate rooms and to beat them but not with severity. If they refrain from these things they have the right to their food and clothing with kindness. Lay injunctions on women kindly, for they are prisoners with you having no control of their persons. You have taken them only as a trust from God (bi amanatillah) and you have the enjoyment of their persons by the words of God, so understand my words, men, for I have told you. I have left with you something which if you will never fall into error—a plain indication, the Book of God and the Practice of His Prophet, so give good heed to what I say. Know that every Muslim is a Muslim's brother, and that the Muslims are brethren. It is only lawful to take from a brother what he gives you willingly, so wrong not yourselves."

International Charter

Talking about the sum and substance of the various human rights and the fundamental freedoms which have been incorporated in the Universal Declaration of Human Rights of 1948, Syed Abdul Latif sums up the position as follows:

"The twin aim of this Declaration is one the one hand to equip the individual to live a free life considered successively as (i) physical organism; (ii) a moral personality; (iii) a worker; (iv) an intelligent being and (v) a member of a community and of a polity, and on the

> other to help the individual so equipped to make his contribution to international amity or the peace of the world..For the student of the Qur'an not one word in the preamble or in the objective of the Charter, and not a single article in the text of the Universal Declaration of Human Rights, will seem unfamiliar."

Under a creed which places man next to God, and brushes aside distinctions of race, colour and birth, and calls upon all mankind to live together as a family of God or as a 'fold' every member of which shall be a shepherd or keeper unto every other and be accountable for its welfare,' the Universal Declaration of Human Rights must follow as a basic corollary, or an extension of the Quranic programme. But a mere declaration of them will not carry humanity far. Several questions call for attention from the Quranic point of view.

The questions he raises concern first the impulse underlying the Charter of the United Nations, and the Universal Declaration of Human Rights adopted in pursuance thereof. Is the scheme in the interest of or for the good of humanity as a whole, or is it a practice to serve the interest of a particular country or group of countries? Secondly, looking at the list of rights covered by the Universal Declaration, he asks if it is possible for any country claiming to be civilized at the present hour to say with confidence that all the rights are observed by it, or that it may serve as a pattern for the rest.

It is obvious that the initiative for implementing them must come from the government or legislature of each country. Is the system of political life in every country such as may place in high office the type of men who may have the urge and the high-mindedness to respect the Declaration and implement its provisions? Lastly, he considers the world order which is the aim of the two documents, and which argues a common purpose acceptable to all the countries of the world. As things stand, the world is divided, broadly speaking, into two camps—the Soviet and the American.

A world arrangement, whatever its form, will be possible only on the basis of some sort of reconciliation between the two contending ideologies, or by building a half-way house for mutual cooperation. Is such a reconciliation possible? He surveys possible answers to these disturbing questions, and records as his opinion that there is a vast discrepancy between the provision of these rights contained in the Universal Declaration and the actual practices of the people of the modern West. In the words of Professor Hitti:

> "Unfortunately during the last decade or two, in particular, the impact of the West has not been entirely for good. There is a striking contrast between the humanitarian ideas professed by Western missionaries, teachers, and preachers, and the disregard of human values by European and American politicians, and warriors; a disparity between word and deed; and overemphasis on economic and nationalist values."

The behaviours of the so-called advanced nations during the last two wars waged on a scale unknown in history; the ability of Western man let loose those diabolic forces which are the product of his science and his machine and which now threaten the world with destruction; their intervention in the Near East, particularly in the handling to the Palestine problem by America, England, France, and other nations, all these have worked together to disillusion this man of the near-East who has been trying to establish an intellectual rapprochement with the West. It is these actions of the West which alienate him and shake his belief in the character of Western man and his morality on both the private and the public levels.

Islamic Viewpoint

It is within the context of such evaluations of the negative impact in any practical terms of the Universal Declaration of Human Rights that we can point the excellence of the strategy with which Islam has enjoined upon its members the obligation to acknowledge and implement human rights. Islam is primarily interested in securing for its believers 'right belief and right conduct,'but in accordance with its teachings the conduct is never right unless it is based on right belief and is consciously willed.

Islam is an enemy of all mechanical actions. One cannot in Islam perform prayers without forming conscious intention to pray; one cannot give zakat (alms) without consciously intending to do so; one cannot fast without forming conscious intention to fast; you cannot go on pilgrimage and perform the prescribed rites without being aware of their significance and without the formation of conscious intention to do so. This 'conscious intention' is the core of the matter and the Prophet said that the niyyat (intention) of the momin (believer) to do the deed, in obedience to the Law of God, was better than mere external conformity with the terms of the conduct prescribed by such law (Al-niyyatui Momin Khairun Mined Amalhi).

Since, it is in the inwardness of his being that such a conscious willing intention can be formed, Islam takes good care to insist that its primary purpose is to produce the Saliheen (righteous people), the Muttaqis (self-controlled people) and the Sadiqeen (people who adhere to truth). It is the transformation of the c[illegible] Adam in man into an expression of the Divine that forms the essence, if not the quintessence, of the strategy of Islam.

The Western world believes that mechanical conformity to the pattern of conduct, prescribed by the law of the state or by some such authority, is sufficient to secure public order and universal peace. In other words, its procedure is to attempt to influence from outside the inner condition of man believing that social, political economic and other institutions are capable of influencing the individual character. It is submitted that this is a fallacious approach; only slaves can be thus handled, not free people.

Islam, on the other hand, begins by inviting man to accept the paramountcy of the power of the Lord, his own servitude and bondage to the will of his Master who is the Sovereign Ruler of the universe; in the last resort it redeems him by prescribing norms of behaviours by which he is to regulate his life. In the words of Professor D. De Santillana:

> "We may agree with the Muslim jurists when they teach that the fundamental rule of law is liberty...God has set a bound to human activity in order to make legitimate

> liberty possible for all; without the 'bounds of God,' liberty would degenerate into licence, destroying the perpetrator himself along with the social fabric."

This 'bound' is precisely what is called law, which restrains human action within certain limits, forbidding some acts enjoining others, and restraining the primitive liberty of man so as to make it as beneficial as possible either to the individual or to society. Whatever their form, these rules tend to the same end and have the same purpose, that is, the public weal (maslahah). Accordingly, law, divine in its origin, human in its subject-matter, has no other end but the welfare of man, even if this end may not at first sight be apparent; for God can do nothing which does not express the wisdom and mercy of which He is the Supreme source. The Qur'an itself provides clear justification for such a thesis:

> "In the name of Allah, the Beneficent, the Merciful. Nay, I swear by this city—and thou art an indweller of this city—and the begetter and that which he begot, we verily have created man in affliction: thinketh he that none hath power over him? And he saith: "I have destroyed vast Wealth" thinketh he that none beholdeth him? Did we not assign unto the parting of the mountain ways? But he hath not attempted the Ascent-Ah, what will convey unto thee what the Ascentis! It is to free a slave, and to feed in the day of hunger an orphan near of kin, or some poor wretch in misery, and to be of those who believe and exhort one another to perseverance and exhort one another to pity. Their place will be on the right hand. But those who disbelieve our revelations, their place will be on the left hand. Fire will be an awning over them."

The title of the surah is Al-Balad or 'the City,' and it represents the condensed essence of the wisdom upon what may be called the subject of civic rights in the context of the development of monotheistic religion. By the word 'City', by which the verse begins, is meant Mecca. The surah is in the nature of a 'charter of freedom' given to man after the prayer of Ibrahim for the foundation of a city by one of his descendants—the Prophet of Islam—had been answered.

It draws attention to the evolution of religion and man from Ibrahim to Muhammad—the entire period of Semitic civilization—and Mecca as its place of birth and completion.

Man has been created to face difficulties, and to help him confront these trials with fortitude he has been reminded that there is some 'power' that is an overseer of his deeds, namely his Lord and Master who sees him through and through. The surah goes on to recount the grace of God to man evidenced by the conferment of powers of sight and of speech.

Furthermore, man has been shown two conspicuous ways and now the choice is his, either to elect to negotiate the way of truth or of falsehood to choose the good or evil deed. Of these two possible choices the path of righteousness consists in siding with the truth and of doing good deeds. This is the uphill or higher way, and the highest deed available to the believer is to 'free a slave'. This constitutes not only physical freedom, but moral, mental and spiritual freedom, as much from other human beings as from one's lower self. It is this freedom from necessity that 'freeing the slave' expresses. This amounts to securing the emancipation of man from virtually all manners of servitude.

It imposes on man a whole range of social duties—freeing the slave, feeding the orphan, caring for 'the poor wretch in misery'—and these duties which confer corresponding rights on all. Over and above these are the duties to believe, and exhort one another to patience and to mercy. Man must believe in the 'Unseen', he must believe in 'all the Prophets' in 'the Angels', in all the 'revealed books' including those that have preceded the Qur'an. Man's ultimate return is to God who is his Creator, and his liability to render account is absolute.

While facing the tests and trials of life, a believer is called upon to be 'patient and to pray' and to show 'compassion and mercy to others'. Those who can adhere to this way of life and exercise their power of choice in conformity with the tenets of the Divine Law are declared to be the 'people of the right hand' and those who disbelieve are characterised as the 'people of the left hand.' It is this distinction which is vital.

Islam presents man with a charter of human liberty within a religious framework which emphasizes the necessity of his being aware of his responsibility and accountability. In the earlier forms of religious belief and practice, the injunctions prescribed to regulate man's conduct were conched as 'absolute commandments', as for instances in the Ten Commandments given by Moses.

In those cases the obedience of the believer was complete if he conducted himself in accordance with the law; at worst even mechanical conformity was enough. But the Qur'an is also the furqan. That is to say it is book that makes exercise of discretion and discrimination possible for man, in that it outlines for him the possible courses of conduct that are open to him as a free agent and invites him to choose the difficult uphill way; to choose the right side with truth and to stand steadfastly against all odds.

Islam makes the believer his brother's keeper, particularly if the brother is helpless, uncared for or unprotected. It extends the sphere of his responsibility by commissioning him to believe, because without proper belief there is no proper conduct. He is, therefore, asked to base his conduct on right belief taught through the revealed Word of God contained in the Qur'an. He is also invited to be a missionary in the cause of Islam, to become a diligent crusader in the cause of inviting his fellow men to the way of patience, to show fortitude and compassion so long as his earthly life lasts.

Should he do all this, he is rightly guided and will be duly rewarded by the grant of Eternal Life; real life as opposed to this life which is only the seed-bed of the Hereafter. That life which is to come is better and eternal; this life exists only to provide the opportunity to win the reward of that life. If he uses this to its full advantage, not only will the believer achieve success here and now, but will also gain the reward of Eternal Life in the Hereafter. If the life of man is to be located in the conceptual framework which results from close study of the Holy Book, the position of man in the scheme of things must be viewed not as though he were a finished product, but rather as an evolving being, in a state of transition.

Broadly speaking, man is to be regarded as one who is here on the earth to spend his time as though it constituted a transitional phase which will one day be brought to an end by the most certain of all events, namely, his death. During this interim phase he cannot, on his own, hope to know the path he should pursue in order to enable himself to reach higher levels of his being.

Just as it is inconceivable, seeing the rose bush embedded in manure and covered in thorns, to imagine the beauty of the rose it will one day produce, it is equally impossible to envisage the final phase of man's evolution in which he is destined to reach his highest fulfillment and expression. As the gardener prunes the rose to encourage yet more beautiful blooms, so process of taqwa in the life of the believer.

Instead of abandoning himself completely to the animal impulses within him he must learn to acquire self-control so that the energy available within him does not exhaust itself on the animal plane of his existence, but is transmuted into higher forms of being capable of surviving the ravages of death and of enjoying the reward of higher, better and eternal life.

Human rights conceived from the anthropocentric perspective are treated by Western thinkers as thought they were no more than an expedient mode of protecting the individual from the assaults that are likely to be made upon him by the authority of the state's coercive power by the unjust laws that may be imposed by the power of the brute majority to deny man the possibility of self-development.

Islam, on the other hand, formulates, defines and protects these very rights by inducing in the believers the disposition to obey the law of God, the practice of his Last Prophet, and to show obedience to those constituted authorities within the realm who themselves are bound to obey the law of God and the practice of the Prophet and conduct man's affairs accordingly.

Furthermore affirmation of those rights is to enable man not only to secure the establishment of those conditions in terms of which the development of man as an individual on the earth may be possible, but also to enable man to so conduct himself inwardly as well as outwardly, that he may be able to obey the Divine Law, that only his Maker is qualified to impose on him. By accepting to live in bondage to this Divine Law, man learns to be free.

Islam terminates the era of revealed religions, declares man free by telling him that no other Prophet hereafter would come, indicates the straight road to be traversed by him, and in the Holy Book provides sufficient guidance to enable him to choose. It is now for him to choose. Depending on the choice he makes, the road he takes will lead him either to Heaven or to Hell.

It is quite impossible within the scope of this chapter to do full justice to all aspects of our subject. But before concluding, there is a question which must be answered. The question so frequently asked by Western scholars is why Islam has insisted so strongly on rewards and punishments? Why the emphasis on Heaven and Hell? The answer to their question turns on the interpretation of freedom.

Islam, a religion of mature minds, gave man complete freedom in the conduct of his life for the first time in history. To this freedom were annexed the consequences of his choice. Given the particular nature of man, true freedom lies only in obedience to God's law; only when he disobeys this law and submits to the rule of the lower passions that stem from his animal nature is man condemned to bondage. It is with this in mind that the Qur'an asks, "have you seen that person who has taken his lower patience as his gods?"

In disobeying God man acts counter to his own nature and reduces himself to slavery. It is too his obedience to God which itself ensures that he shall retain the capacity to be free and responsible. Heaven and Hell are not locations, but merely names for the states of man's being:

> He makes heaven or hell for himself by the way he conducts his life. Rewards and punishments are not imposed from outside but follow as natural consequences of what a man does with his life here below.

God is not some kind of policeman who enforces the law, but His Prophet sent down to help humanity is the warner and guide. He, through the revelation from God, has told us what we must do if we wish to avoid the many pitfalls along the way and make the most of the opportunities which life on earth offers. According to Islam, human action has an objective quality inherent in it, and it is this which overtakes man either as punishment if his conduct be bad, or as reward if it be good.

The Solution

How can we best sum up the contribution Islam can make to the world today? In a lecture delivered by Arnold Toynbee in 1948, under the title "Islam—the West and the Future," he observed that Islam could provide the solution to two of the main problems of the present day, famely those of racial discrimination and of alcoholism. But these are no more than symptoms of a far deeper malaise.

There is neither spiritual nor practical reason why Islam should confine itself to the solution of these issues rather than to other far more deeply-rooted problems now confronting mankind. The mission of Islam is to face all such problems and to offer a solution by showing mankind the true path he should follow to gain salvation in this world and the next.

Let us determine the solution by first of all defining the need. What is mankind's greatest need today? How can Islam meet this need? According to Holy Revelations the basic issue in man's life has been, and will be till the Day of Judgment, the question of worship. Who is to be worshipped and how is He to be worshipped? Let us deal with the first question:

"Who is to be worshipped? Writers and thinkers in the West during the Age of Enlightenment and the Age of Materialism in the 18th and 19th centuries when these ideas were first raised, sought to solve the problem by making it disappear."

Their advice was 'Forget about this issue, it is of no concern whatsoever; live life and enjoy it, if you choose, do not worship anything at all.' By freeing man from the bondage of religion they thought to offer him an unprecedented opportunity of finding happiness on this earth. But their thinking was based on two major illusions. The first illusion was the belief that humanity would attain happiness, and would experience constructive development when it rejected religion.

Indeed the West has progressed tremendously, both technologically and scientifically, since it rejected religion. This very progress fostered the illusion in the hearts of men. They forgot that religion in itself was not the force that held them back, but their own interpretation which, since the Middle Ages in Europe, had obstructed their progress.

However, they overlooked a more important factor—that the scientific and technological progress achieved by Europe after neglecting its religion was not the first, nor even the fundamental ingredient of life. It cannot by itself establish a sound human life.

Only now is the West coming increasingly to realise this, as they recognize that the absence of spiritual values is the main reason behind the anxiety, confusion, madness, suicide, many other psychological and nervous disorders, and the feeling of perplexity and illusion among youth, all of which constitute a threat to the security, peace and welfare of humanity, despite all the material progress achieved during the last two centuries.

The second illusion is the related thought that man can do without worship altogether. This naive illusion is not borne out by our knowledge of man's history from his earliest known origins up to the present time. Whether in the ancient or the modern world 'worship' in some form or the other has never ceased to exist in man's life.

When man says to himself 'I will worship nothing whatsoever', he does not, as he imagines, rid himself of the problem of worship. He merely changes the object of worship, and proclaims himself or his interests as the God to be worshipped and to govern his whole life. Worship is not confined to the offering of prayers, devotions or the submission of offerings, as people appear sometimes to imagine when talking of the subject.

This is a matter of form only. Worship itself is essentially obedience and acquiescence to a certain Being, and the belief that it is our duty to obey that Being. Worship in this sense is an integral part of every man's entirety and existence because it is a component part of himself. Within this context there can be no one who does not worship even man's entirety and existence because it is a component part of himself. Within this context there can be no one who does not worship even though he claims otherwise.

Man is an instinctive worshipper whether or not he chooses or is aware of it. It is only in the nature of the worshipped deity or the way he is worshipped that one man differs from another. Either he worships God, or he worships some other deity or deities by whatever name. His worship of God is either true or deviant, and no sensible man would make false deities the object of his worship.

Having established this fact, the Qur'an proceeds to the other part of the question, namely the explanation of the right way to worship God.It stipulates the uniformity of worship just as it stresses the Unity of God.The correct worship of God is represented in two integral indivisible aspects, namely the maintenance of the rites of worshipping God to the exclusion of any other, and the following of God's revelation in establishing a point of reference for guidance in life.To pray or present offerings to an idol, an object, or a person, is corruptive of religion as well as of worship.The same corruption results from the adoption of a non-godly attitude and practice in life.

There must be unity between man's worship and his attitude towards life. The deity addressed by man in his prayer and devotions is the same deity addressed while studying, earning a living, attempting to better conditions on earth, eating, drinking, copulating, as well as while communicating with his family, with other individuals, with other societies, peoples and states, whether in peace time or during war. Say:

> "Lo! my worship and my sacrifice, and my living and my dying, are for Allah, Lord of the Worlds" (VI. 163).

In all that he does, the constant reiteration of God's name in his heart had the practical effect of recalling to him God's commands, so that he may obey them. In Islam God's commands deal with all such matters and indicate the permitted as well as the prohibited.

When this happens something of considerable significance occurs in man's life. To being with man will be giving due worship to His Creator. Man would never appreciate God as he truly should if he worshipped Him in prayer once during the day and considered this to be the end of it. God says:

> "I created the Jinn and humankind only that they might worship Me"(LI:56).

Meaning by this the wide range of worship which comprises prayer and devotions, living and dying. To do otherwise would be to worship two deities, one in the holy shrine through prayer and devotions, the other (or others, though eventually they culminate into one), through obedience in affairs of everyday life. Allah hath said:

> "Choose not two gods. There is only one God. So of, he only, be in awe."(al-NahlXVI:51).

The ability of the human heart to sense the glory of God and His miraculous powers revealed in the creation of a universe which is such a wonderful model of accuracy, order and uniformity, as well as in the creation of all living objects, will or should lead man to worship this Almighty God in due veneration of His glory and power.

This could never occur through a worship that is pursued from moment to momentand relinquished for the remainder of man's day-to-day living. Regardless of God's reward for this worship, a sense of duty demands that it should be followed as a means of paying others what is due to them.

> Lo! Allah commandeth you that ye restore deposits to their owners. (IV. 58), and who except this Omnipotent God serves disinterested and constant worship?

Yet of His Mercy God is bounteous to those who give Him His due, namely worship in its wider or uniformly comprehensive sense, for He will reward them by eternal life in paradise, and secure their future after death, which, since it is the longer period of man's life, is the worthier to be preserved.

The uniformity of worship during man's span of life influences many important aspects of his living. It gives him first of all an inner security which is nowhere to be found outside the frame of faith. It cannot be obtained either through drugs, drinks, narcotics, leisure or sensual pleasure. All these confirm the state of mind which man wants to evade, but they neither remove nor cure it. Security emanates from faith and the mention of God's name.

As the Qur'an puts it:

> "those who believe, and whose hearts find satisfaction in the remembrance of God: for without doubt in the remembrance of God do hearts find satisfaction."

This security is not a placid resignation to events. Rather, it is the search for the good life wherever it is to be found; the Jihad under God's name to instal God's justice in the world; the opposition to all forms of injustice abhorrent to God; the search for knowledge and instruction. In all these activities the believer will rely on God because everything is moved by and returns back to Him.

The believer, moreover, is confident that God promises only goodness to him, and this is why no anxiety overshadows the earning of a living, the pursuit of study, the Jihad, and the establishment of a civilization, a fact that was once apparent in the early Muslim period.

Until recently, there were writers who acclaimed the present age as the 'age of anxiety', calling it the age of creative anxiety. But they came to realise that it was now more in the nature of a poisonous drug even though taken in the smallest doses. They also realised that the impetuous frantic activity was neither a real nor creative activity. It was only symptomatic of an illness that would soon lead to other consequences, causing man to lose his sense of security and psychological balance. Other writers have said that anxiety is a necessary accompaniment of civilization however damaging or beneficial.

This interpretation lacks scientific precision, since, anxiety goes hand in hand only with a civilization thriving on materialism and neglecting the spirit. This type of civilization lacks the basis for inspiring a true sense of security, and it is this civilization which is responsible for tearing the human soul between two deities, the other who dominates the realities of day-to-day life. This latter deity who accompanies man is more often than not a tough and ruthless one who does not inspire security and stability in his worshippers.

As history shows this was once a flourishing civilization that sensed no pangs of fatal concern because it was secure in the name of God. Uniformity of worship brings together many aspects of man both within his inner self or in his life generally, which present-day deviations have, without justification, torn as under.

It brings together spirit and matter, body and soul. It brings together religion and science, piety and material development, religion and life. Finally, it brings together this life and the Hereafter.

Let us look briefly at each of these unities brought about by Islam. Soul and body or spirit and matter are both or genuine authenticity in the human make-up.

> "Behold, thy Lord said to the angels: I am about to create man from clay. When I have fashioned him (in due proportion) and breathed into him of My Spirit, fall you down in obeisance unto him."

They were brought together inseparably at the birth of man, and the whole of his history is a living confirmation of this fact. But in periods of Jahiliyyah, there is always a tendency to set them apart by directing each on a separate course of its own, and by the exaggeration of one at the expense of the other.

Some pre-Islamic periods emphasised the spirit as the real essence of man and despised the body as an impure object unworthy of veneration. Such an object was entitled only to degrading and tortuous acts. The material aspect of life was also despised as it was nearest to the body, to clay. Other pre-Islamic periods exaggerated the body and sensual pleasure. They considered the body to be the real thing, and the soul only a beautiful shadow that lacked substance. They saw it as a secondary object in man's life or as an inhibitor.

As a result these years of history dedicated a great deal of their interest to material produce and construction and almost completely neglected the spiritual make-up of man. Both attitudes base themselves on a false premise, namely that there is a deep-rooted contradiction between body and soul that can be only conciliated by suppressing one in favour of the other. One either suppresses the body to free the soul, or suppresses the soul in order to attain material emancipation.

But, in reality, in neither case does suppression lead to goodness. The suppression and devitalization of the body runs counter to instinct, resulting in the obstruction of man's energy, material and cultural retardation, poverty, misery, depression, pessimism and despair.

Alternatively, the suppression and blackening of the soul lead to inner worries that can never be satisfied even by the deepest immersion in earthly pleasures which necessarily result in conflict between individuals, communities, states and peoples. These are signs that something counter-instinctive has occurred; the result is a loss of equilibrium in man's life.

Islam, on the other hand, provides the balanced alternative which harmonises soul and body and disposes of any contradiction and conflict between them. Islam never accepted the idea of an irreconciliable situation between these two entities.

It is true that the body and the soul are two different elements but they are integrated in man. Their lack of cohesion is not caused by their mutual existence in the human-being, but by the domination of one by the other, and the consequent loss of the instinctive equilibrium which God bestowed on him:

> "O Man! What has seduced thee from Thy Lord Most Beneficent? Him who created thee, fashioned thee in due proportion, and gave thee a just bias." (V:7).

Moderation or equilibrium lies at the basis of God's creation. But man in his ignorance disturbs this equilibrium. As a result disturbance occurs in the soul well as in the actualities of life, as is testified by events. This idea is expounded in L' Homme Get Inconnu by the scientist-physician Alexis Karel. He indicates:

> "put serious ignorance of the nature of man as well as our neglect of his spiritual aspect, and our setting up of economic, social and political systems based on ignorance, lie at the root of our scientific and cultural progress."

And it is Islam which restores to man the balance and moderation with which he is endowed by God. It puts into effect a simple and realistic though far-reaching measure, namely an invitation to the soul and body to take part in the whole of life.

Prayer is not only a spiritual hymn, it is also a set of movements performed by the body through standing, kneeling and prostration, combined with a conscious mental concentration on the verses recited in prayer. Food, drink and sex on the other hand are not pure body movements, but also represent spiritual aspirations made permissible by mentioning God's name, and performed in strict observance of what is lawful and what is forbidden. In this way, such acts invariably lie between these two poles and is thus included in the integrating system which brings together soul and body, spirit and matter, earth and sky.

A similar split occurred between religion and science. Man has an instinctive disposition to know the secrets of the material world around him, and to subject these to his power. Both dispositions are instinctive and authentic; both are innate. No necessary contradiction, split or conflict exists between them.

Divine Revelation provided no grounds for it, but man's errors have created conflict and dispute between them. This dichotomy occurred in Europe at the beginning or the Renaissance when the Church opposed science and scholars, and threatened to bury, torture and kill people of science such as Copernicus, Galileo and Jordan Bruno.

As time passed, the gap widened and the conflict deepened, until the mere mention of God's name in scientific research was tantamount in the ordinary European's sense to a violation of the spirit of that research and an unwarranted attempt to integrate two irreconciliable attitudes. As Darwin put it:

> "The interpretation of evolution with reference to Providence is an introduction of a metaphysical element into a purely mechanical situation."

This misinterpretation of the nature of the relationship between the two subjects could not help but disturb man's balance and security. It aroused conflict in man's inner self between two genuine elements each requiring satisfaction. When one feels that the satisfaction of one's spiritual needs lies outside the frame-work of science, and that the satisfaction of scientific needs lies beyond the reach of religion, and if at the same time feels that these needs proceed in two separate and diverging directions, one ends by worshipping two irreconciliable deities, each demanding from his worshipper a differing attitude, behaviour and point of view.

For the time being, there is no choice other than to worship the two. Again, man is torn apart, whether consciously or unconsciously. His anxiety is reinforced, and when, as frequently happens, he is forced to choose between them, he succumbs to the deity of science as being more able to satisfy his immediate needs, and abandons the deity of religion as belonging to a world altogether less real and tangible whose existence in any case, he doubts.

Islam in its simplicity eliminates this contradiction again by means of a realistic and simple procedure. The God who man worships in his prayers is the same God who gave man knowledge for the first time, and the same God who invites man still to learning and knowledge.

> "He taught Adam the nature of all things" (p. 31). Read in the name of the Lord who createth. Createth man from a clot.
>
> Read; And thy Lord is the Most Bounteous, who teacheth by the pen. Teacheth man that which he knew not." (XCVI. 1-5).

God invites man to contemplate the secrets of the universe:

> "Behold in the creation of the Heavens and the Earth; in the alteration of the night and the day; in the sailings of the ships through the ocean for the profit of mankind; in the rain which God sends down from the skies, and the life which he gives therewith. To an Earth that is dead, in the beasts of all kinds that he scatters through the Earth, in the change of the winds, and the clouds which they trail like their slaves between the sky and the earth; (here) indeed are signs for a people that are wise." (II. 164).

God taught that He was all that is between the sky and the earth:

> "And hath made of service to you whatsoever is in the Heavens and whatsoever is in the Earth." (XLV. 13).

In order to exploit what is in the Heavens and on Earth by his physical and mental efforts, all that man has to do is to learn the universal law by which God administers this universe:

> "It is He who has made the Earth manageable for you, so traverse ye through its tracts and enjoy of the substance which He furnishes (But unto Him is the resurrection)."

Thus will come the unity of orientation through the Oneness of God.

Human knowledge is not stolen from God despite His will as in the Greek myth of Prometheus. It is a divine gift bestowed on man. Man does not need to disobey God in order to learn. It is God who instructed mankind to learn and to seek knowledge. The Prophet says:

> "The quest of knowledge is an obligation."

Man should not have any sense of guilt when he exploits the resources of the Heavens and Earth for his benefit, nor should he think that he is doing so in rebellion against a Divine Will which seeks to crush and oppress him in the way the relationship between man and God is portrayed in the Greek myth. It is God who harnessed the resources of this universe for the benefit of man and instructed man to settle on the earth.

> "It is He who produced you from the earth and settled you therein."

There is thus no need for man to feel that he is worshipping two opposed gods, each one with conflicting demands on him. In all that man does there is only one God. When man seeks knowledge Allah demands him not to use the fruit of this knowledge in wrongful tyranny over the earth. Man does not feel that he is surrendering to God only out of ignorance of inability, as Julian Huxley claimed in Man in the Modern World. According to Huxley:

> "When man gains knowledge and control over his environment, he rebels against God, making a god of himself."

On the contrary, the more man learns the nearer he becomes to God and to the fear of God.

The erudite among his bondsmen fear God alone." (XXXV:28).

Man prays to God of give him more knowledge:

> "Oh My Lord. Advance me in knowledge." (Taha 114).

Thus even when he is seeking knowledge, man is in his heart always thinking of Allah. He will conduct his life in exploiting the fruits of science for righteous ends with the same assurance and confidence he has in Allah when he offers Him his prayers. In this way, Islam establishes a unity between religion and science and learning, as between religion and life.

In Europe, life was excluded from the sphere of religion through particular circumstances which were not inherent in religion itself. Western man thought of religion as a spiritual relation between man and God, and of life as human endeavour with no relation to God. This is invented by the West, and not revealed by God. It is inconceivable that such a concept could be supported by the words ascribed to the Messiah:

> "Render therefore unto Caesar the things which be Caesar's and unto God the things which be God's."

This is contradictory to the entire concept of religion according to which Allah is the Lord of the heavens and the earth, and Caesar and all men must surrender to the judgment of Allah.

These words should be seen as an instruction by the Messiah to his followers not to declare war against Caesar, but to pay the taxes, he required, till the establishment of a state that would enforce what Allah had revealed, and would subject Caesar himself to the judgment of Allah. There is a similar case in Islam.

Allah told the Muslims in Mecca before the establishment of the Muslim State:

> "Withhold your hands establish worship and pay the poor due." (IV. 77).

No Muslim has understood from this instruction that religion is only a spiritual relation between man and Allah, and that the daily affairs of life should be administered by Caesar or other non-believers in the way they choose. This instruction was for a period of time only, and was followed by the establishment of Muslim society and the Muslim state, thus making life in its entirety subject to the judgment of Allah. This was accompanied by the revelation of detailed legislation governing all aspects of life.

As a result of this wrong interpretation of the scope of religion in the West, life increasingly moved away from religion, until in modern times it was finally excluded completely from its ambit. Politics followed the principles of Machiavelli who justified lying, deception, hypocrisy, dishonesty, killing, murder, fraudulence and trickery, all of which were forbidden in Islam.

Economy was based on the usurious system which is also forbidden in Islam. Social relations were based on social hypocrisy and the hideous isolation of individuals described by Aldous Huxley in Texts and Pretexts, where every man had become an island in itself without any connection with other islands scattered in the ocean of life.

Karel considers that the contravention of innate laws cannot take place without severe punishment, as these laws are as crucial as the Law of Nature itself. The chaos and turmoil now rampant all over the world is the heavy price man has paid for the contravention of the innate laws created by Allah. It is Allah and not man who knows human nature.

How ignorant man is of his nature, as Karel again so rightly observes. Though he has learnt a great deal about the universe surrounding him, his ignorance of himself is profound, since, he sees himself only through his passions and desires. Allah alone knows the innate human nature; He knows what is suitable for it and what is not. He has revealed this religion to guide the life of man as well as his relation with Allah. In a simple yet far-reaching way, Islam establishes the connection between religion and life, and extends this to embrace the hereafter.

Islam presents the true concept of religion. Religion is faith and laws; a faith governing spiritual relations with God, and laws administering the affairs of life in the name of God. In both cases, we are seeking the same God, we worship one God. The Shari'ah as revealed encompasses the whole range of human activity, as well as international relations whether in peace or in war. Thus, politics becomes Islamic politics; economics becomes Islamic economics, social relations become Islamic relations and relations between the two sexes will be organised according to Islam, thought and art become Islamic activities. Islam embraces the whole of life.

Allah who revealed the Shari'ah knows that in man's life there are permanent elements, and others that develop and change. Allah does not want these latter to be petrified or stunted in their growth, therefore, he enacts in his Shari'ah comprehensive and constant principles which, without themselves altering, allow for the process of continuous change through the right interpretation of these laws in their detailed application to new circumstances. This had been the endeavour of Muslim scholars throughout history.

In this way, a constant interconnection is maintained between religion and life. Life will neither be petrified in one form, nor will its development contravene the scope of religion. As Khalifah Omar Ben Abdel Aziz said:

> "The more new problems people have, the more new rules they will find."

It is through this fusion that unity of this life and the hereafter will be achieved. The dichotomy between religion and life led to a separation in the awareness of people of this life and the hereafter. In pursuit of these separate ends they developed two completely unconnected sets of actions, one bearing no relation to the other.

Islam establishes a unity between this life and the hereafter and considers them as a continuous process. Together they constitute one path, the beginning of which is this life and its end the hereafter.

> "But seek, with the (wealth) which God has bestowed on thee, the home of the Hereafter, not forget thy portion in this world". (XXVIII. 77), and "Say who hath produced for His servants and the things, clean and pure, (which he hath provided) for sustenance? Say they are, in the life of the world, for those who believe, (and) purely for them on the Day of Judgment."

In Islam, there is not a single deed which is concerned exclusively with worldly life or with the Hereafter; its purpose is always two fold. Offering prayers, for example, which people may think of as a deed motivated solely by concern for the hereafter, also has its purpose in the worldly life. As God says in the Qur'an,

> "Prayer restrains from shameful and unjust deeds." (XXIX. 45).

Prayer is intended to be offered in the worldly life, and be rewarded in the hereafter. Even the relationship between the sexes, which might be thought of as an exclusively worldly affair, is linked in the consciousness of Muslims with the hereafter. Muhammad said: "You will be rewarded by Allah for copulation with your wives." He was asked: "We do that to satisfy our desire how can we be rewarded for it?" Muhammad replied: "If you satisfy your desires in a forbidden way, wouldn't you be punished for it?" They answered:"Yes we would." Muhammad then said: "If you then satisfy your desire in a permissible way, you must be rewarded."

The result is that this world and the hereafter are interconnected in the awareness of the Muslim individual. In everything he does he commits himself to act in accordance with the revealed Will of Allah. While he conducts his worldly affairs in this life, he will be looking forward to God's reward in the hereafter.

This full integration in the structure of Islam is clearly expressed in a way which has roused the interest of many Orientalists writing about Islam. The English Orientalist Gibb says,

> "The kind of society that a community builds for itself depends fundamentally upon its beliefs as to the nature and purpose of the universe and the place of the human soul within it."

This is a familiar enough doctrine and is reiterated from Christian pulpits week after week. But Islam is possibly the only religion which has constantly and consistently aimed to build up a society on this principle. The prime instrument of this purpose was law.

The Canadian Orientalist Wilfred Cantwell Smith remarks:

> "Observers have noted the paramount position of the community in Islam. Less thought has been devoted to its significance in Islamic history, which is that community in motion, it is well known that Muslim society has a remarkable solidarity, that the loyalty and cohesion of its members are intense. Many have recognised that the community is not only a social group but a religious body; that the 'church and state' are one, to use the inappropriate language of the West."

We would go much further, as has been said, in interpreting this. Yet to stress these facts, to insist upon the centrality of society, is not deny but to interpret our initial emphasis on religion as personal. The community is based on, as it is integrated to, individual faith. Not only is Muslim society held together (as other societies) by common loyalties and traditions, and by a very carefully worked out system of values and of beliefs. Not only is it the product of a superb ideal. It pulsates with the vitality of a profoundly held and deeply personal conviction, a religious conviction that is warm and meaningful for the individual member.

We may say that this society, this community, is the expression of a religious ideal, using 'religious' in the personal sense earlier proposed. As a creed or theological system may be expression in an intellectual form of a personal faith—as is often the case, particularly with Christians—so a social order and its activities are the expression in a practised form of a Muslim's personal faith.

Singularity of the Creator

This integration, which is an expression of the unity of worship and the Oneness of God, is most precious in Islam. It is the real meaning of Shahadah:

"No God but Allah."

It is the most precious gift that Islam can give to humanity in this age; a humanity perplexed, confused and suffering from anxiety through its loss of the unifying element, whether in its theoretical concepts or in its actual behaviour. It seems uncertain in Toynbee's discussion of the possible future contribution of Islam to new manifestations of religion, whether he was aware of this meaning or not.

Whatever the case may be, this meaning does not present ' a new face of religion' as Toynbee and others thought. It is the true meaning of religion revealed by God to mankind. It is the true meaning which materialised in Islam fourteen centuries ago, and was formulated in a concrete way over a long period and in large areas of the world.

Islam provides us with guidance throughout life from cradle to grave, answering their innate questions that consciously or unconsciously press on man in his journey through this world. What exactly is man? What is his role on the earth? What are the limits of his energies? From where have we come? To where will we go after death? For what purpose do we live? How should we organise our life? These are the questions which demand answers. If no convincing and decisive answer is provided, and if that answer is not that right one, it will undoubtedly affect man's psychological stability and his behaviour.

Man will be in a state of crisis. The present world situation is the most obvious example of the extent of this crisis: no further evidence is needed than modern man's present behaviours. What is man? A simple question, yet how difficult for contemporary mankind to answer, and how far their answer from the truth. Is man really an animal as Darwin suggested, or is he a human being? Is he a God as portrayed by Julian Huxley? Does man stand alone as his own creator, as suggested by a book with the title Man Makes Himself? Is he a slave as conceived by other doctrines and theories, and if so, a slave to what?

To an exploiting class as suggested by the materialistic theory of history; to his own body and desires; or to the machine as he came to be under technological progress? What are the potentials of man? What are the limits of reason? Is he able by it alone to understand and explain all things? What is his attitude towards those things which he cannot understand or explain? Should he ignore them, or surrender to them reluctantly? Where does man go after death? Is the end of man's limited life on this earth the end of everything, or is there some form of continuation? What is the purpose of human life? Is it to obtain as much material enjoyment as possible, or is there some other objective, and of what kind? Is it to control nature, or to control others? (Or is it perhaps to co-operate with them?) And to what use should this control be put? To enslave others? To destroy? Or merely to assert ourselves?

On the other hand we desire to control others that we may cooperate with them, the same question arises; to what end will we cooperate? the questions are endless. How should man live? Who will decide the question for him? Philosopher, politicians, dictators, the masses, youths, elders? Or should each man decide for himself as Sartre's existentialist philosophy suggests? Clearly the answers to all these questions and more will determine man's behaviours and the kind of life he will lead on earth.

Contemporary mankind whether in the East or the West has provided a variety of answers. For the most part, they are wrong and misleading. The result is the present unprecedented turmoil and chaos, and the misery of the vast majority of mankind is suffering from, despite the technological and scientific progress which was theoretically to provide humanity with spiritual happiness in addition to material prosperity.

The Role for Man

Islam provides humanity with the right guidance for its journey, and right answers to its persistent questions. Thus assured, man is enabled to set out to achieve his objectives in complete harmony of aspiration, thought, and feeling. Man in Islam is simply man. He is neither God nor animal—the two extremes argued by Huxley and Darwin respectively. His role is to be a Vice-regent on earth; to inhabit it in accordance with the will of Allah. Allah has bestowed on man the talents and abilities necessary for this role. Among them is the ability to learn, the ability to know and distinguish between the path or righteousness and the path of evil, and the ability to choose and pursue one of them. It is because of this ability that man's actions acquire moral value. Man cannot, and should not live without moral values.

There is no single human action which does not fall within the scope of morality. We cannot say that morality has no bearing on politics, science or sexual relations. The only acts that have no relation to morality are the acts of an animal:

> "for an animal there is no choice. Man on the contrary had two alternative courses of action open to him, and he is able to follow one of the two. As a result, all his actions have moral value. If he opts out of the moral choice, behaving like an animal, he will pay the price of his action in misery and perplexity."

We came to be by the will of Allah. We will in the end return to Allah. On the day of resurrection, Allah will question us as to what we did in our worldly life. Those who followed the course of Allah and the way revealed by Him, will later see the paradise of Allah. Disbelievers will end up in Hell:

> "And if as is sure come to you guidance from Me, whosoever follows my guidance, on them shall be no fear, nor shall they grieve. But those who reject faith and belie our signs, they shall be companions of the fire, and shall abide therein." (II: 38-39).

The duty of man of earth is to worship Allah:

> "I have only created jinns and men, that they may serve Me." (LI: 56).

The worship meant is the comprehensive worship already indicated, including not only specific acts of worship but everything that man does. Say:

> "Truly my prayer and my service of sacrifice, my life and my death, are (all) for God, the Cherisher of the world. No partner hath He." (VI: 163-164).

If fulfilled in accordance with Allah's purpose, every act becomes an act of worship. The course humanity should pursue is the course of Allah, since Allah is Lord and man is not; He is the Creator and man is not; Allah is Omniscient and man is not. Wherever man creates laws for himself, he sustains harm and introduces disorder and confusion into his life.

Man can only be truly free and truly equal, when he worships Allah alone, complying only with His Shari'ah. All man-made slogans of freedom and equality will remain illusions with no substance in reality, as long as some men remain the legislators or others.

Such a state of affairs would be consistent with the materialist theory of history. He who owns will be he who rules, while all other people will be his slaves. Feudalists become the rulers and peasants are condemned to servitude; capitalists rule and workers are the slaves; Communism rules, and all people become slaves of the state and are subject to it as their only source for sustenance.

But when Allah is ruler through compliance with Shari'ah, all people, the rulers and the ruled, will be in the servitude of Allah alone, equal in their servitude to Allah, therefore equal in freedom vis-a-vis each other, since all are bound by Shari'ah which has not been made by any of them, and none can alter it to defend his own interests at the expense of others.

When man finds this type of guidance on his journey, he will immediately discover the landmarks of the path ahead of him, and will follow this path. His soul then will not be thrown into confusion; his mind will not suffer bewilderment; his footsteps will be firm and steady.

Man should not demean himself. He is a being greatly honoured by Allah, and should not be humiliated or lose his dignity:

> "We have honoured the sons of Adam; provided them with transport on land and sea; given them for sustenance things good and pure; and conferred on them special favours above a great part of our creation." (XVII:70).

On the other hand, man should not imagine himself greater than he is and out of arrogance turn his back on the worship of God:

> "Nay, but man doth transgress all bounds. In that he looketh upon himself as self-sufficient. Verily, to the Lord is the return (of all)."(XCVI:6-8).

Man should not feel that life is an unrepeatable opportunity, a feeling that leads inevitably to over-indulgence in sensual pleasures. Rather he should avail himself of the reasonable share permitted by Allah, and realise that the excessive pleasure he is seeking without permission from Allah, and realise that the excessive pleasure he is seeking without permission from Allah is not good in itself. Allah did not prohibit this excess in order to torture man, but lest it might discourage him from attaining his ultimate aim, and degrade him from human dignity to the level of an animal.

Moreover, every excessive pleasure that man abandons in his worldly life in obedience to Allah, will be compensated for man if old and his return back to Allah. Man should play his role on this earth with clear vision and awareness. He should not build the world of matter while undermining the spiritual world, neither should he create material facilities as ends in themselves, neglecting the ultimate aims of human existence, which will only be attained by establishing divine justice on Earth, and will only be fulfilled by belief in Allah and by following His course.

It is by presenting this concept to humanity, after providing a true meaning of divinity and worship, the Islam gives humanity the guidance it needs instead of the present fumbling in the dark. We return now to a point raised earlier, namely the question of stability and change in human life.

Darwinism has had a immense influence over Western thought. It has suggested that there are no permanent elements in human life, or in any form of life, throughout the entire universe. To regard any value system such as morality or religion as permanent is, therefore, an unscientific way of thinking and a restriction on human life that should be eliminated.

When we think about it outside the context of local and particular conditions in Europe, and the ensuing conflicts between science, religion, learning and other human activities, we realise that it is the extremist rejection of the permanent values in human life that is unscientific, and that it is this which needs a careful scientific examination unconnected with emotional or historical factors.

The economic, political and social aspects of people's lives do change owing to the constant interaction between human reason and the Universe. This reaction constantly generates more knowledge of the mysteries of the Universe; knowledge which is put to use in harnessing its resources in the service of man. This is true. But what has this to do with constant values in human life? What has this to do, for example, with worshipping Allah?

The necessity of this worship is derived from the fact that Allah is the Creator and the Organiser of this Universe with all therein, including mankind. How does man's discovery of the properties of matter, splitting the atom and its molecule, or sending a rocket to the moon, stars or other planets change this necessary relationship?

The story of Prometheus and his rebellion against God when man learned more about the Universe and harnessed its resources, is a myth and not science. We should note, in the age of science, be dominanted by unscientific stories. To say that man knows himself and his requirements better than Allah is also an emotional statement which lacks the scientific spirit of enquiry.

This is a result of the situation in mediaeval Europe, when the clergy tyrannized on Earth in the name of God in a way that led people to abandon the God of the church in whose name tyranny was practised, and to invent another God—call it Nature or any other name—who had no church, no priests, and who put people under no kind of obligation.

These circumstances were peculiar to Europe and not universal realities or scientific facts. How can we, in the age of science, cling to a concept derived from a specific historical and geographical base, and turn it into a permanent and universal reality on which our life should be based?

The existence of values in the life of man is objective and derived from the fact that he has more than one course open to him; is able to choose and commit himself to a certain course. How this changed by man's discovery of the secrets of the Universe, or by his harnessing its resources?

The abolition of moral values from the life of man—which means a regression to the level of animals or machines—is based on an unscientific concept, presupposing absolute passivity on the part of man. This is true whether we are talking of the psychic determinism preached by Freud and psycho-analysis, or the economic determinism on which the materialist philosophy of history was based. Freud, for example, has not offered a shred of scientific evidence to proved the existence of the Oedipus complex on which his psychological determinism was based.

In the light of the economic determinism propounded by Marx, England should have been the first country in Europe to experience Communism. England is still not a communist state, while the biggest communist blocks in the world, Russia and China, have moved from feudalism to Communism.

The claim that moral values are not permanent, and that they should keep pace with material development, is based on a supposition incapable of scientific testing or proof, namely that innate entity of man develops with material development. There is no evidence of this. We talk, for food, water, clothes, shelter, sex, ownership of property and self-assertion, and we can say with all certainty that the forms of the these things have developed greatly with the passage of time.

However, who can say in a truly scientific sense, that their substance has changed as well? Moral values are concerned with substance, not form. Though the forms of human activity change, the moral values related to this activity are not changeable; they continue to determine, by virtue of their permanency, all the variable forms of human activity from one generation to another.

The permanency of values does not prevent change in form, nor do changes in form require any change in essence. Contemporary humanity went astray when it removed many things from the realm of permanence and pushed them into the realm of evolution without any valid scientific basis.

The most flagrant example of this was placing the issues of religion and morality within and evolutionary context and claiming that man's behaviour had nothing to do with morality. An illustration of this is the assertion that man's sexual behaviour remains outside the scope of morality since it is a purely biological function.

A strange claim, and stranger still to attribute it to the evolutionary process. Sex as a biological relation unrelated to morality had been for millions of years a fact in the world of animals. What kind of evolution is it which takes man millions of years back to the state of an animal and no more? What scientific spirit is this, Darwinism or other, upon which such a concept and its resulting behaviour can be based?

Islam provides us with a decisive judgment on this topic. It teaches us that human life should develop constantly—scientifically, politically, economically and socially but that in its continuous development it should not abandon the constant values derived from the permanent and unchanging facts related to Allah, in his creation of the Universe, life and man. Life based on this concept will be balanced in its movement. It will not become fixed at any one point, not will it set out irrationally on the path to its own destruction.

By providing humanity with these three major concepts—the unity of divinity and of worship, guidance throughout the human journey, the resolution of what is permanent and what is changeable in human life, Islam gives humanity a radical solution to the chief problem now leading to the disorder and confusion we are witnessing". Having fulfilled its primary mission by re-establishing the right concepts, Islam goes on to provide practical solutions to the problems of every day living. Unfortunately, there is no time to deal with these in detail in the present chapter.

FOUR

Various Aspects

In fact, Islamic concept of the fundamental rights has been elucidated by scholars to a great extent by the discussion of the Sovereignty of God, man's covenant of service to God, man's dignified position of vicegerency on earth, man's abiding by the code of conduct of life given by God, the accountability for one's deeds in the Hereafter and the abiding reward or punishment according to the good or bad record of these deeds. However, for further elucidation we are now going to take stock of it from historical, legal and moral aspects.

Historical Aspect

Looked at from the historical aspect the concept of fundamental rights in Islam is as old as man himself. The Creator and Master of man, just as He had supplied air, water, food, light and countless other necessities of life, He had also given him a code of conduct for his life right from the beginning of his life. The Quran furnishes a definite evidence of the fact that long before sending man on earth and honouring him with the envied position of vicegerency on earth, he had been given consciousness of rights and obligations, and with the bestowal of the means of life he had been taught the manner and behaviour in life. The first man coming to this world had started his life not in the darkness of ignorance but in the light of knowledge.

> And He taught Adam the names of all things.
>
> AI Qur'an 11:31

Here it has been said he was taught the names of all things which makes it evident that the knowledge given to man was not defective or incomplete. It was perfect. Man had been taught the names of all those things that he had to deal with in the life of this world. Teaching the names of things does not mean that an inventory of these things was given to him. Rather, every thing concerning their characteristics features, properties, beneficial and detrimental aspects, the way they were to be used and the nature of their relationship with man was fully explained. With the evolution of life, man through his fundamental knowledge, and his instinctive search and enquiry, went on extending the sphere of his knowledge of things, and it still continues. Maulana Maudoodi in his commentary of the Quran writes under this verse:

> "The only way man acquires knowledge is through a mental grasp of their names. So we can say all man's knowledge really comprises the names of things. Teaching Adam the names of these things was virtually imparting knowledge of all those things to him."
>
> Tafheem-al Quran Vol. l.p. 64.

This knowledge of things also essentially included the consciousness of his rights and obligations with relation to these things. That is why we find that during the life-time of Adam when for the first time the problem of -'right' cropped up, it also became evident along with it that man came to have respect for the rights not merely on the basis of his conjecture or intuition but according to the code of conduct given to him by God. Cain, one of the sons of Adam, when he threatened Abel his brother, with murder after the sacrifice offered by him was rejected, received the following answers from his brother thus threatened:

> If thou dost stretch thy hand against me, to slay me, it is not for me to stretch my hand against thee to slay thee: for I do fear God, the Cherisher of the worlds. For me, I intend to draw on thyself my sin as well as thine. For thou will be among the companions of Fire, and that is the reward of those who do wrong
>
> Al Quran V:28:29

His words amply bear out the fact that Abel had full knowledge of God's injunctions regarding respect for human life. He knew well it was a sinful deed, and the perpetrator of this crime would be consigned to Hell. He lost his life for fear of God but did not lift his hand against his brother.

The code of conduct as regards rights and obligations given to Adam in the context of man's relation with God, the servants of God and other creatives, was given to mankind in various ages and regions of the world through the messengers of God from Adam to Muhammad for their guidance. But in every age it was according to the problems and needs of the times, as human society evolved fresh explanations, elucidations and relative commandments. As the sphere of human relations became wider, there were also rules and regulations revealed to strengthen until by the time of the last prophet, Muhammad (Sal'am) this arrangement of education and training had reached its stage of perfection, and it was proclaimed:

> This day have I perfected your religion for you, completed My favour upon you and have chosen Islam as your religion.
>
> Al Quran V:3

This religion, which was perfected when it came to the Prophet Muhammad, had covered long periods of history before that. Let us trace its history with the help of the Quran:

> God did choose Adam and Noah, the family of Abraham and the family of Imran, above all people; offspring one of the other.
>
> Al Quran III-34

That is to say, the system of guidance for mankind, starting from Adam, continued without break through different messengers of God one after the other. The Quran tells us that it was not only that the revealed guidance continued without break but the more important fact is that all the prophets of God called humanity each in his own time, to the same faith without any basic difference. Their mission was the same and they followed and propagated the same code of conduct for human life. And that code of conduct or the way of life was not their own invention, but conferred on them by the Sovereign Who appointed them to the high office of apostleship.

> The same religion has He established for you as that which He enjoined on Noah that which We have sent by inspiration to Thee and that which We enjoined on Moses, and Jesus: namely that you should remain steadfast in Religion (establish the Religion of Allah. Tr.) and make no divisions therein:
>
> Al Quran: 13

This religion was not limited to the reform of beliefs only, but extended from the reform of beliefs to setting right all the affairs of human life, and had detailed instructions for every department of life.

> And We ordained law for him in the Tablets in all matters both commanding and explaining all things, (and said): Take and hold these with firmness, and enjoin thy people to hold fast by the best in the precepts.
>
> Al Quran VII: 145

Now let us hear in legal terms about the rights and obligations, what was this Religion and what were its details:

> And remember We took a covenant from the children of Israel (to this effect) ; Worship none but God; treat with kindness your parents and kindred, and orphans and those in need; speak fair to the people; be steadfast in (establish) prayers; and practise regular charity (Zakat). Then did ye turn back, except a few among you, and ye backslide (even now). And remember We took your covenant (to this effect); Shed no blood amongst you, nor turn out your own people from your homes:
>
> Al Quran 11:83-84

In the same Surah (II) pointing out the revealed commandments and instruction regarding the individual's relations with the rest of the world, it was said:

> Those who break God's Covenant after it is ratified, and who sunder what God has ordered to be joined, and do mischief on earth: cause loss (only) to themselves.
>
> Al Quran 11:27

The same thing has been repeated at another place in these words:

> But those who break the covenant of God, after having plighted their word there to, and cut asunder those things that God has commanded to be joined, and work mischief in the London them is the curse; for them is the terrible Home!
>
> Al Quran X111;226

Explaining these relationships Maulana Maudoodi writes:

> These people sunder those relationships on whose establishment and strengthening depend the collective and individual prosperity, and those that God commanded to be joined. In this short sentence there is such a vast store of meaning that it covers the entire range of man's cultural and moral relationships from that between two individuals to universal international relations of nations. Cutting asunder the relations does not mean only sundering human relationships but all those forms of (unnatural or natural) relations, besides those right and approved by God fall under them since the consequences of unapproved (prohibited) and wrong relation is no different from that of sundering the right ones the corruption of relations between man and the moral and cultural system.
>
> Tafheem-al-Quran Vol.1, p 60-61

This history of the human rights presented by the Quran furnishes definite proof of the fact that the concept of fundamental rights in Islam exists from the time the first man was born. And this also makes it clear what the source of these rights is. They did not come into existence as a result of the mutual bickerings and strife between man and the rulers of the state formed by him and the treaties and contracts made between them. They are **not the** result of the mental exercises of some philosopher or political thinker or legal expert either. Rather they were the endowment of the Creator of man and the true sovereign of His subjects, and are essentially associated with man and his life on earth. They had been determined simultaneously with the creation of man. They have finally been elucidated in the Shariah brought by Muhammad (Sal'am). These rights transcend the limits of time and space. If man were to take off from this abode of his, the earth, and select the moon or some other heavenly satellite, the nature of these rights shall not change. Just as the change of time and space did not bring about any change in his physical build and his natural necessities, the eternal nature of these rights and obligations shall not change either. These rights are absolutely unchangeable and inalienable. The function of the state is not the determination of these rights but their enforcement only.

The westerners assert that the history of the fundamental rights is three or four centuries old. And whatever they have acquired with great pains and after serious struggle, the whole world is being benefitted by it. But the history presented by the Quran before us proves that the day the first man set foot on this earth the fundamental rights formed part of his feeling and consciousness. And their acquirement was not his own achievement but the Sovereign Himself had conferred these rights on him by degrees. Wherever there is an echo of these rights heard, it was the reflection of the inspired teachings that had awakened the consciousness of the basic rights.

In Norman Cousins' book *In God we Trust* published in New York, in 1958, throwing light on the religious beliefs of the Founding Fathers of the American constitution in detail, it has been stated that Benjamin Franklin, George Washington, John Adams, Thomas Jefferson, James Madison, Allexender Hamilton, Saveel Adam, John Jay and Thomas Paine were one and all firm believers in the teachings of Christianity, and their thought was deeply impressed by the beliefs. James Madison defining "Right" says:

> Whatever rights man enjoys is an obligation, a duty of other men enjoined by God. (p. 17).

Similarly, if the British and French constitutions are studied in their proper religious perspective, there too, the real source of the Fundamental Rights can be traced to the religious teachings particularly, the powerful impact of Islam on Europe.

Looked at through the mirror of the history presented by the Quran, Islam alone has the right to use the terms Natural Rights and Birth Rights, since the ambiguity relating to these rights found in the western concept of them, is totally absent here. Islam presents a definite answer to the question who determined these rights, when the western supporters of the theory of Natural Rights could not satisfactorily answer the question raised by Bentham and other critics, what they meant by nature, and which is that authority determining these rights. In other words they wanted to know exactly' what was the sanction behind these rights. Islam presenting the "Natural" and "By Birth" aspects of the rights, in great details, left no room for any such objections.

Legal Aspect

Now let us examine the legal aspect of these rights. A common mistake made in all such surveys is that we keep the western concept of the fundamental rights as the norm before us. We select and prepare a list of all such rights from the Quran as came up to the western norm and are in keeping with its limited sphere of application. The logical result of this trend of thought is that the Islamic concept of rights takes a secondary position and its true features do not come out fully in view.

In the west the sphere of the fundamental rights is confined to the relations between the individual and the state. There the rights conferred on an individual by the state armed with very extensive powers, are regarded as basic. Their nature is defensive and protective, and their basic aim is to protect the helpless citizen from the fully authoritative ruler, oppression and tyranny. The constitution incorporating them shows the individual and the state as parties (opponents) and the position of the constitution becomes that of a compromise between the two, in which the limits of the recognized powers for one and those of the recognized rights for the other are determined. As against this in Islam, the common people and the rulers of their state are not parties at cross purposes with each other. Neither the rights of the citizen have been recognized by the rulers nor the powers of the state have been recognized by the citizens. There is no constitutional document either, between them, prepared with mutual consent and consensus, in which the limits of the rights and powers have been determined as desired. Both these are bound on equal terms by an oath of allegiance to their Lord and Cherisher and true Sovereign. As vicegerents on earth their position is the same (no superiority for either), since vicegerency was not conferred on any individual or a group but on the Muslim Ummah as a whole.

> God has promised, to those among you who believe and work righteous deeds, that He will of a surety grant them in the land inheritence (of power), as He granted to those before them:
>
> Al Quran XX1V:55

This verse amply reveals that the delegated authority vested in man as vicegerent on earth is meant for the Muslims as a whole. That is why Abu Bakr, the first caliph of the Prophet had refused to be called "vicegerent of God", since vicegerency had been conferred on the Ummah as a whole and not on him as an individual. His vicegerency lay in that the Muslim Ummah by free option of their own hand delegated these powers of vicegerency to him. It was in view of this concept of the authority of the caliph that Umar, the second caliph of the Prophet, approved of the title "Amir-al-Mumineeri" (the person conducting the affairs of the state on behalf of the believers with the powers delegated to him by them). And this term remained in voguc in late times also.

The Amir of the believers and the citizens living within the limits of his Emirate, are bound in their respective spheres by the limits prescribed by Allah. Their powers and rights are not mutually recognized but determined by the Sovereig Himself. Both of them are bound to live according to the dictates of the unchangeable and irrevocable constitution based on the Quran and the Sunnah, not even one article of which is negotiable. There is no clash between their rights and powers. These two are such transgential circles which can never cross each other.

Viewed in this perspective the sphere of the fundamental rights in the Islamic State is very extensive. Like the general run of the constitutions of the world this is not confined to the mutual relations of the individual and the state. The sphere of application of the Quranic constitution extends over the entire life of man. The Quranic injunctions are not limited to the relations of the individual and the state but has so regulated the countless relations in the fields of beliefs, devotional acts, morals, social life, culture, economy, polity, judiciary, war and peace and other departments of life, that there is very little left for the state in the sphere of legislation. And even in this limited field, legislation at will cannot be allowed, but is conditioned that every law must conform to the dictates of the Quran and the Sunnah and their general spirit.

Legislation in the Islamic state is a rare thing not a daily occurance. The laws of Islam are not passed in a heated assembly by men who ardently desire the legislation in their interest, against men who oppose it for the same reasons. The laws of Islam are firmly based on the Shariah and are therefore in the interest of people as a whole.

Now the rights reserved for the individual by the Divine Law and the Sunnah of the prophet, in as much as they are part of the constitution, above the legislative powers of the state and attainable through the judiciary are one and all without exception, fundamental rights. These rights do not comprise protection of the life, honour, property, attainments of justice, equality, freedom of expression and freedom of belief, alone but from the terms of suckling a new born babe to the right of a woman to her dower are all included in them as determined by God and His Apostle, and which are inviolable. The Quran has used the term the "limits prescribed by Allah" for the limitations set on man's powers of the legislation. These limits apply both to the individual as well as the state. Whatever Allah has approved for man and allowed him to benefit by it, neither an individual nor the Islamic state nor even the Ummah as a whole can make it prohibited. In connection with these limits prescribed by God, the Quran gives us the following instructions. In the Surah Baqrah (II) after enjoining the relevant commandments, Allah says:

> Those are limits (set by) God: approach not might there to.
>
> Al Quran II:187

Pointing out the characteristics' of the believers Allah says:

> Those that turn (to God) in repentance; that serve Him, and praise Him; that wander in devotion to the cause of God: that bow down and prostrate themselves in prayer: that enjoin good and forbid evil; and observe the limits set by God.
>
> Al Quran IX: 112

The Quran has said in most clear terms that man has no right of legislation where a law given by God exists. Nor has he any right to declare any thing lawful forbidden. All that is required of him is .to obey God and His Apostle:

> Follow (O men!) the revelation given unto you from your Lord and follow not, as friends or protectors, other than Him.
>
> Al Quran V1I:3

> If any fail to judge by (the light of) what God hath revealed they are (no better than). . . . unbelievers. . . .wrong doers. . . . those who rebel.
>
> Al Quran V:47-48-50

> O ye who believe! make not unlawful the good things which God hath made lawful for you, but commit no excess:
>
> Al Quran V:90

> Say: See ye what things God hath sent down to you for sustenance? Yet ye hold forbidden (some things) lawful. Say: Hath God permitted you.
>
> Al Quran X:59

> But say not—for any false things that your tongues may put forth, "This is lawful, and this is forbidden," so as to ascribe false things to God.
>
> Al Quran XVI: 116

Allah did not only put restrictions on legislation by the common people, but did not allow even His Apostle to make any changes where a Divine Law existed:

> Say: "It is not for me, of my own accord, to change it: I follow naught but what is revealed unto me: if I were to disobey my Lord, I should myself fear the Penalty of a Great Day (to come)."
>
> Al Quran X: 15

So when the Prophet took a vow not to taste honey any more to humour certain wives of his. God took serious notice of it;

> O Prophet! why boldest thou to be forbidden that which God has made lawful to thee? Thou seekest to please thy consorts.
>
> Al Quran LXXV1:1

The Prophet had not declared honey forbidden for the Muslims. He could not even think of declaring forbidden what God had made lawful for them. He had himself decided to abstain from it. But since any act of his could become an argument for the Muslims, the error of this decision of his was pointed out to him, that he had no right to declare forbidden even for himself some thing that was made lawful by God.

On the one side this is the state of affairs of the Prophets powers in matters pertaining to God's commandments. But on the other side the Quran also makes it evident that where no injunctions from God exist on any particular issue or the Divine injunction needs elucidation and explanation the opinion of the Prophet is decisive and final. And it will be regarded equivalent to God's injunctions. Since the Prophet is the manifestation of God's political and legal sovereignty his interpretative and legislative position was defined saying:

> He who obeys the Apostle, obeys God:
>
> Al Quran IV:80

> So take what the Apostle, assigns to you, and deny yourself that which he withholds from you.
>
> Al Quran IIX:7

Keeping in view this position of the Quran and the Sunnah if a list of fundamental human rights based on the Quran and the Sunnah is prepared in an Islamic state, it will comprise all those rights that have been determined by god and his Apostle, no matter which department of life they belong to.

What other difference is there between fundamental rights and legal rights than the fact that the former are unchangeable by any measure except through an extraordinary process provided in the constitution itself. They can be attained through the judiciary, and with its help and support, the executive can be kept back from oppression and tyranny. As against this, the legal rights fall in the sphere of usual legislation (common law) and can be amended or cancelled by the state through its legislative powers.

The Difference

Keeping in view this difference between the fundamental and legal rights it is noteworthy that no right conferred by Quran and the Sunnah can be kept out of the list of the fundamental rights, which is beyond the legislative powers of the state, which can be attained through judiciary and in connection with which the Quran and the Sunnah themselves have not conferred on the state any extraordinary powers with which it (the state) can usurp, limit or suspend it under pretext of extraordinary circumstances of emergency. Their exclusion from this life cannot be accepted on the plea that the westerners recognize as fundamental only those rights that concern mutual relation of the individual and the state. This argument can be brought forward only in favour of following the west, but has no weight in the light of the well known legal term fundamental rights and the sense it conveys. The right which enjoys a permanent and eternal position, which the state is unable to change or cancel and is attainable through the judiciary, must of necessity be deemed a fundamental right by any interpretation of law.

If a woman is divorced when she is suckling a baby, the Quran lays down the following code of conduct of rights and obligations between the baby, the divorced mother and her husband:

> The mothers shall give suck to their offspring for two whole years, if the father desires to complete the term. But he shall bear the cost of their food and clothing on equitable terms. No soul shall have a burden, on it .greater than it can bear. No mother, shall be treated unfairly on account of her child. Nor father on account of his child, an heir shall be chargeable in the same way. If they both decide on weaning, by mutual consent, ani' after due consultation, there is no blame on them. If ye decide on a foster-mother for your offspring, there is no blame on you, provided ye pay (the mother) what ye offered, on equitable terms.
>
> Al Quran 11:233

The rights determined for a new barn baby, its mother and father, come under the fundamental rights, since they form part of the constitution of the state, have been determined by the .Sovereign, are attainable through the judiciary, and the state cannot frame any regulation in this matter digressing from the Divine dispensation. The term appointed by the Quran for the suckling of the baby cannot be reduced or increased by the state even by a day. The position of this right of the babe can be gauged by an incident during the time of the Prophet.

> A certain woman, Ghamidiyah by name, came to the Prophet and confessed her guilt of adultery repeatedly (four times it is aid), stating that she was pregnant and wished to be cleansed of this fifth of her sin through stoning to death. The Prophet said to her, "If you insist on your confession, go now and come after delivering the babe". When she returned once again with a babe in her arm, repeating her request to be cleansed, the Prophet told her to suckle the baby and come after weaning. When she came back after weaning the babe, she had brought a piece of bread along, to demonstrate that the suckling period was over and the babe could now subsist on solid food. Thus assured, the Prophet arranged for the care of the child then ordered that she be stoned to death.
>
> Tafheem-al-Quran Vol III.p.336.

This incident reveals that the Prophet postponed the limit set by God in the form of her execution, on the first occasion to save a life, and on the second occasion to allow the full term of the suckling of a baby appointed by God, and ordered it only when he was fully satisfied that the baby had been weaned and could now subsist on food other than mother's milk. Two fundamental rights were involved in this case that of the preservation of life, and the other that of the completion of the period of suckling appointed by God. The Prophet through deferring the enforcement of the punishment of a heinous crime like adultery, made it evident that under the Islamic order, not to speak of a citizen, the rights of even an unborn babe and a suckling one cannot be ignored or tampered with. The pronouncement of the Prophet in this case is a legal precedent, and in such a case the Islamic state can never overlook or override it. That is to say, its legislative power is bound to follow this decision of the Prophet. And it is this restriction which brings the right of a babe to be born and to be suckled for definite period, under the fundamental rights.

Yet another right is determined by this decision of the Prophet's court. The child born out of wedlock shall be deemed innocent, and the Islamic state along with the enforcement of the limit set by God on the parents for their prime, shall arrange for the care and upbringing of the child. That is tantamount to allowing a child, along with the right to be born and to be suckled (for two years), the right of maintenance also. And also that he (or she) shall not be looked down upon but shall enjoy the same position with other normal children.

Now take another right which is usually placed in the sphere of moral rights, but is in reality a fundamental right, as determined by God and His Apostle. God says:

> And that ye be kind to parents. Whether one or both of them attain old age in thy life say not to them a word of contempt, nor repel them, but address them in terms of honour And, out of kindness lower to them the wing of humility, and say: "My Lord! bestow on them thy Mercy even as they cherished me in childhood."
>
> Al Quran XVII:23-24

On the basis of this verse, we now present two decisions, of the Prophet's court which have served as important precedents:

1. Somebody brought case against his parents to the court of the Prophet. He told him that both he and his wealth were his father's. Then the Prophet instructed his father to benefit by his son's 'wealth and in case of resistance he should approach him (the Prophet, and he will be helped against his son.
2. Someone complained to the Prophet of Go-I that his father demanded (his share) of his (son's) wealth. The Prophet asked him to comply and pay him his due. He further explained that his father wanted that he (the son) should surrender every thing he had in his (father's) favour. The Prophet ordered him to do as he (the father) wished. The reporter of this case goes on to say that the Prophet advised the son not to disobey (and displease) his parents. If they demanded that he should leave this world for them, he must comply with their orders.

In the light of the Divine Injunction and the decisions of the Prophet's court, the legists have determined the rights of the parents in great detail, which is proof enough of the fact that this (kind treatment of the parents) is not a mere moral recommendation but a fundamental right which no (Islamic) government can change through exercise of its legislative powers. It cannot give the offspring the liberty of shirking their responsibility of the support and maintenance of the parents.

Now let us take up the case of dower. It is the wife's right that her husband owes to her according to the contract of the marriage. This right of the wife has been determined by the Quran:

> And give the women (on marriage) their dower as a free gift; but if they, of their own good pleasure, remit any part of it to you, take it and enjoy it with right good cheer.
>
> Al Quran IV:4

> Seeing that ye derive benefit from them, give them their dowers at least) as prescribed.
>
> Al Quran IV:24

That is to say, the Quran has declared dower a right of the woman which a husband must pay at all costs. And also that it a woman, of her own free will, were to surrender this right (in part or full), the Islamic state has no right to cancel or even limit it through legislation. So when Umar, the second Caliph, during his period wanted to limit the right of woman's dower and said in his harangue:

"Do not exceed forty Oqiah; An old weight equivalent to 40 drachms. The drachm itself was an old Greek weight equivalent to 3.071 gm. So an Oqiah comes to our present day weight of 122.84 'Umar wanted to bring down the dower of women to 40 Oqiah of silver which would weigh 4913.6 grams, and at the present day market rate of Rs. 40 per 10 gms of silver, even this lowly dower cost a husband Rs. 19,654.00 or about Rs. 20.000/- Tr. of silver in the payment of dower to women. Those who pay more I shall take the excess of his wealth for Bait-al-Mal (the public treasury)."

Immediately on hearing this a tall woman got up and said in a loud tone: "You have no right to do that". And on Umar's asking her to explain her assertion, she said in reply that God had said otherwise in the Quran:

> Even if ye had given her a whole treasure for dower, take not the least bit of it back: would ye take it by slander and a manifest wrong ?
>
> Al Quran IV;20

Umar on hearing this argument said, "The woman is right, the man was in the wrong."

And with that remarks he took back his verdict. The moment his attention was invited to the injunction of the Quran, he desisted from limiting that right. This incident is proof of the fact that in the Islamic state even the right of a woman to her dower is a fundamental right, and it (the state) has no right to cancel, limit or suspend it.

Similarly, all those rights relating to Qisas (life for life and equal for equal), blood money, alimony, inheritance, will, marriage and divorce and matters relating to penalties and fighting, that have been determined by the Quran and the Sunnah of the Prophet. It is not only that the Islamic state has no right to amend these rights but because of the injunction of the Sovereign, it is bound to enforce them. Here these rights are not of a defensive and protective nature, but positive rights, and it is the responsibility of the state to ensure their enforcement exercising all its powers and using all its resources in this work.

The state will have the right to legislate only relating to those matters where the Shariah has not given any injunction. For example, the modern state of today can legislate in keeping with the Islamic principle of legislation in connection with elections, the procedure of the legislative and other assemblies, internal and foreign trade, business transactions, public services like railways, electrical energy, transport, gas, water supply, housing, education, industry, wages, welfare of the government and other servants, workers and peasants and such other matters. The rights determined by these laws shall be called legal rights. These laws shall be framed according to the changing time and space problems and the nature of the conditions and resources. They shall differ from country to country and the change of times, and the resulting rights must also differ due to the difference in laws. For example, the laws relating to acquirement of citizenships can be different in Pakistan and Turkey. But where the rights determined by the Quran and the Sunnah are concerned they are eternal, universal and all-pervasive, transcending time and space, inalienable, outside the sphere of the authority of the state. And wherever in the world an Islamic state comes into existence it is bound to enforce them in toto and as such these rights shall be placed under the "Fundamental Rights".

Here a very pertinent question can be raised that this interpretation of the fundamental rights can be acceptable to the believers only, but can those, who do not believe in God, the Quran and the Day of Reckoning, accept it. What will be their fundamental rights then? Is there going to be any difference between their fundamental rights and those of the Believers?

To answer this pertinent question it is necessary that we try to fully understand the position of non-Muslims in the Islamic State. The Islamic, unlike other states to the world is not a national state. The government there is not normed by any particular nation, race or a linguistic or regional group, so much so that the right of sovereignty does not belong to the Muslims. This is an ideological state. It's Sovereign and Ruler is God Himself. He has fully stated in the Quran through very evident commandments and instructions to tell us about the type of the society He wants to bring into existence on this globe of ours. He has, through His Apostle (Muhammad Sal'am) also presented practically a pattern of His Sovereignty. The government of the Muslims which is termed "Caliphate", is a government through delegated powers that is bound to run the state according to the dictates and limits set by the true Sovereign. The status of the citizens of the Islamic state has two aspects—one as human being and another as Muslims or non-Muslims. The first status is determined by their birth and the other on the basis of belief or unbelief as a result of their own free option. In their capacity as human beings they are all equal in every respect. All distinctions of colour, race, region and tongue are baseless. They have not the least importance in the sight of God. He says:

> He created you (all) from a single Person.
>
> Al Quran XXXIX

In the first verse of Surah Al-Nisa (iv) it has been said:

> O mankind! revergence your Guardian-Lord, Who created you from a single Person, created, of like nature, his mate, and from them twain scattered (like seeds) countless men and women,

At another place it has been said:

> Verily, this Brotherhood of yours is a single Brotherhood, and;
>
> I am your Lord and Cherisher: therefore serve Me (and no other)
>
> Al Quran XXI:92

In the sight of God mankind in its entirety is a single Ummah. Since He is the Creator of them, Muslims and non-Muslims, is their Master and Sustainer in the matter of the rights of all His human creatures. He has conferred equal status. He has enjoined on us (Muslims) the protection of the life, property and honour and dignity of the non-Muslims just as the protection of those of the Muslims. And after declaring this equality on the basis of creation. He divides human being on the basis of their attitude and behaviour, for which they themselves are responsible, into two groups:

> Mankind was one single nation, and God sent Messengers with glad tidings and warnings.
>
> Al Quran 11:213.

> Mankind was but one nation, but differed (later).
>
> Al Quran X:19

That means, the brotherhood of mankind got divided due to its own disobedience and rebellion, some of them, for faking Allah's religion, invented some new creeds for themselves, which resulted in further divisions and sub-divisions of one Ummah. To bring mankind once again to unite by taking to the Religion of Allah, Messengers were sent by God. But due to their own wickedness, they failed to come to this unity. The Divine Message in the form of the Quran is even today calling humanity to unity and integration thus becoming single Ummah. The Quran was not revealed to the guidance of any particular nation and territory but for the guidance of entire humanity. And in the same way, Muhammad (Sal'am), the Apostle of God, was not commissioned as "Mercy to the believers" but as "Mercy for the worlds" (We sent thee not but as a Mercy for all creatures or people.—Al Quran XXI 107 Tr). The rights determined by the Quran for those believing in God and His Apostle are meant for the entire humanity. The message of the Quran is that every one should become a servant of Allah (by total submission to His Will) and should come to deserve their rights, and benefiting by them should live an honourable life in this world. Muslim is not the title of any race or a nation but of all those people believing in Allah's Religion. That is why a person in any part of the world of any colour or race, immediately on declaring his belief in and entering the fold of Islam, becomes entitled to all those rights conferred on the believers by God that born Muslims, through generations, enjoy. Now it is evidently against common sense and most illogical that those recognizing God as their true Sovereign, and the Quran as their code of conduct in life and their constitution, be placed on a par with those rejecting both. Do America, Britain, Russia or any other country make no distinction among those loyal to their constitution and those rejecting it? Such rejectors would not even be allowed to live in those countries. Rather, they would be declared rebels and hanged or exiled. Why then expect the Islamic state to recognize the right of those not recognizing its sovereign and constitution to be included among those who do, and give them equal rights with them? Which of the legal or moral code keeps the rebel on a par with the loyal? This confusion is created by the secular trend of thought and erroneously taking Islam to be a religion having nothing to do with the affairs of the state. But after recognizing God as Sovereign of the state and the Quran and the Sunnah its constitution, there is no room left for this absurd question why Muslims and non-Muslims are not guaranteed the same status in an Islamic state and why the believers in God and those rejecting Him or His sovereignty are not brought on a par?

This aspect of Islam that it not only allows those in rebellion against God and traitors to live within the boundaries of its state in peace and tranquility but in the matters of human rights puts them on a par with the believers. Difference between the loyalists and the infidels lies in that the Muslims on account of their recognizing the political sovereignty of God have been made responsible for its enforcement, when the non-Muslims not recognizing this sovereignty, due to their own rejection of it, have been kept out of it. If they come to believe in God, they would automatically be entitled to the highest post in this set up. But as long as they insist on their rejection of Him, how can Sovereign allow them to participate in the responsibilities of enforcing His injunctions and instructions. He says:

> Is then the man who believes no better than the man who is rebellious and wicked? Not equal are they.
>
> Al Quran XXXII: 18

In another verse it has been said:

> O ye who believe! Take not into your intimacy those outside your ranks; they will not fail to corrupt you. They only desire ruin.
>
> Al Quran 111:118

In a preceding verse of the same Surah it has been said:

> Let not the Believers take for friends or helpers unbelievers rather than Believers:
>
> Al Quran 111:28

The same warning is repeated once again with greater emphasis;

> O ye who believe! Take not for protectors your fathers or your brothers if they love infidelity above Faith: If any of you do so they do wrong.
>
> Al Quran IX:23

Line of Demarcation

This line of demarcation between the believers and unbelievers was drawn by the Sovereign Himself, and does not involve any territorial, national or religious prejudices on the part of the believers. It is their earnest desire, rather they have been commissioned in this world by the Sovereign to take His Message to every one of His servants that he should rid himself of all sorts of bondage by entering the fold of Islam, and share all those rights that have been granted to the believers. Unlike the westerners their trend of thought is not that the world should accept their religion but need not share their political ascendancy and authority. Here is a glimpse of the Muslim trend of thought in connection with the un-believers: Rabi'ah bin'Amir, a companion of the Prophet, addressing Rustam the Persian governor and his courtiers, before the batter or battle of Qadisiyah, said:

> We have been commissioned by God to rid all those servant of His as are anxious to be free men, from, the bondage of men like themselves, and take them away from narrowness of this world to the vast expanse of the life Hereafter and from the excesses of religions to the shade of Justice and Equity under Islam.

If despite this Message of goodwill and glad tidings, an individual or a group persists with its rejection, they themselves are determined to live as Zimmis: literally one living under protection. As a technical term of the Islamic Shariah' the unbeliever who does not accept Islam but is willing to submit to its ideals being enforced in the Muslim state saving only his personal liberty of conscience as regards themselves. Jizya or a kind of poll-tax was levied on- them. There was no amount fixed for it, and in any case, it was symbolical acknowledgment that those whose religion was tolerated would in their turn not interfere with the preaching and progress of Islam. The tax varied in amount and there were exemptions for the poor, for females and the children (according to theorist Abu Hanifa for slaves and monks and hermits. Being a tax on able bodied Zimmis males of military age, it was in a sense a commutation for the military service, when the believers fought in the way of Allah and could be called to arms at a very short notice, and paid Zakat regularly. Moreover, the taxes on Muslims can be enhanced or fresh taxes levied in a national emergency, but not those once levied on Zimmis. However, there should be no misunderstanding that Zimmis have been assigned any lower or secondary position as compared with the believers. As a matter of fact just the reverse is the case. First of all let us consider the word Zimmis itself. It signified those persons safeguards for whose life, property, honour and dignity have been guaranteed. The Islamic state normally takes upon itself the responsibility of the protection of every citizen. But a special term was adopted in connection with non-Muslims in which the element of protection is outstanding. In their case protection and care have been assigned special importance. And it was not a put-up show to impress the world, but the injunctions of God and the Prophet are in fact to this effect. We have quoted above the Quranic verses strictly forbidding Muslims to take into confidence the unbelievers to keep out of harm's way. But here is the other side of the picture. In the matter of justice, emphasizing equality for one and all. God says:

> O ye who believe! Stand out firmly for God, as waitresses to fair dealing, and let not the hatred of others to you make you swerve to wrong and depart from justice. Be just: That is next to piety: and fear God. For God is well-acquainted with all that ye do.
>
> AI Quran V:9

> O ye who believe! Stand out firmly for justice, as witnesses to God, even as against yourselves, or your parents or your kin;
>
> Al Quran IV: 131

A certain member of the Bani Zafar tribe from Ansars, Ta'mah by name, stole the steel armour belonging to another person from Ansars. And to save himself from the punishment of stealing, he entrusted it to the custody of a Jew, and also charged him with theft. His tribe also with one voice, levelled the charge of theft against the Jew and in presenting the case to the Prophet insisted that the Jew be denied the right of his defence on the ground that Ta'mah was a believer and the Jew a polytheist. But before the Prophet could pronounce his judgement after hearing the case. God revealed the true position of the case to him. In a severe warning to the believer bringing a false charge against the Jew, God said in His revelation to the Prophet:

> We have sent down to thee the Book in truth, that thou mightiest judge between men, as guided by God: so be not (used) as an advocate by those who betray their trust. But seek the forgiveness of God; for God is oft-forgiving, Most Merciful. Contend not on behalf of such as betray their own souls; for God loveth not one given to perfidy and crime; they may hide (their crimes) from men, but they cannot hide (them) from God, seeing that He is in their midst when they plot by night, in words that He cannot approve: and God doth compass round all that they do. Ah! these are the sort of men on whose behalf ye may contend in this world; but who will

> contend with God on their behalf on the Day of Reckoning, or who will carry their affairs through! If anyone does evil or wrongs his own soul but afterwards seeks God's forgiveness, he will find God Oft-forgiving, Most Merciful. And if any one earns sin, he earns it against his own soul: for God is full of knowledge and wisdom. But if any one earns a fault or a sin and throws it on to one that is innocent, he carries (on himself both) a falsehood and a flagrant sin. But for the Grace of God to thee and His Mercy, a party of them would certainly have plotted to lead thee astray. But in fact they will lead their own souls astray, and to thee they can do no harm in the least. For God hath sent down to thee the Book and Wisdom and taught thee what thou knowest not before: and great is the Grace of God unto thee.
>
> Al Quran IV: 105-113.

This topic continues and we are told that there is no good in the secrets of people. These verses give us an idea what a heinous sin it is to charge an innocent person even if he is a non-Muslim and to mete him out punishment for a crime that he never committed, and how by intervening through revelation He managed the honourable acquittal of a Jew against a Muslim and all his supporters.

Now let us see what the Apostle of God has to say about the Zimmis:

> Beware! Whoever wrongs a Zimmi, curtails his rights, or puts him to more and harder work than he is capable of, or takes something from him against his consent, I shall personally stand as a complainant against him on the Day of Reckoning.
>
> Abu Daood-Kitab-al-Jehad.

The Prophet never said this about the oppressed Muslims that he would stand up to put their case in the Divine court of justice on the Day of Reckoning. But about the Zimmis he said that if they were oppressed by the Muslims he would be a complainant on their (Zimmi's) behalf. Now it is noteworthy that no Muslim worth the name could even think of oppressing those whose cause the Apostle of God would champion in the Hereafter.

During the period of Abu Bakr's caliphate, the teeth of a woman, who sang satiric verses about Muslims, were extracted as punishment for her highly objectionable activity. When the caliph learnt about it he wrote to his governor, Muhajir bin Ummayyah:

> I have been given to understand that you got two front (ubcusir Tr.) teeth of the woman who ridiculed Muslims in her satiric verses that she went about singing. If such a guilty woman be a believer, serious reprimanding her would be enough and corporal punishment should not be meted out or her disfigurement. But in case of her being a Zimmi woman, what weight does her satire of Muslims carry when we are putting up with their most heinous crime of polytheism. . If only 1 had cautioned you about it earlier, you would have been brought to book for that lapse.

The second caliph, Umar even during death pangs, had the problem of the treatment meted out to the Zimmis, upper most in his thoughts. Almost exhausted as a result of ghastly wounds and profuse bleeding he leaves sound advice for his successor:

"I strongly recommend to my successor in the office of caliphate that those whom the Prophet pledged protection, must be treated sympathetically to honour his pledge to them. They should be protected from harm and they should not be burdened with mor than what they can easily bear."

Not only during the period of the Prophet and the rightly guided caliphs but also during the Umayyid and Abbasid dynasties as well as the Muslim rulers of later days, the protection provided to the non-Muslim minorities with regard to their lives, property and honour and dignity has been recognized by the westerners also. The famous orientalist Montgomery Watt writes:

> In the matter of the benevolent treatment meted out to the non-Muslims the Muslim states have, on the whole, the best record. Benevolent treatment to the non-Muslims was a matter of honour and pride to them. During the

> period of the rightly guided caliphs the protection of the non-Muslim minority paid annual tribute or Jizya in the form of goods or cash according to the agreement. The same amount had to be paid by them in the form of taxes per head. In return for this they were provided protection from foreign aggression and the internal security enjoyed by the Muslims. In those provinces where Zimmis lived, it was the duty of the government to realize Jizya from them and settle the disputes between them and the Muslims. Every minority was perfectly autonomous in their internal affairs. Their religious leader was responsible for the realization of Jizya and it was he who looked after all their internal affairs including the enforcement of their religious laws.

The same author further informs his readers:

> Definite guarantees were provided in all the agreements arrived at during the period of the Prophet of God, that every Zimmi minority would enjoy perfect freedom in its religious affairs. And this freedom was maintained during the later period also. The Christian churches and the Jewish synagogues were projected. Later it was suggested that they should not be allowed to build more places of worship than they already had, but in connection with the Zimmis, this and such other suggested rules and regulations (not included in the earliest agreements) were not put into practice.

This is the position of the Zimmis in an Islamic State. We are going to present in detail the commandments and precedents with regard to the rights of the Zimmis in the following pages; here it was our aim to define the attitude of the Muslim state in connection with them.

Now, where equality of the status of the Muslims and the non-Muslims is concerned, we have the verdict of the Quran before us that the believers and the rejectors are not equal. They are certainly equal with them in as much as they have the common bond of humanity between them, and as human beings they enjoy the same rights that their Muslim compatriots do. And they are equal in this respect too that the rights of both the Muslims and the non-Muslims have been determined by God and His Apostle. Just as the rights of the Muslims are inalienable and irrevocable, so are those of the non-Muslims. If the state cannot tamper with the rights of the Muslims, it cannot amend or cancel the rights of the non-Muslims either. If the Muslims can attain their rights through the judiciary by putting forth the edicts of the Quran and the Sunnah and the precedents of the rightly guided caliphate, the non-Muslims too have the guarantee of attaining their's with reference to the same sources. During the Fatimite regime when some governors wanted to lay hands on the properties of some Christian monks and Jews of Sinai and levied some fresh taxes on them, they approached the government at the centre and presented the documents of the agreements of the past and obtained the court decrees in their favour from Bahram, the vizier of Abdul Majeed Al Hafiz, and Al-Abbas and Talaqi, the viziers of Al-Zafar, in which the governors were directed to respect the old agreements and to strictly abide by the decisions of the rightly guided caliphate. Simultaneously, orders were issued that all new taxes be abolished with immediate effect and the Christians and the Jews be protected and well looked after.

Such examples are found during the Abbasid dynasty and even later period are proof enough of the fact that against the state both Muslims and non-Muslims stand equally protected. And this protection has been provided by Him Whose Entity and Sovereignty the Zimmis do not recognise.

Notwithstanding equality of status from the legal aspect, there is yet a difference between the fundamental rights of the Muslims and non-Muslims. And this difference lies in their political rights. And the reason behind it is neither any discrimination nor religious prejudice, but the peculiar nature of their attitude in the matter of loyalty to the Sovereignty of the Islamic state. The non-Muslims do not recognize the political order of Islam, based on the Sovereignty of God and depending for its constitution on the Quran and the Sunnah, and do not take that oath of allegiance to it which the Muslims do. Since a Muslim believing in God makes a covenant with Him that he will establish His political sovereignty on earth and that he will not only not recognize the sovereignty of any ones else but will efface it even at the cost of his own life, he comes to share the delegated powers conferred by God. Any individual of mankind who makes his covenant with God and takes an oath of allegiance, automatically comes to share these delegated powers. But one who is not prepared to shoulder this responsibility and rejects the sovereignty of God outright, how could he be called to share this authority.

Can any authority delegate its power to an individual or a group that does not recognize its entity and authority? Not withstanding this difference between the Muslims and non-Muslims in principle, Islam has not totally deprived the non-Muslims of the political rights. However, they are not qualified for appointment to the key posts in a Muslim state for which they do not fulfil the essential conditions of taking oath or allegiance to the constitution and its enforcement. In view of this position of non-Muslims, the fundamental rights in a Muslim state will have to be divided into three categories:

1. Those common to the Muslims and non-Muslims.
2. The Relative fundamental rights of the Muslims.
3. The Relative fundamental rights of the non- Muslims.

Among these, the first list will be longest, since God has attached utmost importance to the position of man because of birth. The other two lists shall comprise the rights that accrue to man as a Muslim or a non-Muslim.

Moral Aspect

After taking stock of the history of fundamental rights in Islam and their legal position, let us now take up the moral aspect of these rights. We call only these rights legal which come under the Positive Law, and are enforcible by the executive and attainable through the judiciary, for example the security of life and property and liberty of organization and assembly, and such other rights. But those that are beyond the sphere of the authority of the executive and the judiciary and their enforcement has been left to the conscience and intuition of man, are all moral rights, for example visiting the sick to enquire after their health, aid and support of the needy, entertaining the guests and kind treatment of the neighbours, and the like. That means at the back of the legal rights there exists sanction of the law or the authority of the state, but the enforcement of the moral rights depends on the inner condition of man. Imam Ghazali defining morality, says:

"Morality is the hidden form of the innerself."

Since this inner form of man is beyond the grasp of physical observation and transcends the limited circle of man's knowledge and consciousness., the law did not include it in its sphere of action. Legislation and enforcement of law end at the apparent and observable acts of man. But it has nothing to do with the inner motives behind these acts and the ideas, beliefs and tendencies and leanings that take part in shaping and building the intellectual life of an individual. These things can come up for discussion under morality. And the determination of the human rights under this head is not the job of the legislators but the moral teachers. Maulana Hifzur-Rehman of Seohara, explaining the application of the legal and moral spheres, says:

> The positive law is applicable to the observable acts, but the moral law keeps an eye on acts and the motivating forces behind them, and is applicable to both, so much so that some of those acts which apparently bear good results, the verdict of the moral law on them is that of mischievous, because the motive behind is unhealthy. The positive law is enforced through external forces like officials, army, police, the constitution of the state, jails and modern methods of reform. But the moral law is enforced by the hidden force of the inner self or intuition. The positive law compels the individuals only to the extent of those obligations on which depends the survival of the collection or society, like the protection of and respect for the life and property and other things of that sort. But the moral law compels man to take to virtue and excellence as well as obligations at the same time. And it makes men used to it that their efforts should be on the path of virtue, and as far as possible they should

> strive to attain the highest position they can, on this path."

Our legists, in view of this difference between law and morality, draw a line of demarcation between the legal and moral position of the rights. Allama Syed Sulaiman Nadvi, explaining the Rights due to God and those due to man, says;

> The relation between the Creator and the creatures or God and His servants if related to mental exercise and the state of his heart, it is belief or "creed". And if our body and soul and our goods and property are also involved in this relation, it is service or "worship". The relations between man and man, and man and other creatures, also impose on us certain obligations, which if only legal in nature, are "dealings". But, in case they are not legal but spiritual teachings and instructions, it is "morality."

The same classification of legal and moral is met within the books on jurisprudence. But one important aspect of it is usually overlooked, or divorced from its real context, it is placed under some other head. And that is why the mutual relation between the legal and moral rights fails to be fully explained. According to the general run of the legal and moral principles in the world, this division is in order. But in view of the Sovereignty of God and the position of man as vicegerent on earth, the nature of this classification is entirely changed in Islam. Here legal and moral rights have been determined under the commandment of the one and only Sovereign, and as such the difference here is not that of the law framed by a legislative authority and the moral principles presented by a moral teacher. They do not differ even in the matter of being an enforceable and incapable of enforcement. A Muslim under the covenant with his Lord and Cherisher binds himself to total obedience of God and His Apostle.

> Say: Truly, my prayer and my service of Sacrifice, my life and my death, are (all) for God, the Cherisher of the World.
>
> Al Quran VI: 162.

On the one hand this covenant of loyalty on the part of the servant and on the other the following declaration by God:

> God hath purchased of the Believers their persons and their goods; for theirs (in return) is the Garden (of Paradise):
>
> Al Quran IX : 111

After this covenant and mutual agreement where is the room left for a believer to discriminate between the legal and moral laws and adopt different attitudes towards them. To him every edict of the Quran is a law by itself. He obeys every order of God with equal sense of responsibility. To him legal rights alone are not due and binding, but all those rights coming under morality are equally due and binding. The moral code of conduct ends on establishing a norm of good and evil. Its enforcement is left to the conscience of man, and is voluntary in nature, and nobody is accountable for it in any way. The greatest sanction that can be afforded to it is in any form of social pressure. However, a revolt against it is neither a congnizable offence nor punishable in any court of law. Is this the plight of moral rights under Islam too? Evidently enough the answer is in the negative. The Muslim has to account for every tiny particle without any distinction of legal or moral.

> Then shall any one who has done an atom's weight of good see it! And anyone who has done an atom's weight of evil, shall see it.
>
> Al Quran XCIX : 7-8

When such is the case, why do the jurists classify on the basis of moral and legal bases? On what basis do they make this distinction?

This difference, in Islam, lies in this that individually every Muslim is bound to obey every injunction of his Lord and this duty is of a legal nature since he has to account for every act of his before the Sovereign and it is on the basis of these acts that reward or punishment will be decided for him in His court of justice. There he cannot put up the excuse that, where his own life and his powers were concerned, he was unable to abide by the laws given by God and render his due to Him. But an Amir or Imam has been made responsible for the enforcement of only those rights which he can enforce with the help of his limited knowledge, and understanding and observation based on his senses. These are the rights known as "legal". That amounts to saying that the classification has been undertaken from the point of view of the powers of the government, and not from that of the responsibility and accountability of an individual. For the individual all the rights have a legal position. But considering the limitations of the authority and the responsibilities of the Amir or Imam they get divided into legal and moral. The minimum rights which God has deemed inevitable for making the human society balanced, just, peaceful and prosperous and decent. He made them enforceable through His delegated authority. And in this connection he also gave him the necessary instructions and powers. Those rights which He deemed essential for the building up of the society on the highest moral foundations and the best formation of the individuals' characters for this purpose. He made the individuals singly responsible for their enforcement. And accountability in this behalf He reserved exclusively for Himself. Now, to the extent of the enforcement of the legal rights, the individual and the society both together will be held accountable and punishable in the court of sovereign. But the rights that have been kept out of the sphere of the authority of the state, the individual will still be accountable for them, and to this extent there will be no difference between the legal and the moral rights.

That is to say, in the sphere of the mutual relations of the individual and the delegated authority, the rights on the basis of their observable expression and enforcement, they shall be divided into the legal and moral limits. But where it comes to mutual relations of God and His servant, this division disappears, and all the rights come to have a legal position. To ensure enforcement of the legal rights, God has entrusted them to the state so that if an individual fails in his duty concerning these rights, the state with the powers of the executive and the judiciary may enforce them under compulsion, and let no deserving individual suffer usurpation or injury to his rights. But since the state can discharge this duty only to the extent of observable conduct of people, it was not charged with the legal responsibility of the enforcement of the moral rights. But with the individual it persists. He has not been given the slightest allowance in the matter of enforcing the moral rights however petty in appearance.

Where the government is concerned, it cannot but depend on the statements of the plaintiff, the defendant and the witnesses and the report of the police instead of relying on its direct knowledge, in adjudicating a dispute. All the means of information at its command can encompass the external conduct, having no access whatsoever to the inner self of any person. So in view of these frailties of human beings, the government run by them has been made responsible for the enforcement of the legal rights concerning the external conduct. And even in connection with these rights absolute and final justice has been reserved by God His own court on the Day of Reckoning, since it is possible that in spite of honesty and the best of intentions, due to lack of access to the true facts some of those charged with authority might have failed in dispensing justice. Even the Prophet of God who was the most knowledgeable among men, says about himself:

I am (after all) human. Among those appearing before me for the settlement of their disputes, one party may be more clamorous and clever at exaggeration than the other, and I may decide the case in his favour taking him to be truthful. So if I give somebody what really belongs to his brother, he should not take portion of Hell-fire.

God says:

> They know but the outer (things) in the life of this world:
> but of the End of things they are heedless.
>
> Al Quran XXX:7

Umar, the second caliph, explaining the sphere of action of the government run by men, says:

> During the Prophet's time the Divine revelation always came out with the truth and kept you in your places.
>
> If any one concealed any thing he was exposed and the one who revealed anything against the truth, was also

> caught. You must exhibit the best in you of morality. God knows what is in your breasts. Whoever shows evil on the outside and claims a wholesome innerself, we shall not verify it. And whoever shows a good exterior we shall take him to be good.

In another tradition the same theme is met with in these words:

> Hark ye! When reciting the Quran look only for the reward from Allah, and show it in your deeds. When the revelation was current, we could recognize you through that mirror, since the Prophet of God was amongst us then. Now the revelation has come to an end and the Prophet has left. Now I can recognize you through only those things (norms) I have told you. Hark! Whoever shows goodness we shall take him to be good and form a good opinion of him. And whoever shows evil, he shall be in our bad books and we shall detest him (for evil deeds).

That amounts to saying that even those rights that we term legal, can be enforced only to the extent of human knowledge and perception. They will be finally decided in the Divine Court. That is why Allah Himself kept all those rights that needed for their enforcement knowledge beyond the ken of senses and observation of the innerself, beyond man's limited powers and authority. And making man bound individually for them He has reserved the decision for Himself, since the innerself which is not accessible to human perception is open before God. There are no secrets that are hidden from Him. With His perfect and infallible knowledge He will decide all disputes over rights. And there will be no distinction of moral and legal there (in His court of Justice). He says:

> Know they not that God knoweth what they conceal and what they reveal.
>
> Al Quran II: 77

> But never will they hide a single fact from God.
>
> Al Quran IV:42

For God is witness of all things.

Al Quran XXII: 17

God knoweth well all the secrets of the heart.

Al Quran :119

Since man's motives, aspirations, intentions, thoughts beliefs, in short, nothing is hidden from Him, man's exterior and innerself are clearly before Him, in His court no right shall remain merely "moral right", but all the rights shall be legal rights, and they will be decided according to all the known legal procedures. He will listen to all the wronged ones.

When the female (infant), buried alive, is questioned for what crime she was killed.

Al Quran LXXXI:8-9

He will examine the reports prepared by the guardian angels:

But verily over you (axe appointed angels) to protect you, kind and honourable, all that ye do. Al Quran LXXXII: 10-12

He will call in evidence the tract of land on which a certain incident occurred:

On that Day will she (the earth) declare her tidings. Al Quran XCIX:4

He will give hearing to the statement of the culprit and also the evidence of his own hands and feet:

On the day when their tongues, their feet will bear witness against them as to their actions.

Al Quran XXIV:24

After taking evidence of the prophets and other witnesses He will furnish undeniable proof that -truth had been conveyed to them:

The Prophets and the witnesses will be brought forward:

Al Quran XXXIX:69

And finally the culprit himself will confess that he had been guilty of the crime on his record:

> They will say: Yes indeed: a Warrer did come to us, but we rejected him and said, 'God never sent down any (Messenger)'.
>
> Al Quran LXVII;9

And after they have been convincingly indicted. He will pronounce His Judgement:

> And a just decision pronounced between them; and they will not be wronged (in the least). And to every soul will be paid in full (the fruit) of its deeds; and (God) knoweth best all that they do.
>
> Al Quran XXXIX:69-70

Now just imagine, on what basis the rights that are to come up in the greatest and final court of Justice for decision according to all the known conditions of dispensation of justice, can be termed "moral rights". It is also noteworthy how mutually the moral rights will be examined at the time of hearing in this court. The Quran says:

> When a courteous greeting is offered you, meet it with a greeting still more courteous, or (at least) of equal courtesy. God takes careful account of all things.
>
> Al Quran IV:86

The concluding portion of this verse clearly points to the fact that this is not mere moral recommendation but an injunction, a regulation, and the defaulters shall be called to account in the court of the Sovereign. It is very difficult for a court in this world to determine whether the courteous greeting offered was met with properly or not. So they were not charged with the responsibility of the enforcement of this moral right. But in the court of the Sovereign, the tongue and the hands and the feet themselves shall bear witness whether that method was proper or not, and the heart also shall furnish evidence whether it was full of sincerity or brimming over with the filth of contempt, malice and enmity.

Now let us take up the right in some detail from the Quran and the Sunnah:

> Say: "Come, I will rehearse what God hath (really) prohibited you from": join not anything as equal with

> Him; be good to your parents: kill not your children on a plea of want; We provide sustenance for you and for them; come not nigh shameful deeds, whether open or secret; take not life, which God hath made sacred except by way of justice and law: Thus doth He command you, that ye may learn wisdom. And come not nigh to the orphan's property, except to improve it, until he attain the age of full strength: give measure and weight with (full) justice... no burden do. We place on any soul, but that which it can bear; whenever ye speak, speak justly, even if a near relative is concerned: and fulfil the covenant of God: thus doth He command you that ye may remember. Verily, this is My Way, leading straight: follow it: follow not (other) paths: they will scatter you about from His great path; thus doth He command you, that ye may be righteous.
>
> Al Quran VI: 151-153

All those beliefs and deeds are those for which accountability before God is certain. The sphere of the powers and the scope of hearing of this court (of God) has been fully brought out in Surah Zilzal. (The convulsion-XCIX):

> Then shall anyone who has done an atom's weight of good, shall see it ! And any one who has done an atom's weight of evil, shall see it.
>
> Al Quran XCIX:7—8

Pondering over these verses (VL151-153), we find that polytheism, kind treatment to parents, killing of children, shameful deeds, respect for human life, misappropriation of the property of orphan, honesty in measure and weight, speaking the truth, the covenant of God and following His Straight Path— all these instructions in succession are being given with equal emphasis.

The first and foremost right stressed here is that of God and it is that we must not take other gods, with Him. Ascribing partners to God is a sin absolutely unpardonable. The Quran pronounces that verdict:

> God 'forgiveth not that Partners should be set up with Him; but He forgiveth any thing else, to whom He pleases, to set up partners with God is to devise a sin most heinous indeed.
>
> Al Quran IV:48

In the enforcement of this greatest of rights, the courts and the governments of this world can exercise their power only to the extent of the observable conduct. So when Umar, the second caliph of the Prophet, learnt that people came and offered prayers beneath the tree in whose shade the Prophet had taken the covenant of the Believers (Bai'at-e-Rizwan at Hudaibiyah), he smelt polytheism in this attitude of people and had it felled leaving no trace of it, and remarked:

> O ye people ! I find that you have started worshipping the god Uzza Hark ! After today I would not tolerate anyone coming this way to offer, prayers. If ever I learn of any one doing it I will have' him executed, just as the apostates are executed.

But where things are not as apparent as that, and Uzza, Lat and Manat have found their way to the deepest recesses of the hearts and are snugly seated there who is going to stop and put an end to such polytheism. And if eradication of such hidden heatheism is not possible for any government, will this right of God be deemed a mere "moral right" and be consigned a secondary position to a "legal right". Never! This right is of primary importance according to the covenant between man and God which is the sacred duty of every man, and the rest of the legal and moral rights entirely depend on the recognition and enforcement of this first and foremost right. This is that one right which when neglected and shirked God did not wait for the Day of Reckoning to settle accounts with the criminals and meted out such horrible punishments to them that served as a warning and an admonition to others.

> Say: Travel through the earth and see what was the End of those before (you): Most of them worshipped others besides God.
>
> Al Quran XXX; 42

That is to say when the people as a whole were bent on taking gods other than God and did not listen to the Prophets of God that were commissioned to ask them to desist from their heathenic beliefs and practices and to enforce the commandments of God, He took the command directly in His Own hands and bringing down upon them the scourage of punishment for their evil deeds wiped them off from the face of the earth.

Since the perfect enforcement of this right is totally beyond the powers of man and those of the highest executive or judicial institution founded by him, it will be recognized as a legal right in so far as its external manifestations are concerned. But from the point of view of belief and faith, it will be regarded as a legal right in the society. However, in the court of God this will be the first legal right about which people will be questioned. And that leaves no room for a believer to regard it only as a "moral right."

This was about polytheism, the most heinous crime in the sight of God. But the Prophet of God tells us that every right, no-matter what its significance in our sight, has the same importance. The Prophet says:

> Seest thou one who denies the Judgement (to come)? Then such is the (man) who repulses the orphan (with harshness), and encourages not the feeding of the indigent. So woe to the worshippers who are neglectful of their Prayers, those who (want but) to be seen (of men) but refuse to supply even neighbourly needs.
>
> Al Quran CVII: 1—7

Harsh treatment of the orphan, refusing food to the indigent, are all crimes of a moral nature. But those guilty of them are being given warning and illtidings of ruination in the Hereafter, and told to take heed and not to regard them unimportant; it is on their performance in these fields that their ruination or their salvation and felicity depend. Let us now take another example:

> Ann do good to parents, kinsfolk, orphans, those in need, neighbours, who are near, neighbours who are strangers, the companion by your side, the way-farer (ye meet), and what your right hands possess: for God

> loveth not the arrogant, the vainglorious; (nor) those who are niggardly or enjoin niggardliness on others, or hide the bounties which God has bestowed on them; for we have prepared for those who resist Faith, a Punishment that steeps them in contempt; nor those who spend of their substance, to be seen of men, but have no faith in God and the Last Day: if any take the Evil one for their intimate, what a dreadful intimate he is! And what burden were it on them if they had faith in God and in the Last Day, and they spend out of what God hath given them for sustenance? For God, hath full knowledge of them. God is never unjust in the least degree: if there is any good (done). He doubleth it, and giveth from His Own presence a great reward. Now then if we brought from each people a witness, and we brought thee as a witness against these people! On that day those who reject Faith and disobey the Apostle, will wish that the earth were made one with them but never will they hide a single fact from God;
>
> Al Quran IV:36-42

All these verses relate to the "Moral Rights." But ponder a little over those beginning from "God is never unjust in the least degree" to the end, are all those rights for which we will be called to account, and rewards and punishments pronounced on them, witnesses will be called to furnish evidence, and when there is no flaw left in the legal process, pronouncement will be made on the case.

Here the servants of God have been addressed directly. And the rights pointed out here are such as do not permit division into the legal and the moral. Due to the expressed will of the Sovereign, they are all legal in nature. On what basis can we discriminate between one and another of the rights conferred by the Sovereign as legal and moral? What justification is there for such (arbitrary) classification? At the most what can be said about them is that these rights are beyond the grasp of the state. But are they also beyond the grasp of the Sovereign? If it is not so, how could we be free in either living up to them or neglecting them at our own discretion. And when this freedom is non-existent and not leaving it to our conscience and intention, they have been made obligatory, how can they be regarded as moral rights. They are one and all legal rights. Only this reason that they do not permit the intervention of the state due to its limitations of powers, does not in any way make any difference in their being the injunctions of the Sovereign. Even if we somehow manage to escape from the grip of the human courts and executives, how can we save ourselves from the accountability of the Sovereign's own court?

From among the human beings too, those chosen ones elevated to the highest position conferred on man by God, and who are not dominated by the human sovereignty of limited knowledge and powers, but directly under the sovereignty of the All-knowing and Well-acquainted Sovereign, with them even in this world all moral rights are treated as legal rights in the method of enforcement. So we find that the Prophet who stood at an exalted standard of character by the Grace of his Lord (And thou (standest) on an exalted standard of character—Al Quran LXVIIL4), when on one occasion, while conveying the message of God to the tribal chiefs in a select gathering, on the (untimely) interruption by a blind companion of his, Ibne-Umme-Maktoom, showed signs of disapproval, God at once took serious notice of it and said in a rather admonitory tone:

> (The Prophet) frowned and turned away; because there came to him (interrupting). But what could tell thee but that perchance he might grow (in spiritual understanding)?—Or that he might receive admonition, and the teaching might profit him? As to one who regards himself self-sufficient, to him dost thou attend: though, it is not Thee if he grow not (in spiritual understanding), and but as to him who came to thee striving earnestly, and with fear in his heart, of him wast thou unmindful.
>
> Al Quran LXXX:1-10

Since God had a direct contact with his Apostle through revelation, for the perfect enforcement of a moral right, he was called to account here in this world. But the procedure for the common people is different. Here they are under the domination of a delegated authority, which has been made responsible for the enforcement of legal rights only because of its limited knowledge and information. But when all of them will be there in the presence of their Lord and Cherisher, directly, without any intermediary, the distinction of the moral and legal rights shall have ended and there will be equal accountability for every right.

The discussion so far must have made it quite clear how important is morality in Islam. And how much different are the rights we call moral rights in their sense from the moral rights of the common political terminology of the modern secular world, and how in the final court of justice, the legal and moral rights acquire the same status.

If this position of the rights in the life Hereafter is kept in view, man can develop the highest moral character, and he obeys every divine commandment, not under any external pressure or compelling force but under the urge of his inner self and sense of responsibility, without any hesitation or reserve and with perfect readiness of mind and with a heart full of fear of God, never dividing these commandments into legal and moral spheres. This classification had really to be made with a view to define the limits of the powers of the state, and not to compel man to perfect compliance with same commandments of God and to permit some allowance or indulgence in the case of some others. In the commandments of God conveyed through the Quran all the instructions in connection with beliefs, devotional acts, dealings and moral issues are often met with in the same continuation, intermingled with one another in such a way that there is no room for making any distinction between the external and the inner aspects of man's conduct. The Quran does not split man into an "external man" and an "inner man", but addresses him as an "undivided person" whose mental, physical, emotional and spiritual life is an integrated unity and totality. That is why it was said:

> O ye who believe! Enter into Islam whole-heartedly:
>
> Al Quran 11:208

Explaining this verse Maulana Syed Abul A'la Maudoodi says'

> Which is the same as to say submit your life in its entirety without any exceptions or reserves. Your ideas, your opinions, your disciplines, your manners and habits, your dealings and the course of your action and struggle, must all be made subservient to Islam. Take heed, lest you should divide your life into various compartments, subordinating some to Islam and keeping others away from its sway.
>
> Tafheem al Quran, Vol.I.p.160.

Allah wants total obedience of the whole person. To the extent this obedience was deemed essential for the prosperity and well-being of the individual and collective life and to check confusion and chaos in the human society, it was managed and ensured through laws and the powers of the state to enforce them. But in the life Hereafer the salvation and felicity everlasting shall be decided on the basis of "moral law", since beliefs, devotional acts and the excellence of deeds all come under this law. Viewed from this angle, moral laws and moral rights in Islam have a superiority over the "legal rights", since the code of the Divine court will be that in which the moral aspect has priority and importance. There, the quality of our faith and belief and the sincerity of devotional acts and the inner aspect of our observable acts shall be determined by the "moral laws" alone. Here in this earthly life it is just possible that a person despite his hypocrisy, may pass as a Muslim due to his apparent conduct, and may go on all his life deriving all the benefits of rights, from the Muslims that Islam has conferred on them. But after death his case shall not be decided on the external form of his deeds but on the basis of his inner self, and exactly in accordance with the following unambiguous decision of the Quran:

> For God will collect the Hypocrites and those who defy Faith —all in Hell.
>
> Al Quran IV;140

And in Hell they will be assigned the lowest depths:

> The hypocrites will be in the lowest depths of the Fire: no helper will thou find for them:
>
> Al Quran. IV: 145

This is the unhappy end of those who had offered prayers observed fasts, participated in the Hajj and Jihad (or striving in the way of Allah,) and were found busy in the remembrance of God. But what was the condition of their hearts:

> The Hypocrites—they think they are over-reaching God, but He will over-reach: when they stand up to prayer, they stand without earnestness, to be seen of men, but little do they hold God in remembrance; (they are) distracted in mind even in the midst of it,—being sincerely for neither one group nor another.
>
> Al Quran IV: 142-143

The hypocrites on account of this inner state of theirs, which is entirely of a moral nature, will be the recipients of the severest punishment from God and their observable conduct and deeds which gave them all the rights in this world, will be of no avail to them there, although it was due to these apparent .deeds here in this world that the Prophet of God did not decide that they were unbelievers and never stopped the leaders of the hypocrites like Abdullah bin-e-Ubai, because of their lip service to Islam and showy deeds, from entering and moving about freely among the ranks of the believers.

In the whole of the Quran and particularly in the verses dealing with the Last Day, God has made the inner life of man as the basis of His decisions, which clearly brings out the fact that our salvation depends on what we call "morality." There, not deeds alone (of any sort) but "righteous deeds," shall be our real assets, and this condition of "righteousness" which is here a purely moral issue, will be entirely legal.

The superiority of morality over law can be estimated by a tradition of the Prophet in which he has pointed out that the real mission of his teaching and preaching was for the purpose of perfecting morality. He says:

> I have been commissioned for perfection of morality.
>
> Musnad-e-Ahmad, Baihaqi, Ibn-e-Sa'd

And this is that morality which is supported by the accountability of the Hereafter and its great power of enforcement.

Explaining this relation of law and morality Maulana Mufti Muhammad Shaft says:

> One of the distinctions of Islam is this that, looked at from a wider perspective, its moral instructions are also legal injunctions, since it is on their basis that the reward and the punishment of the Hereafter are to be decided which is of fundamental importance in the life of a Muslim. This creed of the life Hereafter is that which has not only conferred on morality the status of law, but provided support to those, technically termed laws. If you think over the style of the Quran you will, find that with every legal and moral injunction are associated reminders of the concepts of fear of God and provisions for the life Hereafter.

All Rights are God's

After this much understanding of the mutual relation of the legal and moral rights, we shall now take stock of the moral aspect of the rights. Our legists have classified rights in another way under the heading, the "Rights of God" and the "Rights of His Servants." According to this classification, the belief and the devotional acts like Prayers, Fasting and Hajj and such other practices are the rights of God. And all those rights which are mutually due from the servants of God to their brethren are the rights of the servants of God or men, such as security of life and the rights of inheritance, dower and alimony and the like. Some rights are common to both. For example, Zakat being service to God involving man's goods, is a right of God and from a consideration of those deserving (help with) it, it is a right of the servants of God. Similarly, sacrifice which is a right of God inasmuchas it is an offering of life to Him but in relation to the giving away of the hide and the flesh of the animal to the deserving men it is also a right of the servants of God.

But the way the difference of moral and legal rights disappears in the life of a Muslim and in the court of God and all the rights, likewise the division of the rights of God and those of the servants of God ends in the final analysis, and the rights all come to belong to God and from the moral point of view attain that highest position which they are not assigned in any legal order and any moral code of the world.

This classification of the rights of God and the rights of men was meant to determine the direction of the fulfillment of these rights. In other words the rights whose recipient is God they fall under the heading rights of God. And those whose recipient are men are included in the list of the rights of the servants of God. But pondering over the fundamental question of the legal and moral position and justification for them, we have to determine whether man came to deserve these rights on grounds of some struggle or his accepted demands or they have been determined by any social contract, an agreement on the basis of consensus between the people and the government, a constitution framed by man or an agreement between man and man. If there is no such thing, what is the basis for these rights of his. Apparently enough, the only basis for it is the injunction of the Sovereign. It is He Who has determined the rights of every deserving one, and decided the priorities between the rights of these deserving people. About Zakat He says:

> Alms (Zakat Tr.) are for the poor and the needy and those employed to administer the (funds); for those whose hearts have been (recently) reconciled (to truth); for those in bondage and in debt; In the cause of God; and for the way-farer: (thus is) ordained by God, and God is full of knowledge and wisdom.
>
> Al Quran 1X:6Q.

Here, along with pointing out those deserving Zakat, priorities among them have been determined and concluding, it has been said that these rights have been determined by God and their fulfillment has also been ordered by Him. If any one is guilty of a lapse in the matter of these rights he must be aware that none of his deeds is hidden from God.

Similarly, after detailing the rights of various inheritors it has been said.

> These are settled portions ordained by God: and God is All knowing, All wise.
>
> Al Quran 1V:11.

Following this verse the inheritors' portions have been determined and this serial too ends with the following verse:

> Thus it is ordained by God: and God is All-Knowing forbearing.
>
> All Quran IV:12

After detailed injunctions regarding which women are allowed to the believers and which not, it is said:

Thus hath God ordained (prohibitions) against you: (and it is binding on you to observe them).

And after determining the rights of men and women in connection with divorce. Allah says:

> These are the limits ordained by God; so do not transgress them If any do transgress the limits ordained by God, such person wrong (themselves as well as others,) Al Quran 11:229

In connection with rust and Justice it is ordained:

> God doth command you to render back the Trusts to those to whom they are due; and when ye judge between man, and man that ye judge with justice
>
> Al Quran IV:58

The rights of the needy, those who asked and those who failed to get their due, are determined in the wealth of the rich.

> And in their wealth and possessions the right of the (needy) him who asked and him who for some reason was prevented from asking.
>
> Al Quran 1.1:19

In short, taking any one from the rights of God, or those of His servants, and studying the relevant verses of the Quran and every right takes its sanction from the Divine injunction, and its fulfillment has also been ordained by Him .

God did not only determine the rights, but placed Himself as the recipient of every right, so that the person charged with the fulfillment of it may realise that he is offering it not to any one else but to God All mighty Himself. He says:

> Eat of their fruit in their season, but render the dues that are proper (God's share, Tr.) on the day that the harvest is gathered.
>
> Al Quran VI:41

Here, while ordaining the share of His servants in yield of fruit, God associated that share with Himself to bring home to man that whatever he gives to his servants is really His right that He will be fulfilling. He also takes upon Himself the reward for such fulfillment and says:

> So give what is due to kindred, the needy, and the way-farer. This is best for those who seek the countenance of God, and it is they who will prosper.
>
> Al Quran XXX:38.

That means, you may be paying the dues of God or those due to men, the motivating force is the same, and that is obedience to God and seeking His countenance, and through its reward acquiring the facility everlasting. A Muslim offering greeting to his Muslim brother in all sincerity and with love, the motive behind it is never to derive any benefit from him, but through carrying out an order of God he is looking forward to seek His pleasure. And when he is paying out Zakat and Sadqat (charities), he has this end in view. In the collective system of the payment of Zakat, he does not know whom he is going to benefit with his share of Zakat. He entrusts it to the Islamic state as his due to Allah, which in turn spends it on the deserving servants of God. This was the relation in vein between God's and man's rights which prompted Abu Bakr, the first caliph of the Prophet, to declare war in the way of Allah against those who refused to pay Zakat after the passing away of the Prophet. The tribes with holding payment of Zakat were those who subscribed to Islam in all departments, established the (system of) Prayer and were believers in the unity of Allah and the Prophethood of His Apostle.

They had only withheld their goods from the deserving servants of God, thus denying a right ordained by Him. On this occasion many of the Prophet's companions, including even Umar, the great undaunted champion of the Islamic cause and well versed in the finer points of the temperaments of the Faith of God, had expressed his opinion thus:

We should not lake up arms against those who believe in God and His Apostle, but asking them to join hands with us, we should tackle the problem of the apostates with all the forces at our command.

The dialogue between Abu Bakr, the caliph in saddle, and Umar who became his successor, makes it quite evident that the former made no distinction between the rights of God and those of His servants, while 'Umar' was making such distinction, but was finally in agreement with the latter. When after consulting the companions of the Prophet on this issue, Abu Bakr made the forceful assertion:

By Allah! If those refusing to pay Zakat withhold even a rope that they paid during the period of the Prophet, I will wage war against them.

On hearing this Hazrat 'Umar' who was of the opinion that 'fighting against those refusing to pay Zakat was not in the interest of the Muslims, hatted up a bit and said;

> How can we wage war against them when we know that the Prophet of God has definitely told us that he had been ordered to fight against people only so long as they had not pronounced 'There is no god but God and Muhammad is His servant and Apostle." And one who had once announced his belief in this Kalimah, security of his life and property would be the concern of the Muslims, whatever was due from him would be demanded of him. About his intentions only God would call him to account.

Abu-Bakr was not satisfied with the arguments of Umar and said:

> By God! I must fight against those who regard Zakat any the less important than Prayer, since Zakat is the right in goods and the Prophet had said that those entering the fold of Islam shall have to pay all that is due from them.

Umar used to say later:

> Abu Bakr's reply convinced me that Allah Himself had conferred clarity of vision on the issue of those refusing to pay Zakat. And the Truth was with Abu Bakr.

> This incident reveals the important position of the right of His servants determined by Allah, and how it is realizable like the rights of Allah. Refusal to comply with the demand in this connection is tantamount to disobeying Allah Himself. The Quran says:

> Reverence God through Whom ye demand your mutual (rights), and reverence the woman (that bore you): for God ever watches over you. Al Quran IV: I.

Immediately following this verse there is the long series of the rights of the orphans, women, men, the needy, the inheritors and other servants of God. But it has been made very clear in the beginning that every one's right gets its sanction from God, and He is ever watching over you. So fear Him and duly fulfil the rights, or you shall be taken to task in the Hereafter.

> To offer a goodly loan is to help a brother in need. But this loan God has taken upon Himself instead of the person helped, and has promised to repay it with manifold increase and also forgive your sins in return for it:

> If ye loan to God a beautiful loan. He will double it to your (credit), and He will grant you Forgiveness:
>
> Al Quran LI V: 17

At another place it has been said.

> And establish regular Prayer and give regular charity (Zakat); and loan to God a beautiful loan.
>
> Al Quran LXX1II:20

Similarly take the case of spending in the way of Allah. God declares the monetary help offered to any servant of His in need as "spending in the way of Allah", Himself becomes its recipient and promises the best return for it:

Those who spend their substance in the cause of God, and follow not up their gifts with reminder of their generosity or with injury, for them their reward is with their Lord: On them shall be no fear, nor shall they grieve.

Al Quran 11:261

The same thing has been repeated in LVII:10, 18 and 11:272 and in many other verses of the Quran. If a person enters into an agreement with another, written or oral, and brings in Allah as witness, that agreement he makes with Allah, and He watches over the actions of both the parties involved in it for the protection of their rights.

And break not your oaths after ye have confirmed them; indeed you have made God your surety; for God knoweth all that ye do.

AlQuranXVI:91

Similarly, plighting fealty at the hands of the Prophet was declared to be the same as plighting fealty to God:

Verily those who plight their fealty to thee do no less than plight their fealty to God: The Hand of God is over their hands.

Al Quran XLVIIL-10

The great exegetist of the Quran, Abdullah bin-Masood says:

Whenever somebody gives charity (Sadqah), before finding its way to the hands of the needy who asks for it, it touches the hands of Allah and it is He Who remits it to him. Then he recited the following verse:

Know they not that God doth accept repentances from His votaries and receives their gifts of charity.

Al Quran IX: 14

A study of these verses reveals that Allah associating every right, whether the right of God or that of His servants, has conferred such a lofty moral and legal position to it that for a true Muslim no distinctions are left as regards their obligatory nature and their importance. Whenever there is a right due for fulfillment for us, there, with the recipient of that right, God is always associated. To quote the Traditions of the Prophet:

> The Prophet is reported to have said that God will say on Doomsday, 'O son of Adam! I was sick and thou did not visit Me to ask after My health.' He will say: 'O my Lord and Cherisher! How could I visit Thee in Thy sickness? Thou art the Lord of the worlds.' To which God will say: didst thou not know that such and such of My servant was lying in sick bed and thou didst not visit him to ask after his health. Didst thou know that if thou hadst visited him in his sick bed, thou-wouldst have found Me close to him.
>
> Muslim, Reported by Abu Huraira

In another Tradition the same theme is met with in these words:

> The Prophet of God said: "God will say on Doomsday 'O son of Adam; I asked thee for food but thou didst not feed Me.' He will say in reply, 'O my Lord and Cherisher; how could I feed Thee when Thou art the Cherisher and Sustainer of all of us? Allah will say, 'Dost thou not know that such and such of My servants asked thee for food but thou didst not feed him. If thou hadst given him food, thou wouldst have found that food here with Me. O son of Adam! I had asked thee for water but thou didst not give Me water.' To this he will say, 'O my Lord and Cherisher! How could I give thee water to drink when Thou art the Lord and Cherisher of the world. God will say to him, 'Such and such of my servants had asked thee for water but thou did not give him that. If

thou hadst given him water thou wouldst have found that water here with Me'."

Muslim, Reported by Abu Hurairah.

Zakat, Sadqah, giving loans, feeding the hungry, quenching The thirst of the thirsty and entering an agreement with any one, are one and all the rights pertaining to the servants of God. But it is noteworthy how God, associating Himself with every recipient of the right has taken them to the level of the. Rights of God. The famous legist Shatabi says:

"There are two kinds of rights, 'Rights of God and rights of the servants of God.' The latter includes the Rights of Allah also, and those that we term the 'Rights of God' benefit His servants only."

Going a little further, we can say that all rights belong to Allah, and all of them come under service to God. However, all the benefits are derived by the servants of Allah. When a servant of Allah fulfills the right due to Allah, he himself derives all the benefits, since Allah is far above and Independent to need any benefits from any servant of His. When he worships Him he benefits himself in the form of self purification, moulding of the character and perfection of humanity. And when he fulfills the rights due to the servants of God, this benefit becomes two sided. The person fulfilling these rights, having the best character, he is the recipient of honour and respect, ease of conscience, peace of heart and mind and honour and dignity in the Hereafter. And the recipient of the rights on receiving them lives a life of satisfaction and happiness mutual relations of sincerity and love sacrifice and sympathy get strengthened, and in this way the entire human society becomes the cradle of peace and tranquillity and prosperity and security.

Now let us also find out that along with the priorities of right determined by God in this world, what priorities have been provided in this connection in the Hereafter, Anas, a companion, reports from the Prophet:

On the Day of Reckoning there will be three lists of the deeds of men. One of them will be from which not a word will be left by God without taking serious notice of. The second will be that of which little or no notice will be taken. And the third list will comprise those deeds of which not an iota can be forgiven.

The list with forgivable sins will comprise polytheistic practices- That of which God will take no notice is the wrong that an individual has done to his own soul and which is between man and his Lord (such as lapses in offering prayers and fasting and the like). God will forgive sins on this list whomsoever He wills, and he will be saved. But the list of which not a word will be passed over without scrutiny and action will comprise wrongs done by one man to another, save in case of the wronged one having forgiven his tormentor.

(Jama'at Fawaid, Muhammad bin-Sulaiman Ahmaghribi, Vol.11, p.527, Loyalpur, with reference to Musnad-e-Bazaz).

The same tradition has been quoted in *Musnad-e-Ahmed* and *Mustadrak-Hakim* as reported by Ayeshah. The well-known book on Hanafite jurisprudence, entitled *Al Hidayah* under the title Hajj and related mailers, says:

Hajj becames obligatory only when the person concerned is in a Position to provide enough for his defendants to live on during the period of his absence from home, since the rights of the servants to God have priority over those of God, under Hip own injunctions.

Now the question arises why did God give priority to the rights of His servants over His own! The reason is to be found in the fact that by his lapses in fulfilling the rights of God man can do Him no harm, but only wrongs his own Soul and comes to harm. But when he deprives another servant of God, like himself, of a certain right, he injures some interest of his brother which is a factual loss to him. And this is that wrong which is unpardonable in the sight of God, save in case where the wronged persons or groups forgive him of their own free will and choice.

This is the history of rights in Islam, their legal position and their moral status. Unfortunately, this concept is out of the sight of Muslims themselves, and by their own classification of the rights, determined by God, into legal and moral and the Divine and Human rights, have attached greater importance to some and very little or none to others, which is untraceable in any degree in the early period of the Islamic history. In the matter of obedience to God, the unity of character and uniformity was the essence of the lives of the companions of the Prophet. The care they took of their prayers, fasting, Hajj and Zakat, was also devoted to honesty in weights and measures, keeping agreements, help to the brethren in need and such other matters concerning human life, in which each and every injunction from God and His Apostle was respected and duly complied with. Their personality was not divided into compartments (compliance in some and reservations in others) but was a pattern of total submission to the will of their Lord. Shatibi pointing to this spirit of obedience says:

> The classification of Mustahab: Desirable, Preferable or recommendable, Mandoob, that which creates excellence, obligative and Makrooh: Detestable, abhorrent disgusting and Haram (Illegal):
>
> Strictly prohibited, find no place in the Programme of seeking closeness to Allah and purification of the innerself, since the real objective is self purification: whatever helps in this programme is important no matter whether it is Mustahab or obligatory; and that which leads to evil is prohibited, irrespective of its being Makrooh or Haram (strictly prohibited)."

The spirit of the creed of the unity of God is that everything should be done under the commandment of Allah, the way it has been prescribed by Allah, and to seek His countenance alone. The same principle holds in the matter of rights, and according to it, every right, in its determination, enforcement and its consequences at every stage, is associated with God alone.

PART—II

Evolution

FIVE

The Curse of Materialism

Ironically, the secular civilizations have been instrumental in eroding the noble feelings, righteous emotions and moral values of the human race, but even greater destruction has been wrought by the doctrine of social evolution. This doctrine took its birth from materialism. It was fostered by the utilitarian outlook and man's conquest of time and space which lent maturity to it. The doctrine was developed by Kant, Fischter, Hegel, Karl Marx and several other philosophers. With the rise of this theory, wrong took the shape of right and evil became good. Bloodshed, savagery and exploitation of the weak came to be regarded as the highest moral virtues of humanity.

The present chapter cannot admit of a detailed discussion on the subject. I shall, therefore, confine myself to a brief examination of the ideas which have gone into the making of this doctrine. We take up Hegel first, for although the doctrine of social evolution has been extant in the world for several centuries, it was Hegel who with profound conviction and full force of logic presented it to the world as a well-knit system of philosophy.

It is rather a marvel for the student of historiography that this astute German philosopher emphatically refutes Kantian system, yet strives with even greater force and energy to affirm the Kantian theory. He infuses logic into the dull philosophy of Kant and carries the philosophy started by the 'iconoclast' of reason to its final conclusion.'

Avoiding technical intricacies of philosophy, we may explain that in Hegel's view, the evolution of human civilization follows this process: the appearance of contradictions, their conflict and fusion. Each period of human history is a unit and a whole. In a given period, all phases of human life, economic, political, cultural, moral, intellectual and religious ideals are at a particular level. They are all closely interrelated, and they all reflect the age in which they exist. When at the behest of the "Absolute Spirit," the history of mankind advances some steps further, some antithetic ideas, tendencies and doctrines rise from within the body of politics of that age.

An intense conflict between the thesis and antithesis ensues which rages for some time. At last both come to terms. Weak elements on both sides are eliminated and thesis and antithesis merge to from a unity which consists of strong and pure elements of both side. Thus, a completely new system of thought and practice emerges, which in due course of time meets the same fate as its successor. Thus, human civilization continues to advance by this evolutionary process.

In his own terminology, Hegel calls it the Dialectical Process of History. According to this theory, a given period of history is a battleground in which a logical debate and conflict is constantly going on and it is the force of this conflict that propels mankind to further progress. First a thesis appears and then an antithesis arises to challenge the thesis. After a prolonged conflict between the two, the 'Absolute Spirit' brings about a reconciliation between them. Thus, a new entity comes into being which in every respect is better and more comprehensive than its predecessors, for, it contains all the best elements of the preceding entities. Hence each step takes mankind to further advance. This is the Hegelian philosophy of social evolution.

Marx borrowed his philosophical framework from Hegel, but filled in details from his own intuition. He discarded the concept of soul and held that material causes or economic factors were the prime force in the process of historical evolution. Whereas Hegel regards ideas as the most effective power, in Marxian theory, the decisive factor is the material environment and even in this environment the real factors of importance are the means of production.

Hegel thinks that the conflict between thesis and antithesis occurs in the realm of ideas. Marx believes that the main battleground of life is the economic sphere and that it is in this sphere that the destiny of mankind is decided. Economics is the pre-eminent factor in human life and the superstructure of morality, religious doctrines, culture, arts and sciences is erected on the foundation of the economic system. The contours of intellectual and political life in a given period are determined by the various means of economic production in that period. According to Marx, the process of social evolution takes the following course:

> "To begin with a change in the means of economic production takes place, which directly affects the distribution of means of life and the modes of ownership of property. Consequently, all the values of life undergo a change, and a new system comes into existence."

At this stage, a conflict between the new and the old system in the sense of Hegelian dialectics takes place which ends eventually in conciliation and both systems merge to create an entirely new system which contains only the best elements of the preceding systems. Evidently, the emergent system is in every respect superior to former systems. This then is the Marxian view of the process of social evolution.

The third philosopher whose viewpoint lent force to the doctrine of social evolution was Darwin. According to him, all living creatures have a natural tendency towards unlimited growth, development and changing their physical form. But the evolution of various creatures is not determined by any constructive process initiated by providence, but is the result of a destructive process.

The evolution of living creatures does not occur without mutual conflict, famine and death. Darwin reposed implicit faith in Malthusian theory of population and inferred from it that since the number of living creatures multiplies at a faster rate due to availability of food and other necessities for existence, hence each creature is constrained to fight constantly against other creatures in order to preserve his own existence.

In Darwin's view, life is a battleground where at all moments and in every direction the strong are engaged in eliminating the weak in an overall struggle for existence. Only the fittest survive in this struggle and it is really they who deserve all that is best in life. Those who perish in this callous struggle receive a just punishment for their infirmity. In short, this earth, and the means of life on it sustain only those who are the strongest.

There is no room on earth for the weak and the sooner they liquidate their infirm existence from this universe the better. Thus under compulsion of circumstances the process of evolution is initiated and through a constant course of conflict produces higher forms of life. Man too, climbs the high rung of humanity through this complex struggle. Those who emerge victorious from the struggle of existence are pure and the universe belongs to them only.

The theory of social evolution which emerges from a combined view of the doctrines of these philosophers contains the following major principles:

i. The evolution of life takes place through conflict.

ii. Human progress is the consequence of this conflict.

iii. Only the strongest have the right to live and develop in this universe.

iv. Success by whatever means it may be achieved is the main object of existence.

For the moment, I do not intend to point out the intellectual flaws in this doctrine. What I wish to emphasize is that this philosophy instead of humanizing man has actually transformed him into a brute and rather than making this world a heaven of peace, it has changed it into a veritable hell.

The Philosophy

The first impact of the philosophy of social evolution is that man has come to regard material progress as the highest achievement of life, whereas upon a careful consideration it will be found that material development only aids the consciousness of man; it has no creative power of its own. Actually, spiritual power is the prime mover of human consciousness.

It is at this point that the exponents of doctrine of social evolution have committed the greatest blunder. When social evolution means only material development, it necessarily follows that different sections and classes of people should cast morality to the winds and launch a frenzied struggle against each other for expropriating the material means of life, for if they refrained from the struggle, they would perish. This philosophy has produced a permanent fear complex among the people. This savage competitive spirit has enveloped individuals as well as nations, and everyone is scared of the other. This permanent fear complex has developed the vilest qualities among human beings, such as, for instance, selfishness, callousness, avarice, bigotry, faithfulness, corruption and falsehood.

Modern psychologists have established the fact that human actions calculated to make a show of strength spring from a fear complex. Hence ostentations, display of military strength, assertion of superior authority and a craving of power without responsibility are various forms of the same fear complex.

Secondly, this philosophy has plunged the future of humanity into darkness. A philosophy which explains the creation of human ego in terms of time and place can provide man with the knowledge of laws and boundaries of this universe, but cannot liberate man from its cruel fetters. It is for this reason that modern man daily grows pessimistic about his future. The well-known Italian philosopher Croce comments on this problem as follows:

> "The shadow of pessimism covers from time to time the life of the individual and similarly the life of societies; and doubts, fears and despair over the future belongs to all eras of history. But in the years through which Europe is living, that shadow has become wider and darker, philosophers, or people who call themselves philosophers, have become prophets and describe to us, under the guise of philosophical and historical reality, the steep incline, we shall perforce descend...when, as

> frequently happens, we conceive it as a tangle offerces which act outside us and according to their own laws, we have, with the nightmare of these forces, the feelings of helplessness, since, if they are outside us, there is no way of getting among them and of dominating or regulating them. There is nothing left to do then but to speculate, seeking in the external world other forces which may oppose, defeat or check them, and to put our hope in these. But it is uncertain hope, always fearful, because it depends on others and not on us, and, whether fearful or hopeful, we feel ourselves in the clutches of others."[2]

Thirdly, because this doctrine is founded,on the idea that the evolution of man takes place through conflict between hostile forces, hence instead of promoting cooperation among human beings, it has aroused in them a fierce sense of jealousy and competition. This doctrine inculcates in the minds of the people that prosperity and progress in life depend on total commitment to the struggle for worldly gains.

Consequently, it has transformed man into a callous and insensitive creature. This doctrine holds it perfectly natural for the strong to enrich himself at the expense of the weak, by doing so, he proves that only the fittest have the right to survive. Conversely, the weak deservedly suffer persecution and are rightly downtrodden by the strong. Not only has this doctrine turned human beings into savage tyrants, but it has also furnished a rational basis for capitalism and imperialism by endorsing that might is invariably right. Fighting has been a part of human history since long, but before now men considered fighting as evil, though at times a necessary one. This doctrine has baptized war as a definite blessing. In the past, people looked upon a tyrant as an evil-doer.

Today, they laud him as a just man. Max Eastman's comment on the materialistic interpretation of history is, in fact, truly applicable to the whole doctrine of social evolution. He remarks:

> "Notwithstanding their high-sounding claims to humanism, the Marxists have become haughty and

> violent under the influence of this doctrine. The basic assumption of the doctrine is that man attains evolutionary progress through a process of severe and violent conflict. Good and evil in this doctrine are merely names for two material forces and man achieves glory only through a collision between these two forces."[3]

A French author Boris Soyrarine comments:

> "All respect for humanity has been erased from our hearts. Life has lost its real worth and use. At the present time, one has the spirit to eliminate the savagery of the tyrants. Actually, brutishness has reached its zenith."

Referring to the Darwinian theory of evolution another writer Kenneth Walker in his book, *Meaning and Purpose* states that the glories of war described by Trietsechke and Bernhardie is the fruit of the analysis of Darwin's theory of evolution.

In England, which according to the saying of Napoleon is more a land of shopkeepers than of armies, the theory of selection has provided a justification for the worst economic competition and a criminal inelegance on the part of the workers.

Again, this philosophy of life has imparted conviction to the people that movement and conflict of every sort, provided it is materially successful, ensures human evolution. This theory impelled man to worship power and force rather than truth and justice. Man devoted his intellect and skill to the exploration of those means by which he could augment his power and strength.

Aggressive colonialism and oppressive imperialism are mischiefs borne out of this theory. This doctrine represents the darkest period of human history as the most luminous. A famous critic of the Hegelian philosophy, Croce rightly declares that this theory provides instigation for everything, be it conservatism, revolution or restoration.

Similarly, another critic remarks that this doctrine has provided the Marxist writers with an opportunity to justify their stand in every matter. This notion is the major cause of tyranny and oppression in the modern age.

Finally, this theory taught men to repudiate the social significance of religion and morality. It preached that men should exclusively and relentlessly absorb themselves in the struggle for their survival, stability and the grasping of strength and power, wherefrom they may be obtained.

If religion and morality prove useful in achieving this purpose, they should be adopted. If, on the other hand, success is ensured by their repudiation, they should be instantly cast aside. The popularity achieved by the precepts of that high priest of deception, Machiavelli, during the last four centuries has been largely owing to this false doctrine. The following words of Dr. Funk and Goebels represent a true definition of this theory.

> "The sole purpose of all power and strength is to secure the capitation of the enemy by all means, fair or foul. Our movement is perfectly free from moral restraints prescribed by religion. Every act performed for the purpose of dismantling the citadel of colonialism is a moral act."

This, then, is a brief analysis of the components of western civilization and their impact on human life. Modern man is immersed indeed by anxiety. He is at a loss to know why in spite of all the progress in art and sciences and abundance of material provisions, he is still unhappy. The earth yields millions of tons of grain every year, yet, its inhabitants suffer from hunger and privation. Innumerable fountains of knowledge are gushing forth, yet man is still wallowing in ignorance.

In point of fact, the groping for a millennium during the last three or four centuries has led men far astray from their goal. In a New Year message on 1st January, 1935, Iqbal referred to this failure of the secular civilization in the following words:

> "The modern age prides itself in its progress in knowledge and its matchless scientific developments. No doubt, the pride is justified. Today, space and time are being annihilated and man is achieving amazing successes in unveiling the secrets of Nature and harnessing its forces to his own service."[4]

In spite of all these developments, the tyranny of imperialism struts abroad, covering its face under the masks of democracy, nationalism, communism, fascism and heaven knows what else besides. Under these masks, in every corner of the earth, the spirit of freedom and the dignity of man are begin trampled underfoot in a way to which not even the darkest period of human history presents a parallel. He sums up the modern man, equipped with power but lacking in vision, in these striking and beautiful verses:

> Love is denied to him and intellect bites him like a serpent,
>
> He has failed to subordinate intellect to love!
>
> He has succeeded in tracing the course of the stars. But failed to make his way through the labyrinth of his own ideas!
>
> He has got so entangled in the maze of his knowledge,
>
> That to this day he does not know profit from loss.
>
> He ensnared the rays of the sun,
>
> But failed to illuminate the dark night of his life.[5]

Having analysed the ingredients of secular civilization, we shall examine the contemporary social movements which have risen under the patronage of this civilization. Although, these movements bear diverse titles, the spirit which animates them is born of the same mother civilization.

Civil Society in Medina

Having seen the state of Nature and the social and governmental contracts in Medina, we now turn to the civil society. Here, we shall try to see how the individualism of the state of nature which was replaced by the acceptance of Islam by a community of Muslims soon gave way to an organic conception, that is, the individuals who had accepted Islam were yet individual Muslims of Aus and Khazraj, and they had not yet begun to think in terms of a common community and before the coming of the Prophet Muhammad (Peace be on him,) the community of Muslims was like the joint stock company of Locke.

It was like a bundle of sticks which is tied up by a common rope, but every stick keeps up its identity separate. The only common bond of the people of Medina was no doubt acceptance of Islam, but as yet they had not forgotten their individuality. The whole conception, yet, was arithmetical: it was in no sense organic.

It was, therefore, the first task of the Prophet to unite these scattered elements in an organic whole, and to this task he at once turned his attention. Says Wellhausen:

> "The first Arabic community with sovereign powers was established by Mohammed in the city of Medina, not upon the basis of blood which naturally leads to diversity, but upon that of religion which is equally binding on all."[6] Margoliouth also affirms the same thing when he says:
>
> "In the new community all tribal differences were to be sunk, and the theory of the platonic republic, according to which the members of the community should share pains and pleasures to the same extent as the members of one body, is attributed to the Prophet."[7]

Thus, the first care of the Prophet in Medina was to build a mosque, for which he bought a plot of land, though every man offered his land and house free of any charge for the purpose, but the Prophet did not accept them.[8] In the construction of the mosque all worked with the greatest enthusiasm the more so because the Prophet himself was working with them,[9] and they chanted with loud and cheerful voices as they bore along their burdens:

> O Lord! There is no joy but the joy of futurity.
>
> O Lord! Have mercy upon the Citizens and the Refugees.[10]

In this way, the elected President of Medina gave practical proof of the fact that he was but the first citizen and the Prophet showed that he was only like an ordinary mortal, and because he was the representative of God, he has to prove and justify himself as the "First Muslim" as the first servant of God. Thus, for the first time in the history of Medina (and even of all Arabia) the people began to meet on a footing of absolute equality in the mosque five times a day.

A new community had grown up out of heterogeneous and individualistic elements, and as the above couplet has shown, the tribal differentiation of Aus and Khazraj was done away with, for the Citizens of Median began to be called Ansar or helpers, and the people who had migrated and settled from Mecca with the Prophet were called Muhajirin or Refugees.

Covenant of Brotherhood

But still, in the beginning, a greater attachment in the Muslim spirit of brotherhood was necessary between the Ansar and the Muhajirin for the latter were still no more than mere guests of the Ansar as they had forsaken everything of their own—house, wealth and other property at Mecca for the sake of God and their faith. They were, therefore, entirely ill-provided and ill-provisioned.

The Prophet at once created a new Tie of Brotherhood (aqd-i-Muwakhat) between the Ansar and the Muhajirin.'Become brethren every two and two of you,' such ran the command of the Prophet; and he himself 'set the example by taking Ali', or as others say Uthman, for his brother. Accordingly, each of the refugees selected one of the citizens as his brother. The bond was of the closest description, and involved not only special devotion to each other's interests in the persons thus associated, but in the case of de'ath, the 'brother' inherited the property of the deceased."

This covenant or contract lasted only up to the Battle of Badr after which inheritance was allowed to be based on the law of consanguinity as laid down in the Holy Qur'an. This contract of brotherhood makes it definitely clear that while the contract of Locke was meant for the preservation of property, the Islamic contract was based on the idea of the sacrifice of property and this sacrifice was done with the greatest sincerity.

Contract with Jews

After, thus, providing for the two urgent needs of the hour, the Prophet turned his attention to the condition of Medina itself, where another elements could not be ignored. These were the Jews of the three tribes Banu Nadir, Banu Quraiza and Banu Qainua who were not prepared to accept Islam. They came to the Prophet and said:

> "We have come to make a treaty of peace with thee, to the effect that we shall be neither for nor against thee, that we shall aid no one against thee; nor injure any who aids thee; on condition that thou injures neither us nor our friends until we learn what becomes of thy affairs and of those of they people."[13]

The Prophet, complied with their request on condition that they would afford aid to no one against him; nor against any of his companions, neither by word, arms, or cattle, neither openly nor secretly.[14]

This must be pointed out that in spite of all efforts to win over the Jews, they could not be reconciled and from the very beginning were always bent on mischief. Even the Qur'an refers to their adverse activities in a clear manner, for what they could not tolerate was the unification of Aus and Khazraj into one community under the leadership of the Prophet. One Shammas bin Qais (a Jew) set a mischief monger in a meeting of Aus and Khazraj with instructions that he should recall the events of the Battle of Bu'ath. As soon as couplets regarding that battle began to be recited, the extinguished fire of hostility and ravage was rekindled and it took no time to move from verbal hot exchange of words to actual fight and hostility. When the Prophet, on hearing of what was going on, at once appeared on the scene and addressed them to fear God and not to go back to the state of ignorance out of which God had taken them out.

On hearing this, they threw away their implements of war and began to weep and embrace each other. Thus was the unity of the Islamic community maintained in the firm grip of the rope or Covenant of God. They took God to witness that, in case they should fail to keep this agreement and covenant His Lordship would be at liberty to shed their blood, to confiscate their property as well as to capture their wives and children.

A treaty was written for each tribe. Thus, the Prophet associated the Jews in a contract or 'Treaty of Mutual Obligation drawn up in writing between the Refugees and the Believers of Medina on the one hand and the Jews on the other, confirming the latter in the practice of their religion and in the secure possession of their property.'

Religious Toleration

This agreement was, therefore, the First Charter of Religious Toleration in the history of man's political development. It has been preserved in full by Ibn Hashari[15] and is a lengthy document. It begins thus: 'In the name of God, the Compassionate, the Merciful. It is a Covenant (Ahad-Nama) of Muhammad the Prophet of God, on behalf of the believers of Quraish and Yethreb (Medina) and those that are under them[16] and those that may join them and strive with them for the faith. Verily, they form a community apart from the rest of mankind.

Thus, the opening words definitely tell us that the Muslims were now a community and the Holy Qur'an refers to this unity in these words:

> 'Surely, this your community is one community and I am Your Lord, Therefore be careful (of your duty) to me." 23:52.

Wellhausen has expressed this aspect thus:

> "The Community, at the head of which God stands, and the Prophet as God's representative, has power to deliver the shedder of blood over to the avenger, and it is the duty of the community to see that this is done,[17] and in this covenant, as we shall see noted below, it is specifically stated that if a man kills a Muslim wrongfully, the Muslims shall join as one man against him."

The other clauses of this covenant may now be given in brief, to make the above statements clear:

1. The Refugees and the Believers of Medina shall defray the

price of bloodshed among themselves (respectively) and shall ransom honourably their prisoners.

2. Whoever is rebellious or seeketh to spread enmity and sedition, thee hand of every man shall be against him, even if he be a son.

3. No Muslim will kill a Muslim for an unbeliever and non-believer will be helped as against a Muslim. And verily, Allah's Protection is meant for one and all. The Believers are pledged to protect each other against all others.

4. Whosoever of the Jews followeth us, shall have aid and succour; they shall not be injured, not shall any enemy be aided against them.

5. No Unbeliever shall grant protection to thee people of Mecca, either in person or property, nor interpose between the Believers and them.

6. Whosoever killeth a Muslim wrongfully the Muslims shall join as one man against him.

7. The state of peace and war shall be common to all Muslims; no one among them shall have the right of concluding peace with, or declaring war, against the enemies of his co-religionists.

8. The Jews who attach themselves to our commonwealth shall be protected from all insults and vexations; they shall have an equal right with our people to our assistance and good offices.

9. The Jews shall contribute with the Muslims and join with them in defending Medina against a common enemy.

10. The Jews of the various branches of Awf, Najjar, Harith, Isham, thalaba. Ans and all others domiciled in Medina shall form with the Muslims one composite nation, i.e. one people with the Believers.

11. The Jews will profess their religion as freely as the Muslim theirs.

12. The interior of Medina shall be sacred and inviolable for all those who join this covenant.
13. All true Muslims shall hold in abhorrence every man guilty of crime, injustice or disorder.
14. Controversies and disputes shall be referred for the decision of Allah and His Prophet.
15. None shall join the men of Mecca or their allies; for, verily, the engaging parties are bound together against every one that shall threaten Medina. War and peace shall be made in common. And verily! Allah is the protector of the righteous and the godly, and Muhammad is His Prophet.

Free Church of Free State

From this brief summary of the covenant, it is clear, that it does not merely assert the unity and oneness of the Muslim community, it even asserts the unity of the City State of Medina itself, for the Jews and the Unbelievers also have been considered to form one nation with the Muslims, and they had equal obligations in the defence and the maintenance of peace in Medina.

Moreover, the fact Medina was made inviolable makes it clear that the Divine Laws of Peace had now been promulgated with full force in a land of war, turmoil and anarchy. Lastly, the tolerance that was granted to the Jews for the first time established a 'Free Church in the Free State of Medina', and it was the first charter of freedom of conscience and of religious worship in the history of the world.

The Prophet, thus reconciled the various parties in the city and introduced law, order and peace among its various elements. The covenant with the Jews was the crowning contract in the edifice of contracts which established the City State of Medina. Thus, in the words of Amir Ali, "the contract constituted the Prophet as 'the chief Magistrate of the nation, as much by his prophetic mission as by a virtual compact between himself and the people."[18] Dr. Hell regards this contract (ordinance) as a piece of fare statesmanship and of far-reaching importance"[19] of rare statesmanship because it was the only way of reconciling the tribe and the best means of Meccans with the united support of the whole of Medina; and of far-reaching importance because it made the Prophet the sole guiding power in a land which had known no common superior. Nicholson thus estimates the significance of this event:

> "Ostensibly a cautious and tactful reform, it was in reality a revolution. Mohammed dared not strike openly at the independence of the tribes, but he destroyed it, in effect, by shifting the centre of power from the tribe to the community, and although the community included Jews and pagans as well as Muslims, he fully recognised what his opponents failed to foresee, that the Muslims were the active and must soon be the predominant partners in the newly founded State".[20]

The City State of Medina was founded on the basis of various contracts, and 'Islam thus became what, in theory at least, it has always remained a political as well as a religious system.'[21] The First contract was the contract with God and this was the acceptance of Islam which every Muslim has to individually utter the 'Kalima' of faith: there is no god but God and Muhammad is His Prophet. Then the Second Contract was a contract for the Protection of the Prophet—not only as God's representative on Earth but also as their own elected ruler.

The Third Contract was the confirmation of the Second Contract by the whole of the Muslim population of Medina; and the Fourth Contract with the Jews was not merely a charter of toleration for freedom of belief and conscience, it was also a contract for the creation of a composite nation or community for common defence and protection. The Republic of Medina (of which the elected President was the Prophet) was thus recognised 'organic even though the whole process of its creation was individualistic and therefore contractual.'[22]

Islamic State

It is a recognised principle of modern political philosophy that the theory of contract assumes a mechanical way of creating a state and it makes it a mere manufacture, but it is now universally held that the state is not contracted or made, it grows. And here, in the City State of Medina we have said that it is by contract that the state has been made 'organic' (and that too in a double sense); for it is primarily a Muslim state, the Muslim community was already one and every Muslim was an inseparable part of the whole, as it was the greatest sin to shed the blood of a brother Muslim; and if it was a common state of all the peoples of Medina, they were solemnly bound , 'under the protection of God which extends to one and all' to defend the common state against all foreign dangers, and internally too, its soil was made inviolable and free from all bloodshed. This was the Islamic City State of Medina made 'organic' by contracts and to this day both the ideas of contract and the unity of the community[23] continue to be the central features of Muslim religious life.

The idea of contract was therefore, never a fiction in Islam. As has already been shown, the making of contract was a historical reality in Arabia. But in political philosophy, it is not only Kant who has called 'contract' an 'idea of reason', modern critics have tried to make it even unreal and unnecessary in those who are the real classical writers of this theory. They have tried to show that these writers—Hobbes, Spinoza, Locke and Rousseau—have expressed their political ideas. Through the medium of the contract, not because it was essential for their political philosophy, but because it was the prevalent mode of expressing[24] political ideas in terms of contract. Thus, says Vaughan, "of the four philosophers in question, Locke comes nearest in principle of accepting the theory of contract."

But he rejects it in terms; and, even when in substance he seems nearest to it, he inserts so many limitations, he puts in so many hostile amendments, that, in the net result, he is much farther from it than, at first sight we might be tempted to imagine. Of the remaining three, one Spinoza accepts it in words but in fact, takes away with one hand what he professes to give with the other. The two that are adjudged as one in the interest of absolutism and the other in that of the sovereign people reject it root and branch.[25]

According to Vaughan, Locke was only a half-hearted social contract writer. But Joad has absolved Locke also of this irrelevancy absolutely in these words: "But the social contract theory, in the form in which Locke maintained it requires us to suppose that the abolition of Government involves man's relapse into a personal condition would admittedly be a condition of peaceable and socially disposed persons, and it would not be the same as the condition introduced by society, since it is the establishment of government which puts an end to this condition and establishes the condition of society. Such, at least are the contentions of the social contract theory as Locke states it.

It is difficult in the light of these contentions to see how society could survive the abolition of government; yet that it does so, is precisely what Locke, in making his distinction between society and government, maintains. This social contract theory is however, no sense essentional to Locke's political philosophy. [26] Thus, critics have freed all the four political philosophers from being social contract witers, even though they have been the classical writers of this theory. This means that critics have made them what they had never thought about their own writings.

Contractual Organicity

In the Islamic conception of the State, as we have already seen, the 'contract' (social and governmental) is a reality just as much as the conception of the community is organic. "The Islamic State may, therefore, fittingly be called a 'contractual organism"[27] in the words of Fouillee, a modern French writer. The defect of the contract theory is that it makes the state a plaything of individual caprice even though it emphasises the 'consent' as the basis of the state; the defect of the organic theory is that though it emphasises the interdependence of the individual and the community, it entirely belittles individuality and the individual is made unreal. Both these defects are not to be found in the Islamic state.

A Muslim has to individually make a contract with God; but at the same time, he is an inspirable part of his community of which he is an equal member. Thus, the individual in the Islamic state is both individuality and his dependence upon the community.

This explains the full significance of the conception of contractual organicity in Islam.

Abolition of Slavery

Aristotle maintains that slavery is based on nature, and that certain races are intended to be subject. Whether this be true or not, it would be useless to hope for the abolition of slavery in Muhammadan countries under present conditions. Whether the Prophet of Islam could have abolished slavery altogether among his followers is very doubtful and his prescriptions regarding the just and humane treatment of this unfortunate class, taken all in all, are praiseworthy.

On the other hand, there is nothing whatsoever in Islam that tends to the abolition of this curse. As Muir has well said, "Rather, while lightening, he riveted the fetter. There is no obligation whatever on a Muslims to release his slaves."[28]

Acquisition of Slaves

"The greatest of all divisions, that between a free man and slave, appears as soon as the barbaric warrior spares the life of his enemy when he has him down, and brings him home to drudge for him and till the soil." The two main causes of slavery are want and war, and of these two it may be said that the acquisition of slaves was chiefly connected with warfare. (In Sura 47 Muhammed commands his followers thus, i.e. verse 4.f.):

> "When ye encounter the Unbelievers, strike off their heads; until ye have made a great slaughter among them; then bind (the remainder) in fetters. And after this give (the later) either a free dismissal or exact a ransom, until the war shall have laid down its arms."

The usual expression for female slaves in the Qur'an as we have already seen is that which your right hands possess. Muhammed says nothing in the Qur'an regarding the purchase of slaves. According to Islamic law, a slave is:

1. a person taken captive in war, or carried off by force from a foreign hostile country, and being at the time of capture an Unbeliever.

2. the child of a female slave whose father is (a) a slave, or (b) is not the owner of the mother of the child, or (c) is the owner of the mother, but who does not acknowledge himself to be the father.

3. a person acquired by purchase.

War and slavery, as one would expect, is also closely bound together in the Old Testament. In Num, chap. 31, the Children ol Israel are commanded to wage a war of vengeance against the Midianites. And in verse 7, ff, we read:

> " And they warred against Midinian, as the Lord commanded Moss, and they slew every male... (9) And the Children ol Israel took captive the women of Midian and their little ones, etc."

As far as strangers were concerned, the Israelites were allowed to buy, sell, or transfer their male an female slaves. So, we read in Lev. 25, 44 ff.:

> "And as for thy bondmen, and thy bondmaids, which thou shalt have; of the nations that are round about your, of them shall ye buy bondmen and bondmaids. (45) Moreover, the children of the strangers families that are with you, which they have begotten in your land; and they shall be your possession[30] (46) And ye shall make them an inheritance for your children after you.[31] to hold for a possession, of them shall ye take your bondmen for ever."

As among the Muhammadans slaves consist partly of children of female slaves, and partly also of those that are acquired, so in the Old Testament we have the two expressions:

> "He that is born in the house, and he that is bought with money."

This shows us that among the Israelites as among the Muhammadans, the number of slaves might be multiplied by birth. This, of course, is true of all peoples who trade in slaves; since the slaves are the "possession" of their masters, their children also belong to them.

A further agreement between the Muhammadan and Old Testament laws consists in the limitation of slaves to foreigners. In Lev. 25, 39.ff.we read:

> "And if thy brother be waxen poor with thee, and sell himself upto thee; thou shalt not make him to serve as a bond servant: (40) as a hired servant, and as a sojourner, he shall be with thee; he shall serve with thee unto the year of jubilee: (41) then shall he go out from thee, he and his children with him. (42). They shall not be sold as a slave is sold."[32]

And so with the Muhammadans, who are strictly forbidden to take believers as slaves, thee Muhammadan like the Israelite is to regard his fellow-believer as a brother.[33]

Among the Babylonians, however, it was otherwise. Slaves were recruited both from within and without. If a son, whether natural or adopted, sinned against his parents, his father could see him as a slave. And likewise the husband had the right to dispose of a quarrelsome wife for money. Also the captured enemy naturally took the position of a slave, especially did the white (light complex-ioned) slaves from Gutium and Shubarti at that time appear to be much desired.[34]

Treatment with Slaves

We have already seen how the Prophet in the Qur'an insists upon the just and humane treatment of the widow and orphan. And a like treatment is demanded by him also for slaves; and that in accordance with his teaching that all men belong to God, and are therefore in a certain sense alike. So, we read in Sura 16,73:

> "God hath caused some to excel others in worldly possession; Yet those thus excel do not give of their wealth unto those whom their right hands possess (their slaves) so that both may have an equal share thereof. Do they, therefore, deny the beneficence of God.?" Also Sura 4, 40:
>
> "Honour God, and associate none with nil" and show kindness unto parents, relations, orphans, the poor, the neighbour who is of kin to you, and he who is not,[35] and to

> your trusted friends, and the traveller and to those whom your right hands possess for God loveth not the arrogant and the proud."

In the year before his death, the Prophet, during a farewell pilgrimage at Mina, delivered an address to his followers, in which, among several other injunctions, we find the following:

> "And your slaves! See that ye feed them with such food as ye eat yourselves, and clothe them with the like clothing as ye wear yourselves; and if they commit a fault which ye are included not to forgive, sell them; for they are the servants of the Lord, and are not to be tormented.'[36]

If Muhammed could not abolish slavery, he has certainly done what he could to secure for slaves a humane treatment. And if present-day Muhammadans disregard his injunctions, it is not fair to hold the Prophet himself responsible for it.[37] Also, as already observed, it must not be forgotten that the legislation of the Qur'an was enacted for a seventh-century people.

The position and treatment of slaves among the ancients in different lands naturally differed in accordance with the character of the various people, as well as the character of the slaves themselves, that is whether they be foreign or inland born. And there was also a difference of treatment by the same people at different times.[38]

But if the enactments of the Prophet were only faithfully observed by his followers, the treatment of slaves in Muhammadan countries would in all cases compare very favourably with what it was among the ancients. Also the treatment of slaves, as enacted in Muhammadan law, taken all in all, can only be regarded as just.

As we have already seen in the case of adultery, female slaves were held to be less guilty than free women, and consequently their punishment was to be less severe. And especially did the law enact that they should be sufficiently supported, and not made to suffer.

On the other hand, it must be remembered that slaves, like any other property, were transferable. A Muhammadan has the right to sell his concubine, as long as he has no child by her.[39] And even if he has a child by her, he can always deny the paternity (although this does not often happen). And in any cases, the slave would have to continue to serve him, and be his concubine, that is unless he, when she has born a son to him, presents her with her freedom by way of compensation.

Emancipation of Slaves

The founder of Islam not only insisted upon the humane treatment of slaves, but also that it should be made possible for them to secure their freedom, when they have shown themselves worthy of it by their conduct. Accordingly, the emancipation of slaves among the Muhammadans must be regarded as a meritorious act[40]. Sura 24, 33 reads:

> "And those of your slaves who desire a deed of manumission, write it for them, if ye have a good opinion of them, and give them of the wealth of God, which he has given you."

The manner in which this emancipation is brought about in Muhammadan countries varies. Sometimes complete and immediate emancipation is granted to a slave gratuitously, or for a monetary compensation to be paid later. This is done by means of a written document, or by a verbal declaration in the presence of two witnesses; or again by the master presenting the slave with the certificate of sale obtained from the former master. Also, in conformity with the Prophet's demand in Sura 24, 33.

Future emancipation is sometimes agreed upon to be granted on the fulfillment of certain conditions; or more frequently, upon the death of the owner. In the latter case the owner cannot sell the slave with whom the agreement has been made.[41] Also, as the owner cannot alienate by will more than one-third of the whole property that he leaves, the law ordains that, if the value of the said slave exceeds that portion, the slave must obtain, and pay to the owner's heirs the additional sum. We shall see further on that for certain offence, such as manslaughter, etc., the freeing of a captive is reckoned in part-punishment.[42]

It is not impossible that Muhammad (PBUH) to some extent, at any rate, was acquainted with the Old Testament enactments concerning the emancipation of slaves. While, however, the Old Testament deals only with the emancipation of Israelite slaves, who has become bondmen through debt, Muhammad speaks of the emancipation of all slaves.

Sources

1. Bertrand Russel, History of the Wertern Philosophy.
2. Benedotto Croce, Politics and Morals, George Alien and Unwin, London, 1946, p. 136.
3. Ibid.
4. Iqbal, New Year's Message broadcast from the Lahore Radio Station on 1st January, 1938; see Vahid, Thoughts and Reflections of Iqbal, Ashraf, Lahore 1946, p. 373.
5. K. G. Saiyldain,Iqbal's Educational Philosophy, Ashraf, Lahore, 1960, 5th edition, pp. 142-43.
6. Wellhausen, Historians, History of the World-Article, ND, p. 291.
7. Margoliouth, Muhammadanism, p. 75.
8. Al Baladhuri, (Hitti's Translation), p. 19.
9. Ibn Khaldun, p. 53; Raudatus Safa, p. 251.
10. Muri Life of Mahomet, 1894, p. 168,/fen Hisham, p. 176.
11. Muri(1894 edition) p. 1671; Ibn Khaldun, p. 62; Abul Fida, p. 301. Raudatus Safa notes that this brotherhood was created between Mahajirin and 45 Ansar (p. 261) The Translation of Zaidan (named as Tamaddun-i-Islam), Part-1, by Shaikh Ghulam Muhammad that I possess gives one more Contract which I do not find in otheibooks. Before the creation of this Fraternal Contract, the Prophet hadirought about a written Contract between the Ansar and the Muhajirin in which they had declared themselves to be one nation (Qaum) (p. 47). It was after this Contract of one nationhoodthat brotherhood between two and two was made. Zaidan says that this Contract occurs in Iban Hisham in full but this translation has omitted all that part of it. But such a Contract seems to be feasible because in

the Contract with Jews Muslims are treated as one community or nation (Qaum).

12. Raudatus Safa, p. 261.
13. Ibid., pp. 255-56.
14. For further details, seethe Holy Qur'an translated by the late M. Mahumudul Hasan and M. Shabbir Ahmad 'Uthmani', pp. 80-81.
15. Ibn Hisham, pp. l79-SO;Ibn Khaldun, pp. 53-61, see also Muir, pp. 177-78, and Amir Mil's Spirit of Islam, pp. 54-55.
16. "Those under them, means those unbelievers in Medina who had not yet accepted Islam but were a hopeless minority.
17. Historians: History of the World, p. 291.
18. The Spirit of Islam, p. 55.
19. Hell, Arabian Civilisation, p. 23.
20. Nicholson, A Literary History of the Arabs, p. 173.
21. Arnold, Preaching of Islam, p. 32.
22. Vaughan, 'It is manifest that the idea of Contract naturally lends itself to an individualist theory of the State,' p. LVIDu Contract Social-Modern Language Texts, Longmans, 1918.
23. The Prophet said: 'None of you shall be a Momin (faithful) until wish the same thing for a brother Muslim what you wish for your own self.'(Bukhari); Abu Susa reports that the Prophet said: 'A Momin is like a building for another Momin for one of its parts is a source of strength to the other, and then he crossed the fingers of both his hands (to suggest that union is strength). (Bukhari).
24. The Contract of Rousseau by Cole (Everyman's Library), p. IX.
25. Vaughan, Du, Contract Social, p. LXV.
26. Joad, Guide to the Philosophy of Morals and Politics, p. 492.
27. Coker, Recent Political Thought, p. 412.
28. SirW. Muri, "The Qur'an, its Composition and Teaching," p. 58.
29. Tyior. Anthropology, p. 434 ff; also Hastings, D. B., Vol. 4, p. 461.
30. "Possession" esp. of land and landed property (Gen. 17, 8, etc):

then also, as here, of persons.

31. So also with the Babylonians, Die Sclaven drafting one Eriaubnis ihers herrn nicht die Schoole varlassen and gingen bei dem Tode

des Besitzers one writers in die hande science Erben Uber. "- Meissner. "Beitrage zum altba by to nischen Provatrcht: p. 5; See also Meissner, "Aus d. Altatabably. Recht" ("Alter Orient", VII, I), p. 8f.

32. This law, however, can only be regarded as an ideal. That Israelites could be taken as slaves and in fact, were often so taken, usually on account of debt, we find from such passages as 2 Kings, 4,1; Ex. 21.

33. See Syed Ameer Ali, The Personal Law of the Mahommedans, p. 37f.

34. Meissner, "Beitrage zum altbaylonischen Privatrecht, "p. 6.

35. "The person who is one's neighbour, but who belongs to another people," Lana, Lex.

36. Muri, Life of Mahomet, Vol. I, London, p. 486.

37. Prof. Fischer says, "Dass man sich die Lage der Sklaven in Heutigen Muslimischen Landern im allgemeinen nicht zu schlimm vorstellen darf, hat, abgeschenvonandern(S.Z.B. Lane, "Moder Egyptians,: p. 168), besonders Snouck Hurgronjegezeigt ("Mekka," 2. p. 18ff). Bei meinem zweimaligen Aufenthalte in Marokko have ich gleich-fallsdenEindruckjewonnendass die lage der Muslimichen Sklaven nur formell von der christlicher Dienerverschieden its." Cf. also Doughty, "Arabia Deserta, " I. p. 554; "The condition of the slave is always tolerable and is often happy in Arabia; bred up as poor brothers of the sons of the household, they are a manner of God's wards of the pious Mohammedan householder who is army [properly 'my uncle'] of their servitude and buy ['my father']...It is not many years 'if their houselord fears Allah; before he will given them their liberty; and then he sends them away not empty; but in pland Arabia (where only substantial persons are slave holders) he good man will marry out his free servants, male and female, endowing them with somewhat of his own substance, whether camels or palm stem's.

38. As regards the Babylonians cf, Meissner, "Beitr.Z.Altba, Privatrecht," p. 6f.," Der Sclave war each altably lonischem Reechte kein Mensch, sondern eine Sache, welche man stickwise berechnete; deshalb ward von hm immerals I, SAG ardu-\ Stuck (eightlich Kopf-caput geredet, und aus eben dem Grunde wird auch nie derName seienees Vaters Genannt. Von den Freien Waren sie Schon ausserlich druch ein eingle branntes Mal unterschienden, haubing, usd besonders

whol, wenn sie als Ausereisser bekannt waren, trugen sie sogarKetten.. ....Aiich dieTodesstrafknnote naturlich one witeres gegensie ange wandt werden..Trotzdeem die Sclaven ihern Herrn absolute rechtlos regenuberstanden, wird das Verhaltnis zqischen Herrn und Diener gewohnilich ein recht freundliches gewesen sein. Die Sclavin war gewohnlich dieNebenfran ihres Gebieters..der ihre kinder zu erzi-ehdn verpfichete war...Ingleicher Weise wird auch der Sclave gut behandeltwordensein; je es kam sogarvor, dass Sclaven adoptiert wurden..Ein anderer Weg, die Freiheit zu eriangen, war der Loskauf durch Geld (imptiru)." Also as regards the Israelites, cf. Guthe: Bibelworter bunch,' art. "Sklaven." Deraltests Haussklave..hatte eine sehr angesehence Stel lung and unter Urnstanden Erbrecht (gen 15, 2f.). Even Sklvin knnote duch den Herrn Zur Gattin and Gebie-terin des Hauses rehoben werden. Man gab den Sklaven Weiber aus den eigenen Tochterni, Chron. 2m35 und den Sklandlung von Sklaven, aur die Luc. 12, 46 ff, an spielt, ist romisch order herodeisch, nichtisrealeitisch."

39. Cf, Hammurabi & 119.-"If a debt has seized a man, and he has handed over for the money a maidservant who has borne him children, for the money the merchant paid to him, the owner of the maid shall pay (back) and he shall ransom his maid.

40. Sachau, "Muh,Recht. "p. 131.

41. See Lane, "Modern Egyptians, "p. 155f; also Sachau, "Muh. Recht," p. 13 Iff.

42. Margoliouth, Mohammed, p. 46 If.

SIX

Problems and Issues

As per Islamic view, the concepts, analogous to human rights have certain precursors in heritage of philosophy and theology, but human rights lack precise equivalents in medieval fiqh (jurisprudence). In fiqh, the category haqq al-ad, the right of the individual Muslim, was used to distinguish cases in which legal actions against a wrongdoer were left to the discretion of the injured party or parties from other cases belonging to the category of the right of Allah, haqq Allah, in which prosecution was mandatory and was to be undertaken by the government.

One settled fiqh principle corresponding to a modern right was the right of the owners of property to seek legal right against interference with their property. Rather than constructing doctrines or proposing institutions designed to curb the powers of the ruler or to protect the individual from the ruler's oppression, Islamic legal thought long concentrated on defining the theoretical duties of believers, including rulers, vis-a-vis Allah.

According to the prevailing perspective, rulers had the obligation to rule according to shari'ah law; their subjects were to obey them unless ordered to do something constituting a sin. The development of institutions that could place real curbs on rulers' despotism or make them accountable to those whose rule was neglected. Rebellion was commonly proposed as the remedy for tyranny.

To deal with the practical problems of protecting rights and freedoms, Muslim intellectuals and statesmen began to adopt the principles of European constitutionalism in the nineteenth century.

In the latter half of the twentieth century, after the common acceptance of the principles of constitutionalism, the related question of the compatibility of international human rights principles with Islamic doctrine was raised.

The strongest influence on Muslim's ideas came from French concepts and legal principles developed during the Enlightenment and the French Revolution. These included the first great statement of modern human rights, the 1789 Declaration des Droits de I'Homme et du Citoyen, and the 1791 French Constitution, as well as concepts of public liberties.

In the areas of the Muslim world ruled by Britain, which lacked a written constitution expressly guaranteeing specified rights, the models were democratic freedom as developed in the common law tradition and Britain's system of parliamentary government.

Many nineteenth-century officials, diplomats, and writers from Muslim countries played roles in disseminating European ideas of constitutionalism and public liberties. They included the Egyptian Shaikh Rifa an Raff al-Tahtawi (1801-1891), an al-Azhar scholar who studied at French legal and political institutions in Paris from 1826 to 1831. He prepared a report on concepts of political rights, the rule of law, liberty, equality, and the ideas of the Enlightenment, and translated the French Constitution into Arabic; in 1839 his report was translated into Turkish.

Persian diplomat Mirza Malkom Khan (1833-1908), who educated in Paris and had lived in Turkey, later becoming Persian ambassador to Great Britain, wrote extensively on European concepts of government, the rule of law, and liberty, claiming that these could be reconciled with Islam. In the Ottoman realm, the literary figure Namik Keman (1840-1888) was prominent in disseminating ideas of rights and freedom and the notion of their compatibility with Islam.

Doctrines vs Modernity

In the nineteenth century clashes between inherited Islamic doctrines and modern norms regarding rights came on the question of the equality of Muslims and non-Muslims before the law. The issue was joined as European powers pressed for the elimination of the disabilities traditionally placed on non-Muslims.

A fundamental pact announced in Tunisia in 1857 under European pressure guaranteed equality for all before the law and in taxation as well as complete security for all inhabitants irrespective of religion, nationality, or race. Tunisia was the first Muslim country to promulgate a constitution, doing so in 1861 and affirming the rights established in the pact; however, the constitution was suspended by the French Protectorate (1881-1956).

In Tunisia as in many other Muslim countries, the independence struggle against European domination accentuated people's consciousness of the importance of rights and democratic freedom. After independence, the 1956 Tunisian Constitution stated that the republican form of government was the best guarantee of "human rights."

The most important early reforms in the direction of realizing rights were undertaken in the Ottoman Empire, which had many non-Muslim subjects and which, owing to its military and economic vulnerability, was also exposed to pressures from European powers. The hatt-i-serif of 1839, reinforced by the hatt-i humayun of 1856, was part of a series of modernizing reforms in the Tanzimat period that aimed to establish the security of life, honour, and property, fair and public trials, and equality before the law for all Ottoman subjects irrespective of religion. The principle of non-discrimination based on language and race was added by the hatt-i-humayun. In 1840, the new penal code affirmed the equality of all Ottoman subjects before the law.

By mid-century, reformist pressures prompted the adoption of the 1876 Ottoman Constitution, which contained a section on hukuk-i-umumiye, or public liberties, of Ottoman subjects, providing for equality regardless of religion, free exercise of religions other than Islam and freedom of worship, inviolability of personal freedom of worship, and guarantees against arbitrary intrusions, extortion, arrest, or other unlawful violations of person, residence, or property.

There were also provisions for freedom of the press, association, and education. This constitution was suspended in practice and not revived until after the Young Turk Revolution in 1908, a central goal of which was reviving the constitution and establishing the equality of all Ottoman citizens. The Young Turk's reforms expanded constitutional rights protection, prohibited arrests and searches except by established legal procedures, abolished special or extraordinary courts, and guaranteed press freedom. Turkey's second republic saw in 1861 the promulgation of a constitution that undertook in its preamble to ensure and guarantee "human rights and liberties" and made men and women equal.(Article 12)

In the area of free exercise of religion, conditions were imposed to safeguard the policy of secularism adopted by Mustafa Kemal Ataturk (1881-1938), the first President of the Turkish Republic. Article 2 of the 1982 Turkish Constitution proclaimed Turkey to be a law-state that respects human rights.

In Republican Turkey the energetic pursuit of Kemalist secularism, beginning in 1925, led to the repression of various Islamic groups, especially dervish orders. In Soviet Central Asia, the atheistic policies of the Soviet Union curbed the religious freedoms of the Muslim populace until the collapse of the Soviet state in 1991.

Suppression of Islam and denial of religious freedom also occurred under the Marxist regimes that ruled Albania from 1945 to 1991 and Afghanistan from 1978 to 1982. Elsewhere in the twentieth century regimes with secular orientations often indulged in harsh persecutions of Islamic fundamentalists.

Popular agitation against the despotism of the Qajar Shah culminated in Persia's first constitution in 1906-1907. Persia's Shi'i clerics were divided about the religious legitimacy of constitutionalism and its attendant rights provisions. The Supplementary Constitutional Law of 1907 included Islamic qualifications of two rights provisions; publications were said to be free except where heretical or harmful to Islam (Article 21) and the study and teaching of science, education, and art were to be free except as prohibited by religious law (Article 18). Moreover, ministers in the government wre required to be Persian Muslims

(Article 58). However, the country's inhabitants were to enjoy equal rights before the law (Article 8).

After the 1978-1979 Islamic Revolution in Iran, official spokesmen invoked Islam as the reason for the clerical regime's hostility to international human rights, which they often dismissed as products of an alien, western cultural tradition; however, Iran did not repudiate its ratification of the International Covenant on Civil and Political Rights.

The 1979 Iranian Constitution in Article 20 expressly provided that all citizens enjoyed human, political, economic, social and cultural rights according to Islamic standards; Article 4 provided that Islamic principles prevailed over those in the constitution. Notwithstanding the reference in Article 20 to economic, social, and cultural rights, the concern seemed to be with using Islamic criteria to curb civil and political rights-many of the latter being expressly limited by Islamic criteria. The principle of equality and equal protection for women and religious minorities were breached in many ways.

In the name of implementing Islamic criminal justice, the regime irnored principles of criminal procedure designed to protect the rights of the accused both before and during trial, as well as prohibition of cruel and inhuman punishment. Religious minorities and individuals and groups opposed to clerical rule or the regime's religious ideology were excluded from the political process and were often subject to harsh persecution.

Islamic and Western concepts were combined in the Afghan Constitution produced between 1921 and 1924. For example, all inhabitants were to be equal before the government without distinction of religion and sect, and it was provided that all Afghans would be equal before the Shari'ah and the laws of the State. Nonetheless, Hindus and Jews (the only recognized non-Muslim communities) were required to pay thejizyah, the poll-tax traditionally imposed on dhimmis (protected non-Muslims), and to wear distinctive emblems.

By the end of the twentieth century all Muslim countries had adopted constitutions containing some or all of the rights principles set forth in international human rights law. The 1989 Algerian Constitution was noteworthy for its guarantee of equality before the law regardless of gender (Article 28), fundamental liberties and human rights (Article 31), and human rights advocacy (Article 32). Like most Muslim countries, however, Algeria retained Islamic personal status rules and constitutional provisions according Islam a privileged status, perpetuating the ambiguous relationship between religious and constitutional norms.

Fiqh survived longest as the official law of the land in Saudi Arabia. However, changes inaugurated in 1922 suggested that the country might be moving gradually towards a governmental system that would accord at least limited recognition to rights and constitutionalism, albeit subject to Islamic criteria. The principle that Islam entails on human rights was adopted in the Basic Law of Government promulgated by the Saudi Arabian regime in 1922; Article 26 provided that "the State protects human rights in accordance with the Islamic Shari'ah."

What the Shari'ah limits on rights would entail was not defined. The basic law provided for many citizen entitlements in the area of social welfare, but only a few rights in the political or civil area were recognized. These included the provision that no one should be arrested, imprisoned, or have his action restricted except as provided by law (Article 36); chat homes should not be entered or searched save in cases specified by statutes (Article 37); that communications should not be confiscated, delayed, read or listen to except in cases defined by statutes (Article 40); and that private property must be protected and could only be taken for the public interest and with fair compensation (Article 17).

Women's Rights

One of the areas where the clash between inherited Islamic principles and international human rights norms was most acute was that of women's rights. Although conservatives propounded the nation that full equality for women violated Islamic precepts, feminists argued that it was patriarchal attitudes and inadequate study of the Islamic sources that led to the notion that Islam required keeping women in a subordinate position.

Already in the late nineteenth century liberal writers like the Egyptian Qasim Amin (1865-1908) had propounded the thesis that certain problems facing Middle Eastern societies—despotism, moral degeneration, and the degraded status of women—were not intrinsic to Islam but were the products of corrupting influences and social customs. While not advocating full equality for women, Amin demanded that women's rights should be enhanced. He also linked the cause of women's freedom to the realization of freedom and rights for citizens in general. Feminists such as the Egyptian Huda Sharawi (1882-1947) became prominent advocates of women's rights and emancipation.

One of the boldest attempts to reconcile Islam with full equality for women was offered by al-Rahir al-Haddad, a Tunisian graduate of al-Zaytunah, who in 1930 published Imra 'atunafi al shari'ah wa-al-mujtama (Our Women in the Shari'ah and Society), which propounded the idea that Islam had envisaged a progressive emancipation of women; he advocated the reform of Islamic laws to eliminate obstacles to male-female equality in the domestic as well as the public sphere. For the boldness of its thesis, the book was condemned with particular vehemence by conservatives and its author denounced as a heretic.

Unequivocal support for full equality for women came from Kemal Ataturk, who in the wake of the Turkish war of independence proclaimed that women had the right to be equal; he subsequently took measures to remove the disabilities imposed by Turkish custom and Islamic law—without attempting to reconcile his reforms with Islamic precepts.

In the Arab world, the most dramatic reforms was embodied in the Tunisian Law of Personal Status of 1956 promulgated by President Habib Bourguiba. Presented as an Islamic law, the code undertook bold reforms improving women's status, such as abolishing polygamy and establishing equal rights for men and women in divorce.

Into the late twentieth century, Muslim countries preserved laws that discriminated against women and denied them full civil and political rights, often in the face of constitutional provisions mandating the equality of all citizens. In general, laws afforded women considerable equality outside the family; it was in the area of personal status that discriminatory features taken from fiqh were retained. Saudi Arabia was notable for its reliance on Islam to justify its refusal to grant women rights and freedoms widely enjoyed elsewhere in the Muslim world.

Few Muslim countries ratified the 1979 Convention on the elimination of all forms of discrimination against women, and those that chose to rectify did so subject to reservations regarding various central provisions. The reservations made by Bangladesh, Egypt, Libya, and Russia were specifically justified by their need to adhere to Islamic law.

Human Rights Movements

Independent, non-governmental organizations founded for the defence of human rights have spearheaded campaigns to improve respect for human rights in Muslim countries. One of the earliest Muslim human rights organizations was established by Moroccans in December, 1933 in the Spanish-controlled enclave of Tetouan as an affiliate of a Spanish human rights organization.

A human rights group with Islamic affiliations, the Iranian Committee for the Defence of Freedom and Human Rights, was formed with the participation of several religious figures; it aimed primarily at achieving democratization and the elimination of torture and in camera political trials. A central participant was Mehdi Bazaragan (b. 1907), a proponent of Islamic liberalism who went on to become Iran's first prime minister immediately after the Islamic Revolution. He and his associates later suffered persecution when their stance on human rights put them at odds with the central regime.

Human rights organizations in which educated professionals were prominent proliferated throughout the Muslim world in the 1980s in the face of daunting obstacles and dangers. One of the most important was the Arab Organization for Human Rights, which, like the overwhelming majority of independent human rights organizations, espoused the human rights programmes.

Muslim States and International Human Rights Law

It was in the aftermath of World War II that the modern international formulations of human rights were produced, setting standards that became incorporated in public international law. Muslim countries were among the founding members of the United Nations, whose 1945 Charter called for respect for human rights and fundamental freedoms; all Muslim countries eventually joined the UN.

Aspects of the Universal Declaration of Human Rights passed by the General Assembly in 1948 provoked criticism for representatives of Muslim countries, although in the end only Saudi Arabia failed to support its passage.

Muslim nations different greatly in their willingness to ratify the human rights conventions subsequently drafted under UN auspices. Muslims sometimes charged that international rights norms had a Western or Judeo-Christian bias that precluded their acceptance in the Muslim milieu.

In terms of the compatibility of international rights norms and Islamic law, the alleged conflicts centred around civil and political rights; problems of the compatibility of Islam with economic, social, and cultural rights were rarely raised. The principles of freedom of religion—notably the right to convert from Islam to another faith—and the full equality of persons regardless of sex or religion seemed to pose particular problems.

The Charter of the Organization of the Islamic Conference (OIC), an international organization founded 1973 to which all Muslim countries belong, indicated in its preamble that the members were "reaffirming their commitment to the UN Charter and fundamental human rights." In 1980, however, the OIC issued the Cairo Declaration on Human Rights in Islam, which diverged significantly from international human rights standards; it was not made clear how this declaration was to be reconciled with the conflicting obligations undertaken by OIC members in ratifying international human rights covenant or in their individual constitutional rights provisions, which in many cases corresponded to the international norms.

Like the many other self-proclaimed "Islamic" human rights schemes that proliferated from the 1960s onward, the OIC declaration extensively borrowed terms and concepts from the International Bill of Human Rights, presenting a hybrid mixture of elements taken from Islamic and international law. The OIC declaration asserted that "fundamental rights and universal freedom in Islam are an integral part of the Islamic religion," but proceeded to insert 'Islamic' qualification and conditions on the rights and freedom guaranteed under international law—in conflict with international human rights theory, which does not permit religious criteria to override rights. Representative provisions included the rule in Article 24 that all the rights and freedoms stipulated in the declaration were subject to the Shari'ah, without defining what limits this would entail.

There was no provision for equal rights for all persons regardless of sex or religion. Instead, Article I stated that "all human beings are equal in terms of basic human dignity and basic obligations and responsibilities (not 'right'), without any discrimination on the grounds of race, colour, language, sex, religious belief, political affiliation, social status or other considerations." Article 6 further provided that "woman is equal to man in human dignity" ['not rights'], but it imposed on the husband the responsibility for the support and welfare of the family. In contrast, Article 13 provided that men and women were entitled to fair wages "without discrimination." Article 5 provided that on the right to marry there should be "no restrictions stemming from race, colour or nationality," but did not prohibit restrictions based on religion.

The provisions regarding religion did not aim at neutrality : Article 2 stated that Islam was the religion of unspoiled nature and prohibited "any form of compulsion on man or to exploit his poverty or ignorance in order to convert him to another religion or to atheism." Article 9 called for the State to ensure the means to acquire education "so as to enable man to be acquainted with the religion of Islam."

The favoured treatment of Islam carried over to freedom of speech, with Article 22 (a) stating that expressing opinion freely was allowed "in such manner as would not be contrary to the principles of the Shari'ah. Article 22 (c) barred the exploitation or misuse of information "in such a way as may violate sanctities and the dignity of Prophets, undermine moral and ethical values or disintegrate, corrupt or harm society or weaken its faith." Article 18 stipulated a right to privacy in the conduct of private affairs, in the home, in the family, and regarding property and relationships. Article 15 set forth "rights of ownership to property acquired in a legitimate way, barring expropriation except for the public interest and upon payment of immediate and fair compensation."

Noteworthy by their absence were provisions calling for the observance of democratic principles in political systems and guarantees of freedom of religion, freedom of association, freedom of the press, and equality and equal protection of the law. Although torture was prohibited in Article 20, there were no provisions explicitly endorsing international rights norms in the area of criminal procedure—only the vague assurance in Article 19 that the defendant would be entitled to "a fair trial in which he shall be given all the guarantees of defence." Since Article 25 stated that the Shari'ah "is the only source of reference of the explanation or clarification of any of the articles of this Declaration."

"The possibility was left open that a trial would be deemed 'fair' as long which were historically underdeveloped in the area of criminal procedure. There was no principle of legality per se. The provision in Article 19 that there should be no crime or punishment except as provided for in the shari'ah seemed to open the door to the application ofta'zir (discretionary) penalties, as well as rules regarding hadd crimes. Article 2 prohibited taking away life except for a reason prescribed by the Shari'ah. Reflecting the third world setting in which Muslim nations elaborate their position on rights, Article II prohibited colonialism and stated that "people's suffering from colonialism have the full right to freedom and self-determination."

In sum, the OIC Declaration suggested that the official approach of Muslim countries to civil and political rights was distinguishable from that of non-Muslim countries by reason of their reliance on Shari'ah rules.

Governments and individuals throughout the Muslim world continue to take many positions on human rights that are by self-designation 'Islamic.' Given the variety of approaches and principles involved, it is evident that Muslim opinion remains divided on the relationship between international human rights principles and the Islamic legal heritage, and on the compatibility of the two.

In conclusion, one cannot but view the future with some apprehension. If Muslims persist in their acceptance of the absence of social justice among them, if they continue to separate worship in the mosque from the social justice to be observed in lands where the spirit of Islam is to be sown, and to separate the places of prayer from business and industry; if they uphold the hypocrisy of a worship without soul, showing themselves "mean towards those who needs help," then woe betide them in this world, and woe betide them in the Hereafter, even if they are not among those whom the Qur'an says "neglect their prayers."

Charter of Human Rights

Having seen the failure of the constitution in safeguarding the fundamental rights on the national level, let us now have a look at the measures undertaken to ensure their protection at the international level and find out how far they have succeeded in their objective.

The world charter of Human Rights declared by the General Assembly of the United Nations on December 10, 1948, is so to say, the zenith of human efforts in this context. This charter comprises 30 sections which are as follows:

1. All men are born free and are equal in status in the matter of dignity and rights.
2. Every individual without any discrimination on the basis of race, colour, sex, language, religion, political or other views, national and social status, properties, birth or any other aspect or distinction of any sort whatsoever shall be equally entitled to the rights and freedoms mentioned in this charter.

3. Every individual has the right to live, to remain free, and to protect his life.
4. No body shall be enslaved or subjugated. Slavery and slave-trade in every form shall be prohibited.
5. No person shall bed made the target of violence, tyranny and oppression, inhuman and derogatory treatment or punishment.
6. Every individual as such shall enjoy a certain recognized status in the eye of law.
7. All persons shall be deemed to have equal status in the eye of law, and enjoy equal legal protection without any discrimination.
8. Every persons shall have the right to effective legal action through a tribunal with adequate authority against any laws, made in contravention of the fundamental rights granted under any law or constitution.
9. No body shall be punished without justification, with imprisonment, confinement, or exile.
10. Every one shall have equal right of open just hearing by a free, independent and imparital trtibunal for the determination of his fundamental right and obligations or for his acquittal from the charges levied against him.
11. (1) In case of a penal offence every individual shall have the right to be deemed innocent so long as he is not proved a criminal in an open court where he shall have all the guarantees for his defence and proving himself guiltless.

    (2) No body can be held guilty of a punishable crime for any intentional or unintentional act of his, which is not in fact punishable under any national or international law.
12. There shall be no intervention in any individual's privacy, domestic life, familial affairs, and correspondence, nor his dignity and honour shall be violated.

13. (1) Every individual shall have perfect freedom of movement and residence within the limits of his own state.

    (2) Every individual shall be free to go abroad and to come back to his own country.

14. (1) Every individual shall have the right to seek asylum in other countries to save himself from tyranny and violence.

    (2) However, this right shall not be available to persons trying to save themselves from cases of a non-political nature or actions against the principles and objectives of the United Nations Organisation.

15. (1) Every individual shall be entitled to the right of citizenship.

    (2) No individual shall be deprived of the right of citizenship nor deprived of the right of changing his citizenship nationality.

16. (1) Every adult man or woman shall have the right of marrying and having a home of his (or her) own without any distinction of race, citizenship (nationality) or creed.

    (2) Marriage shall be contacted with the free consent and approval of husband and the wife.

    (3) Family is the basic natural unit of the society, and is entitled to complete protection from the society and the state.

17. (1) Every individual shall have individually, or in association with others, right to own property.

    (2) No one shall be deprived of the ownership of property without a just cause.

18. Every individual shall enjoy the freedom of thought, conscience and faith and this right includes the rights of change of faith giving expression to his faith and to the preaching of faith and worship.

19. Every individual has the right of self-expression and it includes the right of holding any opinion and getting ideas and information as well as conveying them, without any intervention and with any means and without consideration of the frontiers.

20. (1) Every individual has the right of peaceful assembly and organization.

    (2) Nobody can be compelled to be associated with any particular organisation.

21. (1) Every individual has the right to participate, in the government of his country directly or through the elected representatives.

    (2) Every one has equal right of getting a government service in his own country.

    (3) The real basis of the authority of the 'government shall be the will and desire of the people which shall be manifested through elections in the form of free voting and secret ballot.

22. Every individual shall have the right of social protection for life with dignity and building up his personality and, through national effort and international cooperation and according to the resources of the state concerned shall be entitled to economic, social and cultural rights.

23. (1) Every individual shall have the right to work, to take to a profession of his own choice, to secure better and fair conditions of work, and security against unemployment.

    (2) Every individual without any discrimination, shall be entitled to equal wages for equal amount of work.

    (3) Every individual has the right of getting better and fair remuneration for his family ensuring a dignified living and if necessary, some other means may also be provided for his social security.

(4) Every individual shall have the right of forming trade unions and participating in them for safeguarding his interests.

24 Every individual shall have the right to rest, entertainment, reasonable fixation of working hours, and leave with pay.

25. (1) Every individual has the light to maintain a reasonable standard of life for his own health and prosperity and that of his family, which includes security of food, clothes, residential space, medical aid, essential service, unemployment, sickness, disability, widowhood, old age and such other conditions.

(2) Maternity and suckling period shall be deemed deserving of special attention and help. And all babies, whether born in or out of wedlock, shall receive equal social security.

26. (1) Every one has the right to receive education.

(2) The goal of education shall be the perfect building up of man's personality and inculcating deep respect for human rights and freedoms.

(3) The parent shall have the option of selecting the type of education their children should have.

27. (1) Every individual has the right to freely participate in the cultural life of the society, to receive his share of the entertainment provided by the sciences and arts, and to be benefited by the fruits of the scientific progress.

(2) Every individual has the right of the protection to the material or moral fruits of his scientific, literary or technical creative work.

28. Every individual has the right to pass his life in a social and international atmosphere ensuring the benefits given form of the rights and freedoms conferred by this charter.

29 (1) Every individual has certain obligations too, imposed by the society, observing which makes possible the free and perfect freedoms of other people.

(2) In connection with the rights and freedoms every person shall confine himself to those limits as ensure the rights and freedoms of other people.

(3) These rights and freedoms cannot be used against the aims and objects and principles of the United Nations Organisation.

30. No part of this charter shall be so interpreted as to acquire for any state, group or individual the right of engaging in an activity through which these definite rights and freedoms may be sabotaged.

The rights and freedoms declared in this Charter have been later divided into two portions. Under one list, economic social and cultural rights have been brought together and in the second list are included the civic rights and those of the State. The General Assembly approved these two covenants and left it to the discretion of the member states to sign them in case they voluntarily recognized these rights.

The UN Commission for Human Rights has done some further work in this connection. In 1959 it issued a declaration relating to the rights of children and in 1963 for the prevention of racial discrimination. The General Assembly adopted various covenants and resolutions in 1948 for the prevention of genocide, in 1951 for the security of migrants and exiled persons, in 1952 for the rights of women, in 1957 for the determination of the nationality of married women, in 1951 for the total prohibition of slavery and putting an end to it and in 1965 for the condemnation of racial discrimination in South Africa.

The special institutions of UN such as the International Labour Organization (ILO), United Nations Educational Scientific and Cultural Organization (UNESCO), International Rehabilitation Organization (IRO) and the High Commissioner for the displaced persons, have also done considerable work for the determination and protection of human rights.

But what is the outcome of these splendid efforts of the world charter of Human Rights and United Nations' Organization and its subsidiary institutions? Has this charter really redeemed man from the clutches of oppression, tyranny and dictatorship and Fascism so that he can now breathe in a free atmosphere and is in a position to be benefited by his rights? The true position of this Charter and the helplessness of the United Nations' Organization is very well brought out by the Western thinkers and international legal experts themselves.

> In 1947 the Commission adopted a report on the subject of implementation which reversed its previous attitude on the matter. It laid it down as a general rule that the Commission recognises that it has no power to take any action in regard to complaints concerning human rights.

It means that even a year prior to the declaration of the charter it was decided that it would have no legal status. If any country wishes to do so, it may go ahead with its enforcement voluntarily, otherwise it may consign it to that waste paper basket. Hans Kelson comments on it thus:

Judged strictly from a purely legalistic perspective, the provisions of the Charter do not impose upon the members any binding obligation to recognise and protect these human rights and freedoms to which reference is made in preamble or in the text of the Charter. The language used by the Charter does not allow for the interpretation that the members are under any legal obligation to grant human rights and freedom to their subjects.

What the charter has conferred on an individual to remove the high handedness of the states, Kerl Mannhein writes:

> The Charter does not confer upon the individuals the legal possibility to appeal to International Court and specially to the Principal Judicial organ of the United Nations, the International Court of Justice, in case one of the rights or freedoms proclaimed in the preamble or referred to in the text of Charter is violated. The statute of the court stipulates expressly in Article 34 that only states may be parties in cases before the court.

Exposing the real position of the economic and social rights, mentioned in the charter. Dr. Raphael says:

> The so-called economic and social rights, in so far as they are intelligible at all, impose no such universal duty. They are rights to be given things, things such as a decent income, schools, and social services. But who is called upon to do the giving? Whose duty is it? When the authors of the United Nations' Declaration of Human Rights assert that 'everyone has the right to social security', are they saying that everyone ought to subscribe to some form of world-wide social security system from which each in turn may benefit in case of need? If something of this kind is meant, why do the draft United Nations covenants, which are supposed to implement the Universal Declaration, make no provision for instituting such a system? And if no such system exists, where is the obligation, and where the right? To impose on men a 'duty' which they cannot possibly perform is as absurd in its way, though perhaps not as cruel, as bestowing on them a Right' which they cannot possibly enjoy.

A.K. Brohi says about these rights:

> But the rights in the current on economic and social rights are not rights in the accepted sense of the term in the reality, they are merely principles of social and economic policy. That incidentally explains the reason why two separate covenants had to be drawn up by the commission instead of one.

He has hinted at the two different ideological camps of the world, which do not only follow diametrically opposite policies but have totally different concepts of rights.

Having had an idea of the UN charter of Human Rights and the helplessness of the UNO, let us now see what a western thinker has to say about it in his frustrating analysis of the future possibilities:

> It cannot therefore be asserted that the legal protection of human rights has a bright future under the United Nations. The Organisation is made up of groups of states

> each with different conceptions of democracy and of the relationship between the state and the individual. Certain rights and freedoms are considered by the Western countries as fundamental to civilized society. These rights, they claim, constitute foundations for real democracy. The communist states, on the other hand, hold that no rights and freedoms are fundamental. According to them, the state is the creator of all rights and is entitled to make regular their enjoyment in the interest of society as a whole. Finally, many of the underdeveloped countries whose ambition is to achieve very quick economic and social developments, see in guarantees of the traditional civil and political rights and freedoms an obstacle to the attainment of desirable economic and social objectives. Having regard to all these differences, it is not surprising that the United Nations has been unable to achieve substantial results in the field of human rights, nor is it realistic to expect it to do so in the very immediate future.

A study of the Charter of Human Rights and the comments on it amply reveal the fact even man's collective efforts at the international level could not secure full guarantees of a dignified and respectable life for him. He is just as helpless before the excesses of the government to-day as he was in the days gone by. Rather, the ever-increasing sphere of the activities and the powers of the state have rendered the fundamental rights and civil liberties meaningless. The value of the Charter of Human Rights is no more than a beautiful document. A list of rights has certainly been made out very carefully but not one of these rights has any sanction and enforcing power at its back. It neither imposes any legal restraint on the states to prevent them from denying the fundamental rights to their citizens, nor provides for any forum to seek legal remedy for the restoration of the usurped rights of an individual. Thus, the charter is a totally useless and undependable document in protecting human rights. The maximum good that it has done to humanity is to establish a norm of human rights and has conferred on the world brotherhood of mankind a progressive consciousness of the protection of fundamental rights, has stressed the importance of the individual, and with its help and guidance the newly emancipated countries, when formulating their constitutions, find it easier to decorate the formal chapter of the fundamental rights. The status of this charter is only moralistic having no weight and no value from the legal point of view. As the protector of fundamental rights the strength and importance of this charter can be gauged from the fact that the international organisation concerned with the affairs of political prisoners, the Amnesty International, alone has brought on record in its published report for the year 1975-76, that 113 countries out of the 142 member states were found guilty of serious violation of the fundamental rights, and there has been a disturbing increase on the universal plane in the improper use of power, unjustified arrests, political incarcerations, coercion and violence and incidences of death penalty, muzzling of the press, curtailment of the powers of the judiciary, enforcement of the dictatorial ordinances and even laws.

PART—III

Practice

SEVEN

Fundamental Rights

All human beings, whether they belong to this country or that, whether they are a believers or unbelievers, whether they live in a forest or in a desert, have certain basic human rights simply because they are a human beings. We have seen, too, that it is the duty of every Muslim to recognize these rights. They are:

I. The Right to Life

The first and foremost basic right is the right to life. The Holy Qur'an lays down:

"Whosoever kills a human being, without any reason like manslaughter, or corruption on earth, it is though he had killed all mankind." (5:32)

The propriety of taking life in retaliation for murder or for spreading corruption can be decided only by a competent court of law. During a war it can be decided only by a properly established government. In any event, no individual has the right to decide such questions by himself. As the Holy Qur'an makes clear:

"Do not kill a soul which Allah has made sacred except through the due process of law." (6:151)

Homicide is thus distinguished from destruction of life carried out in the pursuit of justice. The Prophet, blessings of Allah and peace be upon him, has declared homicide as the greatest sin after polytheism. A Tradition of the Prophet reads: "The greatest sins are to associate something with God and to kill human beings."

In all these verses of the Qur'an and the Traditions of the Prophet the word 'soul' (nafs) has been used in general terms without any indication that citizens belonging to one's own nation or the people of a particular race or religion should not be killed. The injunction applies to all human beings.

The 'Right to Life' has been given to man as a whole only by Islam. You will observe that reference to human rights in constitutions or declarations in many countries clearly implies that these rights are applicable only to the citizens of that country or to the white race. For example, human beings were hunted down like animals in Australia and the land was cleared of the aborigines for the white man. Similarly, the aboriginal population of America was systematically destroyed and the Red Indians who somehow survived this genocide were confined to reservations. In Africa, human beings were also hunted down like wild animals. Contrary to this partial concept of human rights, Islam recognizes such rights for all human beings.

II. The Right to the Safety of Life

Immediately after the verse in the Holy Qur'an which has been mentioned in connection with the right to life, God says:

> "And whoever saves a life it is as though he had saved the lives of all mankind." (5:32)

There can be several forms of saving man from death. If a man is ill or wounded it is your duty to get him medical help. If he is dying of starvation, it is your duty to feed him. If he is drowning, it is your duty to rescue him. We regard it as our duty to save every human life, because it is thus that we have been enjoined in the Holy Qur'an.

III. Respect for the Chastity of Women

The third important element in the Charter of Human Rights granted by Islam is that a woman's chastity must be respected and protected at all times, whether she belongs to one's own nation or to the nation of an enemy, whether we find her in a remote forest or in a conquered city, whether she is our co-religionist or belongs to some other religion or has no religion at all. A Muslim may not physically abuse her under any circumstances. All promiscuous relationships are forbidden to him, irrespective of the status or position of the woman or of whether she is a willing partner to the act.

The words of the Holy Qur'an in this respect are: "Do not approach (the bounds) of adultery" (17:32). Heavy punishment has been prescribed for this crime, and no mitigating circumstances are indicated. Since the violation of the chastity of a woman is forbidden in Islam, a Muslim who perpetrates this crime cannot escape punishment whether he receives it in this world or in the Hereafter.

This concept of the sanctity of chastity and the protection of women can be found nowhere else except in Islam. The armies of the Western powers need the daughters of their own nations to satisfy their carnal appetites even in their own countries, and if they happen to occupy another country, the fate of its womenfolk can better be imagined than described.

But the history of the Muslims, apart from individual lapses, has been free from this crime against womanhood. It has never happened that after the conquest of a foreign country the Muslim army has gone about raping the women of the conquered people, or, in their own country, the government has arranged to provide prostitutes for them.

From the point of view of Islam, not only the woman but also the man possesses chastity. A man who perpetrates rape or adultery spoils not only the chastity of the woman, but his own as well.

IV. The Right to a Basic Standard of Life

Speaking about economic rights, the Holy Qur'an enjoins its followers:

> "And in their wealth there is acknowledged right for the needy and destitute." (51:12)

The wording of this injunction shows that it is categorical and unqualified. Furthermore, this injunction was given in Makka where there was no Muslim society in existence and where the Muslims came in contact mostly with disbelievers.

The clear meaning of this verse is that anyone who asks for help and anyone who is suffering from deprivation has a right to share in the property and wealth of a Muslim: irrespective of whether he belongs to this or to that nation, to this or to that country, to this or to that race. If one is in a position to help and a needy person asks for help or if one comes to know that he is in need. then it is one's duty to help him.

V. The Individual's Right to Freedom

Islam has categorically forbidden the primitive practice of capturing a free man to make him a slave or to sell him into slavery. On this point the unequivocal words of the Prophet (blessings of Allah and peace be upon him) are as follows: "There are three categories of people against whom I shall myself be a plaintiff on the Day of Judgement. Of these three, one is he who enslaves a free man, then sells him and eats this money".

The words of this Tradition of the Prophet have not been qualified or restricted to a particular nation or race, or to followers of a particular religion. The Europeans take great pride in claiming that they abolished slavery from the world, though they had the decency to do so only in the middle of the last century. Before this, the Western powers had been raiding Africa on a very large scale, capturing free men, putting them in bondage and transporting them to their new colonies. The treatment which they meted out to these unfortunate people was worse than that given to animals. Accounts in Western books themselves bear testimony to this fact

Slave Trade of Western Nations. After the occupation of America and the West Indies, traffic in slave trade continued for three hundred and fifty years. The African ports where the Africans were brought from the interior and put on ships came to be known as the Slave Coast. In the course of only one century (from 1680 to 1786), the total number of free people who were captured and enslaved for the British Colonies amounts, according to the estimate of British authors, to 20 million. We are told that in the year 1790,

75,000 human beings were captured and sent for slave labour in the colonies. The ships which were used for transporting the slaves were small and dirty. These unfortunate Africans were thrust into the holds like cattle and many of them, were chained, one on top of the other, to wooden shelves on which they could hardly move because they were only eighteen inches apart. They were not given proper food, and if they fell ill or were injured, no attempt was made to provide them with medical treatment.

Western writers themselves state that at least 20 per cent of the total number of people who were captured for slavery and forced labour perished while being transported from Africa to America. It has also been estimated that the total number of people who were captured for slavery by the various European nations during the heyday of the slave trade was at least one hundred million. This is the record of the people who denounce Muslims for recognizing the institution of slavery. It is as if a criminal is pointing the finger of blame at an innocent man.

Position of Slavery in Islam. Islam tried to solve the problem of the slaves that were already in Arabia by encouraging people to set them free. Muslims were told that freeing slaves would mean the expiation of some of their sins. Freeing a slave of one's own free will was declared to be an act of such great merit that the limbs of the man who freed a slave would be protected from hell-fire—one for each limb of the slave freed.

The result of this policy was that, by the time the period of the rightly-guided Caliphs was reached, all the old slaves of Arabia had been liberated. The Prophet (blessings of Allah and peace be upon him) alone liberated as many as 63 slaves. The number of slaves freed by Aisha was 67; Abbas liberated 70; Abd Allah bin Umar liberated one thousand; and Abd al-Rahman purchased thirty thousand and set them free. Other companions of the Prophet liberated a large number of slaves, the details of which are given in the traditions and books of history of that period.

The problem of the slaves of Arabia was thus solved in under 40 years. After this the only slaves left in Islamic society were prisoners of war captured on the battlefield. These were kept by the Muslim government in question until their own government agreed to receive them back in exchange for Muslim soldiers captured by them or arranged the payment of ransom on their behalf. If the soldiers they captured were not exchanged for Muslim prisoners of war, or their people did not pay their ransom money to purchase their liberty, the Muslim government distributed them among the soldiers of the army which had captured them.

This was a more humane way of disposing of them than penning them like cattle in concentration camps and taking forced labour from them and, if their womenfolk were also captured, setting them aside for prostitution. Islam preferred to spread them through the population and thus bring them in contact with individual human beings. Their guardians, in addition, were ordered to treat them well.

The result of this policy was that most of the men who were captured on foreign battlefields and brought to the Muslim countries as slaves embraced Islam and their descendants produced great scholars, imams, jurists, commentators, statesmen and generals. So much so that later they became rulers of the Muslim world.

Today prisoners of war throughout the world are exchanged on the cessation of hostilities. This is a practice which has been learnt from Islam. But treating well prisoners who cannot, for one reason or another, be exchanged, has not been learnt. Can anyone tell us, for example, the fate of the thousands of prisoners of war captured by Russia from the defeated armies of Germany and Japan in the Second World War? No one knows how many thousands of them are still alive and how many thousands of them perished due to the hardships of the Russian concentration and labour camps. It is doubtful if, even in the times of the ancient Pharaohs of Egypt, such harsh labour was exacted from the slaves who built the pyramids as was exacted from the prisoners of war in Russia who developed Siberia and other backward areas of the country.

VI. The Right to Justice

This is a very important and valuable right which Islam has given to man. The Holy Qur'an has laid down: "Do not let your hatred of a people incite you to aggression" (5:3). "And do not let ill-will towards any folk incite you so that you swerve from dealing justly. Be just: that is nearest to heedfulness" (5:8). Stressing this point the Qur'an again says: "You who believe stand steadfast before God as witness for (truth and) fair play" (4:135)

The point is thus made clear that Muslims have to be just not only to their friends but also their enemies. In other words, the justice to which Islam invites her followers is not limited to the citizens of one's own country, or the people of one's own tribe, nation or race, or the Muslim community as a whole; it is meant for all human beings.

VII. The Equality of Human Beings

Islam not only recognizes the principle of absolute equality between men irrespective of colour, race or nationality, it makes it an important reality. Almighty God has laid down in the Holy Qur'an: "O mankind, we have created you from a male and female." In other words, all human beings are brothers. They all are the descendants from one father and one mother. And we set you up as nations and tribes so that you may be able to recognize each other" (49:13). This means that the division of human beings into nations, races, groups and tribes is for the sake of distinction, so that people of one race or tribe may meet and be acquainted with people belonging to another race or tribe and co-operate with one another.

This division of the human race is neither meant for one nation to take pride in its superiority over others nor for one nation to treat another with contempt. "Indeed, the noblest among you before God are the most heedful of you" (49:13). That is, the superiority of one man over another is only on the basis of God-consciousness, purity of character and high morals, and not colour, race, language or nationality. People are therefore not justified in assuming airs of superiority over other human beings. Nor do the righteous have any special privileges over others.

This has been thus exemplified by the Prophet (blessings of Allah and peace be upon him) in one of his sayings: "No Arab has any superiority over a non-Arab, nor does a non-Arab have any superiority over a black man, or the black man any superiority over the white man. You are all the children of Adam, and Adam was created from clay." In this manner Islam established the principle of equality of the entire human race and struck at the very root of all distinctions based on colour, race, language or nationality.

According to Islam, God has given man this right of equality as a birthright. No man should therefore be discriminated against on the grounds of the colour of his skin, his place of birth, the race or the nation in which he was born.

Malcolm X, the leader of African Negroes in America, once launched a bitter struggle against the white people of America in order to win civil rights for his black compatriots. But when he went to perform the pilgrimage, he saw how the Muslims of Asia, Africa, Europe and America were all wearing the same dress and were all hurrying towards the mosque and were offering prayers standing in the same row. He realized that this was the solution to the problem of colour and race, and not what he had been trying to seek or achieve in America. Today, a number of non-Muslim thinkers openly admit that no other religion or way of life has solved this problem with the same degree of success as Islam.

VIII. The Right to Co-operate and not to Co-operate

Islam has prescribed a general principle of paramount importance and universal application. The Holy Qur'an says: "Co-operate with one another for virtue and heedfulness and do not co-operate with one another for the purpose of vice and aggression" (5:2). This means that the man who undertakes noble and righteous work, irrespective of whether he is living at the North Pole or the South Pole, has the right to expect support and active co-operation from Muslims. But he who practises vice and aggression, even if he is our closest relation or neighbour, does not have the right to our support and help in the name of race, country, language or nationality, nor should he expect Muslims to co-operate with him.

The wicked and vicious person may be our own brother, but he is not of us, and he can have no help or support from us as long as he does not repent of his ways. On the other hand, the man who is doing deeds of virtue and righteousness may have no kinship with Muslims, but Muslims will be his companions and supporters, or at least his well-wishers.

Rights of Citizens

We have discussed human rights in general. We turn now specifically to the question of the rights of citizens in an Islamic state. As these rights are more extensive than the general human rights which have been described earlier, they need separate treatment.

I. The Security of Life and Property

In the address which the Prophet (blessings of Allah and peace be upon him) delivered on the occasion of the Farewell Hajj, he said: "Your lives and properties are forbidden to one another till you meet your Lord on the Day of Resurrection." God Almighty has laid down in the Holy Qur'an: "Anyone who kills a believer deliberately will receive as his reward (a sentence) to live in Hell for ever. God will be angry with him and curse him, and prepare dreadful torment for him" (4:93). The Prophet (blessings of Allah and peace be upon him) has also said about the dhimmis (the non-Muslim citizens of a Muslim state): "One who kills a man under covenant (i.e. a dhimmi) will not even smell the fragrance of Paradise" (Bukhari and Abu Dawud).

Islam prohibits all killing except that done in the due process of law. This is referred to in the Qur'an as bi'l-haqq ("with the truth"). During wars or insurrections, only a just and righteous government, which follows the shan'a, can decide whether the taking of a life is justified.

These weighty decisions may not be left in the hands of a court which has become heedless of God's will and is under the influence of the administration. Such judiciary may miscarry justice. Nor can the state seek justification in the Holy Qur'an or Traditions if it murders citizens because they oppose unjust policies and actions or criticize it for its misdeeds; equally, the state has no right to hire assassins to kill innocent people and then protect the assassins from the just retribution of the courts. The very existence of such a government is a crime and none of the killings carried out by it can be called "execution for the sake of justice", as the Holy Qur'an puts it.

Along with security of life, Islam has with equal clarity conferred the right of security of ownership of property. The Holy Qur'an goes so far as to declare that the taking of people's possessions or property is prohibited unless done by lawful means: The law of God categorically declares "Do not devour one another's wealth by false and illegal means" (2:188).

II. The Protection of Honour

The second important right is the right of citizens to the protection of their honour. In the address delivered on the occasion of the Farewell Hajj, the Prophet (blessings of Allah and peace be upon him) not only prohibited Muslims taking the life and property of other Muslims, but also any encroachment on their honour, respect and chastity. The Holy Qur'an lays down:

(a) "You who believe, do not let one (set of) people make—of another set.

(b) Do not defame one another.

(c) Do not insult by using nicknames.

(d) And do not backbite or speak ill of one another" (49:11-12)

This law is superior to the Western law of defamation- (Jader Islamic law, if it is proved that someone has attacked the honour of a another person. then, irrespective of whether the victim is able to prove himself a respectable and honourable person, the culprit will be punished The interesting fact about the Western law of defamation is that the person who files suit for defamation has first to prove that he is a man of honour and public esteem and during the interrogation he may be subjected to scurrilous attacks and accusations by the defence counsel to such an extent that the court hearing may be more damaging than the attack on his reputation which originally led him to the court. In addition, he also has to produce witnesses to testify in court that the defamatory accusations have damaged his reputation in their eyes.

Good gracious! What a subtle point of law and what an adherence to the spirit of law! How can this unfair and unjust law be compared to the Divine law? Islam has declared defamation a cnme irrespective of whether the accused is a man of honour, or whether the words used have actually disgraced the victim and harmed his reputation. Under Islamic law it is sufficient to prove that the accused said things which according to common sense, could have damaged the reputation and honour of the plaintiff.

III. The Sanctity and Security of Private Life

Islam recognizes the right of every citizen in an Islamic state to no undue encroachment on the privacy of his life. The Holy Qur'an has laid down the injunction: "Do not spy on one another" (49:12). "Do not enter any house except your own homes unless you are sure of their occupants' consent" (24:27). The Prophet (blessings of Allah and peace be upon him) went to the extent of instructing his followers that a man should not enter even his own house suddenly or surreptitiously. He should somehow indicate to those inside that he is entering so that he may not see his mother, sister or daughter in a condition in which they would not like to be seen, nor in which he himself would like to see them.

Peering into the houses of other people has also been strictly prohibited so much so that there is the saying of the Prophet (blessings of Allah and peace be upon him) that if a man finds another person secretly peering into his house, and he puts out his eye or eyes as a punishment, he will not be liable to prosecution.

The Prophet (blessings of Allah and peace be upon him) has even prohibited people from reading the letters of others; indeed, if a man is reading his letter and another man casts sidelong glances at it and tries to read it, his conduct becomes reprehensible. These are examples of the sanctity of privacy that Islam grants to individuals.

On the other hand, in the so-called modern civilised world we find that not only are the letters of other people read and censored, but even that photostat copies are retained for future use or blackmail. Bugging devices are secretly fixed in houses so that conversations taking place behind closed doors can be taped. In other words, in many spheres of life individuals have no real privacy.

This prying into the life of the individual cannot be justified on moral grounds by a government saying that it needs to know the secrets of potentially dangerous persons. The basis of this philosophy is the fear and suspicion with which modern governments look at those of their citizens who are intelligent and dissatisfied with official policies. This is exactly what Islam has called the root cause of mischief in politics. The injunction of the Prophet (blessings of Allah and peace be upon him) is: "When the ruler begins to search for the causes of dissatisfaction amongst his people, he spoils them" (Abu Dawud). The Amir Mu'awiya has said that he himself heard the Prophet saying: "If you try to find out the secrets of the people, then you will definitely spoil them or at least you will bring them to the verge of ruin."

"Spoiling" people is what happens when secret police are spread all around a country looking into their affairs: men begin to look at one another with suspicion, so much so that they are afraid of talking freely in their houses lest some word should escape from the lips of their wives and children which may put them in embarrassing situations. In this manner, it becomes difficult for a common citizen to speak freely, even in his own house: society begins to suffer from mutual distrust and suspicion.

IV. The Security of Personal Freedom

Islam has laid down the principle that no citizen may be imprisoned unless his guilt has been proved in open court. To arrest a man only on the basis of suspicion and to throw him into prison without proper court proceedings and without providing him with a reasonable opportunity to produce his defence is not permissible in Islam.

It is related in the Traditions that the Prophet (blessings of Allah and peace be upon him) was once delivering a lecture in the Mosque, when a man rose and said: "O Prophet of God, for what crime have my neighbours been arrested?" The Prophet appeared not to hear the question and continued his lecture. The man rose again and repeated the question. The Prophet again did not answer and continued his lecture. The man rose for a third time and repeated the question. Then the Prophet ordered the man's neighbours to be released.

The reason why the Prophet had not answered when the question was asked twice earlier was that the police officer who had carried out the arrest was present in the Mosque; if there had been valid reasons for the arrest, he would have got up to give them. Since the police officer did not, the Prophet ordered that the arrested persons should be released. The police officer was aware of Islamic law and therefore he did not get up to say: "The administration is aware of the charges against the arrested men, but they cannot be disclosed in public. If the Prophet inquires about their guilt in camera I will enlighten him." If the police officer had made such a statement, he would have been dismissed then and there. The fact that the police officer did not give any reasons for the arrests in open court was sufficient for the Prophet to give immediate orders for the release of the arrested men.

The injunction of the Holy Qur'an is very clear on this point. "Whenever you judge between people, you should judge with (a sense of) justice" (4:58). And the Prophet (blessings of Allah and peace be upon him) said: "I have been ordered by God to dispense justice between you." This was the reason why the Caliph Umar said: "In Islam no one can be imprisoned except in pursuance of justice." The words used here clearly indicate that justice means due process of law in open court.

If a government suspects that a particular individual has committed a crime or is likely to commit an offence in the near future, it should give reasons for its suspicion before a court of law and the culprit or the suspect should be allowed to produce his defence. If good reason for suspicion is proved, he should be informed of how long he will be kept in preventive detention.

In all such circumstances, it is essential that the public hear the charges brought by the government, as well as the defence made by the accused, and thus have the opportunity of seeing that the due process of law is being carried out.

The correct method of dealing with such cases in Islam is exemplified in the famous decision the Prophet (blessings of Allah and peace be upon him) made before the conquest of Makka. The Prophet was making preparations for the attack on the city when one of his companions, Hatib bin Abi Balta'a, sent a letter through a woman to the authorities in Makka informing them of the impending attack. The Prophet came to know of this through a Divine inspiration. He ordered 'Ait and Zubair: "Go quickly on the route to Makka, at such and such a place, you will find a woman carrying a letter. Recover the letter from her and bring it to me." So they went and found the woman exactly where the Prophet had said. They recovered the letter from her and brought it to the Prophet.

This was indeed a clear case of treachery. In fact, one cannot think of a more serious crime during a time of war than giving a military secret to one's enemy. What could have been a more suitable case for a secret hearing than one into the betrayal of a military secret? But the Prophet summoned Hatib to the open court of the Mosque of the Prophet and in the presence of hundreds of people asked him to explain his position with regard to the letter addressed to the leaders of Quraysh.

The accused said: "O God's Messenger (may God's blessings be on you) I have not revolted against Islam, nor have I done this with the intention of betraying a military secret. The truth of the matter is that my wife and children are living in Makka and I do not have my tribe to protect them there. I had written this letter so that the leaders of Quraysh may be indebted to me and may protect my wife and children out of gratitude." Umar rose and respectfully submitted: "O Prophet, please permit me to put this traitor to the sword." The Prophet replied: "He is one of those people who took part in the battle of Badr and the explanation he has advanced in his defence would seem to be acceptable."

Let us look at this decision of the Prophet in perspective. It was a clear case of treachery and betrayal of military secrets. But the Prophet acquitted Hatib on two counts. Firstly, that his past record was clean in that he had fought at the battle of Badr when there were heavy odds against the Muslims. Secondly, his family was in fact in danger in Makka. In such circumstances it was sufficient punishment that his secret offence became public and that he was disgraced and humiliated in the eyes of the Believers.

The attitude and activities of the Kharijites in the days of the Caliph Hazrat Ali are well known to students of Muslim history. They used to abuse the Caliph openly, and threaten him with murder. But whenever they were arrested. for these offences, 'AIT would set them free and tell his officers: "As long as they do not actually perpetrate offences against state, the mere use of abusive language or the threat of use of force are not such offences for which they can be imprisoned." The Imam Abu Hanifa has recorded following saying of the Caliph Hazrat Ali, "As long as they do not set out on led rebellion, the Caliph of the Faithful will not interfere with them." On another occasion, 'He was delivering a lecture in the Mosque when Kharijites raised their special slogan there. 'He said: We will not deny the right to come to the mosques to worship God, nor will we stop your share from the wealth of the state, as long as you are with us (and support us in wars against the unbelievers) and we shall never take military action it you as long as you do not fight with us."

One can visualize the opposition which 'All was facing: more violent and vituperative opposition cannot be imagined even in a present-day democratic state, but the freedom that he allowed to the opposition was such that no government has ever since been able to give to its opposition.

V. The Right to Protest against Tyranny

Amongst the rights that Islam has conferred on human beings is the right to protest against a government's tyranny. The Qur'an says: "God does not love evil talk in public unless it is by someone who has been injured thereby" (4:148). This means that God strongly disapproves of abusive language or strong words of condemnation, but that the person who has been the victim of injustice or tyranny has the right to protest strongly against the injury that has been done to him.

This right is not limited to individuals. The words of the verse have general application. If an individual or a group of people or a party usurps power and, after assuming the reins of authority, begins to tyrannize individuals or groups of men or the entire population of the country, then to raise the voice of protest is the God-given right of man. Trying to usurp this right is tantamount to rebellion against God. The talisman of Section 144 may protect such a tyrant in this world, but it cannot save him from hell-fire in the Hereafter.

VI. Freedom of Expression

Islam gives the right of freedom of thought and expression to all citizens of an Islamic State on condition that it is used for propagating virtue and not for spreading evil. This Islamic concept of freedom of expression is far superior to that of the West. Indeed, the right to freedom of expression to propagate virtue and righteousness is not only a right, but an obligation. Anyone who tries to deny this right to his people is openly at war with God, the All-Powerful. It is equally a right of and an obligation on an individual to attempt to stop evil, whether this evil is perpetrated by an individual or by a group of people or the government of one's own country or the government of some other country. Over and above this, he should openly condemn the evil and point to the morally correct course which should be adopted.

The Holy Qur'an has described this quality of the faithful in the following words: "They enjoin what is proper and forbid what is improper" (9:71). By contrast, describing the qualities of a hypocrite, the Qur'an says:

"They bid what is improper and forbid what is proper" (9:67). The main purpose of an Islamic government has been defined by God in the Qur'an as follows: "If we give authority to these men on earth they will keep up prayers, and offer welfare due, bid what is proper and forbid what is improper" (22:41). The Prophet has said: "If any one of you comes across an evil, he should try to stop it with his hand (using force): if he is not in a position to stop it with his hand then he should try to stop it by means of his tongue (meaning he should speak against it). If he is not even able to use his tongue then he should at least condemn it in his heart. This is the weakest degree of faith."

The obligation to try to persuade people along the paths of righteousness and away from the paths of evil is incumbent on all true Muslims. Any government which deprives its citizens of this right is in direct conflict with divine injunction. Such a government is then not in conflict with its people, but with God: it is trying to usurp that right of its people which God has conferred not merely as a right but as an obligation.

VII. Freedom of Association

Islam has also given people the right to freedom of association and formation of parties or organizations. This right is subject to certain general rules. It should be exercised for propagating virtue and righteousness and never for spreading evil and mischief. We have not only been given this right to spread righteousness and virtue— we have been ordered to exercise it. Addressing the Muslims, the Holy Qur'an declares:

"You are the best community which has been brought forth for mankind. You command what is proper and forbid what is improper and you believe in God" (3:110).

This means that it is the obligation and duty of the entire Muslim community to enjoin people to righteousness and virtue and forbid them to do evil. If the Muslim community as a whole does not perform this duty then "let there be a community among you who will invite (people) to (do) good, command what is proper and forbid what is improper, those will be prosperous" (3:104). This clearly indicates that if the community collectively begins to neglect its obligations, then it is absolutely essential lor there to be at least one group within the community prepared to meet them.

It is ironic that in a Muslim country the assembly and association that has been formed for the purpose of spreading evil and mischief should also have the right to rule over the country and the association and party which has been formed for the purpose of propagating righteousness and virtue should live in perpetual fear of harassment and of being declared illegal. Conditions here are the reverse of what has been prescribed by God. The claim is that we are Muslims and that this is an Islamic State, but the work that is being done is directed to spreading evil, to corrupting and morally degrading and debasing people, while there is active and effective hindrance on the work being carried out to reform society and point people to righteousness. Moreover, the lives of those who are engaged in spreading righteousness and checking the spread of evil and wickedness are made intolerable.

VIII. Freedom of Conscience and Conviction

Islam gives the right to freedom of conscience and conviction to the citizens of an Islamic State. The Holy Qur'an has laid down the injunction:

"There should be no coercion in the matter of faith" (2:256). Although there is no truth or virtue greater than Islam, and although Muslims are enjoined to invite people to embrace it and advance arguments in favour of it, they are not asked to spread this faith by force. Whoever accepts it does so by his own choice. Muslims welcome such converts to Islam with open arms and admit them to their community with equal rights and privileges. But, equally, Muslims have to recognize and respect the decision of people who do not accept Islam: no moral, social or political pressures may be put on them to change their minds.

IX. Protection of Religious Sentiments

Along with freedom of conviction and freedom of conscience, Islam guarantees the individual that his religious sentiments will be given due respect and that nothing will be said or done which may encroach on this right. It is ordained by God in the Holy Qur'an: "Do not abuse those they appeal to instead of God" (6:108). These instructions are not limited to idols and deities—they also apply to the leaders or national heroes of the people. If a group of people hold certain convictions and certain persons in an esteem which you feel is not deserved, then it is not justifiable in Islam for you to use abusive language to them and thus injure their feelings. Islam does not prohibit people holding debate and discussions to be conducted in decency. "Do not argue with the people of the Book unless it is in the politest manner" (29:46), says the Qur'an. This order is not limited to the people of the Scriptures, but applies with equal force to those following other faiths.

X. Protection from Arbitrary Imprisonment

Islam recognizes the right of the individual not to be arrested or imprisoned for the offences of others. The Holy Qur'an has laid down this principle clearly: "No bearer of burdens shall be made to bear the burden of another" (6:164). Islam believes in personal responsibility. We ourselves are responsible for our acts, and their consequences cannot be transferred to someone else.

It is a matter of great regret and shame that we are seeing this just and equitable principle, which has been framed by the Creator and Nourisher of the entire universe, being flouted and violated before our eyes. So much so that if a man is guilty of a crime or if he is a suspect, his wife is also liable to arrest. Indeed, things have gone so far that innocent people are being punished for the crimes of others.

To give a recent example, a man in Karachi was suspected of being involved in a bomb-throwing incident. In the course of police investigations he was subjected to horrible torture to try to extract a confession from him. When he insisted on his innocence, the police arrested his mother, his wife, daughter and sister and brought them to the police station. They were all stripped naked in his presence, and he was stripped naked before their eyes so that a confession of the crime could be extracted from him. It appears as if for the sake of investigation of crime it has become proper and legal to strip innocent womenfolk of a household in order to bring pressure on a suspect.

I would here like to ask what right such tyrants—who perpetrate these crimes against mankind—have to tell us that they are Muslims or that they are conducting the affairs of the state according to the teachings of Islam. They are flouting a clear law of the Holy Qur'an by stripping men and women naked. They disgrace and humiliate humanity—and then they claim that they are Muslims.

XI. The Right to the Basic Necessities of Life

Islam has recognized the right of the needy to assistance. "And in their wealth there is acknowledged right for the needy and the destitute" (51:19). In this verse, the Qur'an has not only conferred a right to every man who asks for assistance in the wealth of the Muslims, but has also laid down that if a Muslim comes to know that a certain man is without the basic necessities of life, then, irrespective of whether he asks for assistance or not, it is his duty to give all the help that he can.

For this purpose, Islam does not depend only on voluntary charity, but has made compulsory charity, its third pillar, next only to the profession of faith and worship of God through regular prayers. The Prophet (blessings of Allah and peace be upon him) has clearly instructed us: "It will be taken from their rich and given to those in the community in need."

In addition, it has also been declared that the Islamic State should support those who have nobody to support them. The Prophet has said:

"The Head of State is the guardian of him who has nobody to support him" (Abu Dawud, Tirmidhi). The word which is used by the Prophet has a wide range of meanings. It is the duty and the responsibility of the state to support and assist orphans, the old, the unemployed and the sick if they have no one to help them. If a dead man has no guardian or heir, it is the duty of the state to arrange for his burial. A true Islamic State is therefore a true welfare state.

XII. Equality Before the Law

Islam gives its citizens the right to absolute equality in the eyes of the law. As far as Muslims are concerned, there are clear instructions in the Holy Qur'an and Hadith that in their rights and obligations they are all equal: "The believers are brothers (to each other)" (49:10). "If they (disbelievers) repent and keep up prayer and pay the welfare due they are your brothers in faith" (9:11), The Prophet has said that: "The life and blood of Muslims are equally precious" (Abu Dawud. Ibn Maja). In another Hadith he has said: "The protection given by all Muslims are equal. Even an ordinary man of them can grant protection to any man." In another more detailed Tradition of the Prophet, it has been said that those who accept the Oneness of God, believe in the Prophethood of His Messenger, give up primitive prejudices and join the Muslim community and brotherhood, "then they have the same rights and obligations as other Muslims have." Thus there is absolute equality between converts to Islam and born followers of the Faith.

This religious brotherhood and the uniformity of their rights and obligations is the foundation of equality in Islamic society. The position of non-Muslim citizens in an Islamic State has been well expressed by the Caliph AIT: "They have accepted our protection only because their lives may be like our lives and their properties like our properties" (Abu Dawud). In other words, their lives and properties are as sacred as the lives and properties of Muslims. Discrimination based on class was one of the greatest crimes that, according to the Qur'an, Pharaoh used to indulge in:

"He had divided his people into different classes," ... "And he suppressed one group of them (at the cost of others)" (28:4).

XIII. Rulers are not Above the Law

Islam insists and demands that all officials of an Islamic State, from most senior to most junior, are equal in the eyes of the law. None of them can claim immunity from it. The most humble citizen has the right to file a legal complaint against the highest executive in the land. The Caliph Umar said: "I have myself seen the Prophet, may God's blessings be on him, taking revenge against himself (penalizing himself for some shortcoming or failing)." On the occasion of the battle of Badr. when the Prophet was straightening the rows of the Muslim army, he hit the stomach of a soldier in an attempt to push him back in line. The soldier complained, "O Prophet, you have hurt me with your stick." The Prophet immediately bared his stomach and said, "I am very sorry, you can revenge by doing the same to me." The soldier came forward and kissed the abdomen of the Prophet and said that this was all that he wanted.

A woman belonging to a high and noble family was arrested in connection with a theft. The case was brought to the Prophet and it was recommended that she be spared punishment. The Prophet replied: "The nations that lived before you were destroyed by God because they punished the common man for their offences and let their dignitaries go unpunished for their crimes: I swear by Him (God) who holds my life in His hand that even if Fatima, the daughter of Muhammad, had committed this crime, then I would have amputated her hand."

During the caliphate of Umar, Muhammad the son of Amr bin al-As, the Governor of Egypt, whipped an Egyptian.The Egyptian went to Madina and lodged his complaint with the Caliph, who immediately summoned the Governor and his son. When they appeared before him the Caliph handed a whip to the Egyptian plaintiff and asked him to whip the son of the Governor in his presence. After the Egyptian had taken his revenge, Umar said to him: "Give one stroke of the whip to the Honourable Governor as well. His son would certainly not have beaten you were it not for the false pride that he had in his father's high office." The plaintiff submitted: "The person who had beaten me, I have already avenged myself on him." 'Umar said: "By God, if you had beaten him (the Governor), I would not have checked you from doing so. You have spared him of your own free will." Then he ('Umar) turned to Amr bin al-As and said angrily: "O Amr, when did you start to enslave the people, though they were born free of their mothers?"

When the Islamic State was nourishing in its pristine glory, the common people could equally lodge complaints against the caliph of the time in the court and the caliph had to appear before the qadi answer the charges. And if the caliph had any complaint against any citizen, he could not act without first referring the case to the court of law.

XIV. The Right to Avoid Sin

Islam confers the right on every citizen to refuse to commit a sin or a crime; if any government or administrator orders an individual to do a wrong, he may refuse to comply. Not only is his refusal not an offence, the giving of an order to one's subordinates to commit a sin or do a wrong is itself an offence and such a serious one that the officer who gives it, whatever his rank, is liable to summary dismissal.

These clear instructions of the Prophet are summarized in the following Hadith. "It is not permissible to disobey God in obedience to the orders of any human being" (Musnad of Ibn Hanbal). In other words, no-one has the right to order his subordinates to act against the laws of God. No offender may seek to prove his innocence or escape punishment by saying that the offence was committed on the orders of a superior. If such a situation arises, the person who commits the offence and the person who orders it are equally liable to criminal proceedings.

XV. The Right to Participate in the Affairs of State

According to Islam, governments are representatives (khalifa) of the Creator of the universe; this responsibility is not entrusted to any individual or family or to any particular class or group of people, but to the entire Muslim community. The Holy Qur'an says: "God has promised to appoint in which the right of every individual Muslim is neither more nor less than the right of any other person.

The method recommended by the Holy Qur'an for running the affairs of the state is as follows: "And their business is (conducted) through consultation among themselves" (42:38). According to this principle, it is the right of every Muslim either to have a direct say in the affairs of the state or to have a representative chosen by him and other Muslims to participate in the running of the state.

Under no circumstances does Islam permit an individual or a group or party of individuals to deprive the common Muslims of their rights or usurp powers of the state. Nor does Islam regard it as right and proper for an individual to put on a false show of setting up a legislative assembly and by means of such tactics as fraud, persecution, bribery and so on, get himself and men of his choice elected to the assembly. This is not only treachery against the people whose rights are illegally usurped, but also against the Creator who has entrusted Muslims to rule on earth on His behalf, and has prescribed the procedure of an assembly for exercising these powers.

The shura or legislative assembly should embrace the following principles:

1. The executive head of the government and the members of the assembly should be elected by free and independent choice of the people.
2. The people and their representatives should have the right to criticize and freely express their opinions.
3. The real conditions of the country should be brought before the people without suppression of fact so that they are in a position to judge whether the government is working properly or not.
4. There should be adequate guarantee that only those people who have the support of the masses should rule over the country and those who fail to win this support should be removed from their position of authority.

Rights of Enemies

Before the advent of Islam the world was ignorant of the concept of humane and decent rules of war. The West first began to develop this concept through the works of the seventeenth century thinker, Grotius. But the actual codification of 'international law' in war began in the middle of the nineteenth century. Prior to this, all forms of barbarism and savagery were perpetrated in war, and the rights of those in a war were not even recognized, let alone respected.

The 'laws' which were framed in this field during the nineteenth century or over the following period up to the present day cannot be called laws in the real sense of the word. They are only conventions and agreements, because nations do not regard them as binding unless, of course, their adversaries also agree to abide by them. In other words, these civilized laws imply that if our enemies respect them, we shall also respect them, but if they ignore them then we shall ignore them, too. Arrangements which depend on mutual acceptability cannot be called 'laws'. This is the reason why so-called 'international law' has been constantly flouted and ignored.

Law of War and Peace in Islam

The rules which have been framed by Islam to make war civilized and humane are in the nature of law, because they are the injunctions of God and His Prophet (blessings of Allah and peace be upon him) which are followed by Muslims in all circumstances, irrespective of the behaviour of enemy. It would be instructive to research into how well the West has adopted the laws of war given by Islam fourteen hundred years ago; and, even after their adoption, how well the West has managed to attain those heights of civilized and human warfare behaviour which Muslims have reached through the blessings of Islam.

Western writers have often asserted that the Prophet (blessings of Allah and peace be upon him) borrowed his teachings from the Jews and Christians. It is sufficient here to recommend the reader to refer to the Bible so that he can see what methods of war are recommended by the sacred Book of these Western claimants to civilization and culture.

We have examined in some detail the basic human rights that Islam has conferred on man. Let us now look at the rights and obligations Islam recognizes for an enemy.

Rights of Non-combatants

Islam has drawn a clear distinction between combatants and non combatants in an enemy country. As far as the non-combatant population is concerned—women, children, the old and the infirm - the instructions of the Prophet are as follows: "Do not kill any old person, any child or any woman." "Do not kill the monks in monasteries" and "Do not kill the people who are sitting in places of worship."

During a war, the Prophet saw the corpse of a woman lying on the ground and observed: "She was not fighting. How then came she to be killed?" From this statement of the Prophet, the exegesists and jurists have drawn the principle that those who are non-combatants should not be killed during or after a war.

Rights of Combatants

Now let us see what rights Islam has conferred on the combatants.

I. Torture by fire

In the Hadith, there is a saying of the Prophet that: "Punishment by fire does not behove anyone except the Master of the Fire." The injunction deduced from this saying is that the adversary should not be burnt alive.

II. Protection of the wounded

"Do not attack a wounded person", said the Prophet. This means that wounded soldiers who are not fit to fight, nor actually fighting, should not be attacked.

III. Prisoners of war should not be slain

"No prisoner should be put to the sword" —a very clear and unequivocal instruction given by the Prophet.

IV. No one should be tied to be killed

"The Prophet has prohibited the killing of anyone who is tied or is in captivity."'

V. No looting and destruction in the enemy's country

Muslims have been instructed by the Prophet not to pillage or plunder or destroy residential areas, nor harm the property of anyone not fighting. It has been narrated in the Hadnh: "The

Prophet has prohibited the Believers from loot and plunder" His injunction is: "The loot is no more lawful than the carrion". Abu Bakr Siddiq used to tell soldiers on their way to war: "Do not destroy the villages and towns, do not spoil the cultivated fields and gardens, and do not slaughter the cattle."

Booty of war from the battleground is altogether different. It consists of the wealth, provisions and equipment captured from the camps and military headquarters of the combatant armies and may legitimately be appropriated.

VI. Sanctity of property

Muslims have been prohibited from taking anything from the general public of conquered country without paying for it. If the Muslim army occupies an area of the enemy country, it does not have the right to use the things belonging to the people without their consent. If the army needs anything, it should purchase it from the local population or should obtain permission from the owners. Abu Bakr Siddiq used to tell Muslim armies being dispatched to the battle front that they should not even use the milk of the milch cattle without the permission of the owners.

VII. Sanctity of a dead body

Islam has categorically prohibited its followers from mutilating the corpses of their enemies, as was practised in Arabia before the advent of Islam. It is said in the Hadith: "The Prophet has prohibited us from mutilating the corpses of the enemies." The occasion on which this order was given is highly instructive. In the battle of Uhud, the disbelievers mutilated the bodies of the Muslims who had fallen on the battlefield by cutting off their ears and noses and threading them together to put round their necks as trophies of war. The stomach of Hamza, the uncle of the Prophet, was ripped open by the Quraysh and his liver was taken out and chewed by Hinda, the wife of Abu Sufyan, the leader of the Makkan army. The Muslims were naturally enraged by this horrible sight. But the Prophet asked his followers not to mete out similar treatment to the dead bodies of the enemies.

This great example of forebearance and restraint should be sufficient to convince any reasonable man that Islam really is the religion sent down by the Creator of the universe; if Islam allowed human emotions free rein, this horrible sight on the battlefield of Uhud would have provoked the Prophet to order his followers to mutilate the bodies of their enemy in the same manner.

VIII. Return of corpses of the enemy

In the battle of Ahzab a renowned enemy warrior was killed and his body fell into the trench which the Muslims had dug for the defence of Madina. The unbelievers presented ten thousand dinars to the Prophet and requested that the dead body of their fallen warrior be handed ever to them. The Prophet replied: "I do not sell dead bodies. You can take away the corpse of your fallen comrade."

IX. Prohibition of breach of treaties

Islam has strictly prohibited treachery. One of the instruction that the Prophet used to give to Muslim warriors when sending them to the battlefront was: "Do not be guilty of breach of faith." This order has been repeated in the Holy Qur'an and the Hadith again and again. There is a famous incident in the peace treaty of Hudaybiya who, after the settlement of the terms of the treaty, Abu Jandal, the son of thee emissary of the unbelievers who had negotiated the treaty with the Muslims came bound and blood-stained to the Muslim camp crying for help. The Prophet told him: "Since the terms of the treaty have been settled, we are not in a position to help you. You should go back with your father. God will provide you with some other opportunity to escape this persecution"

The entire Muslim army was deeply touched and worried at the plight of Abu Jandal and many of them were moved to tear the bonds, when the Prophet declared "we cannot break the agreement." not a single person came forward to help the unfortunate prisoner: so the unbelievers forcibly dragged him back to Makka. This is an unparralel example of the observance of the terms of agreement by Muslims: Islam can show many similar examples.

X. *Rules about declaration of war*

It has been laid down in the Holy Quran: "If you apprehend breach of treaty firm a people, then openly throw the treaty at their faces" (8:58). In this verse, Muslims have been prohibited from opening hostilities against their enemies without properly declaring war against them, unless of course, the adversary has already started the aggression. Present-day international law of war, but since this is a man-made rule, it is often disregarded, Muslim laws, on the other hand, have been framed by God and not be disregarded.

This is a brief sketch of those rights which 1400 years ago Islam gave to man, to those who were at war with each other and to the citizens of its state. It reinforce and strengthens our faith in Islarn when we realize that even in this modern age, which makes such loud claims of progress and emancipation, the world has not been able to produce more just and equitable laws than those given 1400 years ago. On the other hand, it is saddening to realize that Muslims, nonetheless, often look for guidance to the West. Even more painful is the realization that, throughout the world, rulers who claim to be Muslims have made disobedience to their God and the Prophet, the basis and foundation of their government. May God have mercy on them and give them true guidance.

EIGHT

In the Modern Age

So far, we have examined the theoretical bases of society as they are outlined in the Qur'an and the Traditions, and we have looked briefly at Muslim society as it evolved in the course of history. It now remains for us to ask: Is it possible today to renew something similar to that form of Islamic life for the present and for the future? It is not sufficient that Islam should have been a living force in the past; it is not enough that it has produced a sound and well-constructed society in the time of the Prophet and in the age of the Caliphate.

Since that distant time, there have been immense changes in life—mental, economic, political, and social. There have even been material changes on the Earth, and in its powers relative to man. All these things must be carefully considered before an answer can be given to our question. There is also the further consideration which cannot be overlooked in any discussion which is directed to a practical and particular end, rather than to a theoretical and general; we must discover why it was that the spread of the Islamic spirit came to a halt in matters of political and economic theory only a short time after the era of the Prophet. Was this the longest possible span of life which the inner spirit and resources of Islam could command? Before dealing with these two considerations, we must emphasize the following truths:

> "That Islamic society today is not Islamic in any true sense." We have already quoted a verse from the Qur'an which can not in any way be honestly applied today:
>
> "Whoever does not judge by what Allah has revealed is an unbeliever."[1]

In our modern society, we do not judge by what Allah has revealed; the basis of our economic life is usury; our laws permit rather than punish oppression; the poor-tax is not obligatory, and is not spent in the requisite ways. We permit the extravagance and the luxury which Islam prohibits; we allow the starvation and the destitution of which the Messenger once said:

> "Whatever people anywhere allow a man to go hungry, they are outside the protection of Allah, the Blessed and the Exalted."

The Imam Ibn-Hazm also delivered a fatwa[2] on the same subject, to the effect that if a man dies in starvation in any town, the people of that town are regarded as having killed him, and the blood-money may be demanded of them. We permit this and similar things which have long been the subject of vain protest. Yet, the Qur'anic text is undeniably applicable to such things.

It refers to the existence in our modern society of such laws as those which permit usury, adultery, and refusal to pay the poor-tax, which thereby prove themselves to be in opposition to the divine laws laid down in the Qur'an. So long as Muslim society adhered to Islam, it manifested no weakness and no tendency to abdicate its control of life. It was when it fell away from Islam that these things took place. Emphasis on this fact will compensate for the idle aspersions which Western scholars have cast on our faith, and which they have evidenced from history.

These aspersions have been taken up by some in the East who were either gullible or mercenary, and have been the cause of the sullying of hundreds of pages by such men, under the claim of being liberal thinkers and accurate scholars. This is nonsense, and can only serve as a pretext for the false, the gullible, or the mercenary mind. We may now return to treat the two considerations whose discussion we deferred until we had noted the above points. We may start by answering the second question, why did the spread of the Islamic spirit come to a halt a short space after the time of the Prophet? Here again, we must emphasize two historical facts:

"This halt was only partial, never complete. It took place only in a limited sphere, that of politics."

The tolerant Caliphate became a tyrannical monarchy:

"The public funds were made accessible to the monarch, his relatives, his courtiers, and his flatterers, while they became inaccessible to those who had a true claim on them by the laws of Allah and His Messenger. But the remainder of the teachings of Islam remained in force; the charity and benevolence, the mutual help and responsibility tolerance and freedom of conscience and human equality, the payment of the poor-tax and the alms, and all the other positive and negative ordinances of Islam—all these continued in force to a greater or a lesser extent in many Muslim communities. " The Shari'a even continued in force as the system of civil law until the nineteenth century, when we introduced French law, thus giving the coup de grace to another tie which bound us to the beliefs of Islam.

The change which overtook the system and the development of politics—a partial change, as we have just said—was the product of an unfortunate mischance, as we have already contended. The mischance was that the control should fall into the hands of the Umayyads, first in an indirect way in the reign of Uthman, and later quite openly in the reign of Mu'awiya. If we are to be fair to Islam we cannot hold it responsible for the Umayyads; for it was injured far more by this clan of the Quraish than by the fiercest of its enemies.

It is certain that, if the life of Umar had lasted several years longer, or if Ali had been the third Caliph, or even if Uthman had become Caliph when he was twenty years younger, then the course of Islamic history would have been very considerably changed. For the policy which Umar enunciated was:

(a) to take excessive wealth from the rich and give it to the poor;

(b) to equalize the stipends assigned to the people, as had been the practice under Abu-Bakr.

If Umar had done this, there could have been no opposition to a policy so consistent with Islam. Umar's conscience was above all question, as was his zeal for the faith; the reverence in which he was held for his fidelity to the faith was similarly above the attacks of jealousy and doubt.

If this programme had been carried out by Umar, it would have restored economic and social equity to the Islamic world, and the civil war would have been averted at its very beginning, or, at the least, would have been postponed for a long time. Or if Ali had succeeded Umar, he would have guided the people in Umar's policy, whatever might have been the position of the Quraiship, who had more self-confidence in dealing with Ali than they had in dealing with Umar.

In this case, the matter would not then have come to the stage of rebellion or civil war. The Umayyads would not have later aspired to power; for their nobles had no high standing in Islam because of their early conversion or their renown in the early wars; they were only among the "forced" converts who embraced Islam at the conquest of Mecca, when the success of the new faith was already assured. Under such circumstances they could have held office in the army or in provinces, but with no special reason for holding or being kept out of office, such as they gained in thirteen years under the reign of Uthman.

But it will be asked: How were the Umayyads able to effect such a speedy revolution during a period of turmoil in Islam? Does this not indicate that the Islamic system is unsteady by nature, or at least unsuited to permanancy? Does it not indicate that by nature Islam provides no adequate safeguards against such revolution? We must here take account of the conditions of the Islamic state in that age, and we must reckon not only with factors of external power, but also with those of internal agitation.

The truth is that, at that stage Islam was in a ferment, and the really strange thing is that the Umayyads did with it only as much as they could. For "the fact is that the astonishing speed of the conquests, to which history can produce no parallel, added to Islamic society a huge territory, teeming with various races and skills, intellects and languages, systems, traditions, and heritages.

However strong the spirit of Islam may have been, and however powerful in suppressing all these heritages, an element of time was essential before all this new material could be homogenized, before a change could be wrought in the old moral ideas, the rooted traditions, the cherished social systems and customs. Thus, the Umayyad attack on the spirit of Islam just at this juncture took place at a unique point of time; if it had been stayed for a space, it could never have accomplished all that it did.

We have seen that the bulk of Mu'awiya's support lay in Syria, a conquered country, rather than in Arabia itself. Those of his supporters who did hail from the Peninsula, such as Amar ibn al-As, were of a nature akin to Mu'awiya himself, men who trampled down the moral element in their reckonings, who justified the means by the end, and who justified the end simply on the grounds that they desired it.

As for the suggestion that the Islamic system does not provide by nature adequate safeguards against revolution, for one thing we must bear in mind that this system was assailed by revolution before it had properly struck roots; and for another thing we must remember that in practice no system has any such real safeguards. Where, for example, are the safeguards of democracy in Europe? This is a strongly entrenched system, which has achieved a definite form, and which has had time to establish itself and to spread its influence over a long period into every quarter of life.

Yet, where were its safeguards at the time of the Nazi revolution, or the Fascist, or the Spanish? Or again take the institution of free speech in the United States, whose people fled from Europe to form a free society—where are its safeguards? Today a few newspaper and radio companies can hold a monopoly of both information and opinion, and can forbid any contrary opinions to find their way to the eyes, the ears, or the thoughts of the people.

The truth is that any suspicion that the Islamic system does not afford safeguards against revolution is due to ignorance of what is practically feasible in any system. It betrays also an ignorance of the true facts of Islamic history; we have the evidence of the minor rebellion in the Hejaz, and of the great rebellion against Uthman; we have the evidence of the Qarmatian rebellion and of many others, all of which were directed against exploitation, arbitrary power, and class distinctions. The spirit of Islam has continually and successfully resisted all such things, in spite of the grievous injuries which it has suffered at their hands throughout thirteen hundred years.

The spread of the spirit of Islam, then, was not halted because that spirit was unable to establish itself, nor because it was found inadequate to cope with the demands of the life. As we shall shortly see, this spirit has been continuously operative in many of the aspects of life and society. The halt in its spread was the product of an unfortunate mischance at a unique point of time. And it was when that mischance brought to Islam a Caliph who retained something of the true spirit of the caliphate in the person of Umar II, that the spread of Islam became again apparent, and the government again truly Islamic. But then the times were not propitious for such a truly Muslim Caliph to restore what had been destroyed, or to establish the roots of Islamic traditions in the political system.

But, nonetheless the attempt of Umar II does give us a clear indication that the inner power of Islam was really strong and capable of application in very different times. For his attempt followed the oppressive and evil age of the Umayyads, and it indicated clearly that a renaissance of Islamic government was possible, and not out of question.

We must repeat our contention that even when the spread of the Islamic spirit came to a halt in the realm of politics—though even here it was only a partial halt—it still continued to operate in other aspects of both social and individual life. It continued to realize many of its ideals, and to achieve many of its aims; indeed even to the present day it is still effective in such spheres as are not strongly under the influence of politics. As the Frenchman, Gouilly, says in Islam and the Great Powers:

> "The number of Muslims in Madagascar is not less than three quarters of a million. Most European authorities explain the spread of Islam in the native villages by the

> fact that it is a unifying religion which ensures for the negro an equality and justice for which he longs; it emancipates him finally from the bondage of priesthood and superstition, and even from the nightmare of evil spirits."[4]

H.A.R., Gibb writes in Whither Islam?:

> "Islam still has it in its power to render a conspicuous service to mankind. There is no other society which can show such a record of having united various races in one unity based on equality. The great Islamic community in China, and the still smaller community in Japan, all show that Islam has still the power completely to reconcile such divergent elements as those of race and class. If ever the opposition of the great states of the East and West is to be replaced by understanding, this can only be done through the medium of Islam."[5]

Muslims' Conduct during Crusades

The conduct of the Muslims during the Crusades showed the full inspiration of the strong spirit of Islam, as it rose superior to worldly considerations, treachery and ruthlessness. It showed a belief in the unity of mankind and the relationship of humanity beyond all differences of faith, and above all temporal and ephemeral enmities. Saladdin was not the only one whom the history of the Crusades has recorded as being of the true and lofty Islamic spirit; rather would this description apply to all the Muslim armies which took part in these long and bitter wars. And this remained true despite the foul deeds of the Crusaders. These may be exemplified in the fall of Jerusalem on the fifteenth of July, 1099 A.D. (492 A. H.), during the first Crusade.

The Muslims sought refuge and sanctuary in the Aqsa Mosque, but the Crusaders followed them inside and dispatched them with their swords, so that blood flowed through the sacred precincts in a flood. In this act, the Crusaders violated a solemn treaty which their leader had made with some of the Arabs.[6] This was only one example of the barbarity of the Crusaders, involving as it did a violation of their honour, punishment of the living, and retaliation on the infirm and the children.

Even after that, when fate turned against the barbarians, their treatment at the hands of the Muslims was imbued with the Islamic spirit, which was strong enough to check the desire for vengeance in Muslim hearts, and to keep them within the bounds of humanity and religion.

Again, within our own times, the recent war against the Jewish settlers in Palestine had revealed the penetration of the Islamic spirit. Even after the long interval during which Muslims have been divorced from the spirit and traditions of their faith, these have proved effective in keeping the Arab forces from taking vengeance for the most horrible and inhuman crimes committed by the Zionists in the Holy Land. They have been effective in keeping Muslim armies tme to the lofty tradition which their religion has maintained for fourteen centuries, and that in the tnidst of a constant record of inhumanity.

While we are discussing the inner vitality of Islam, we must not overlook the succession of disasters and calamities, both internal and external, to which Islam has been subjected throughout its long history. Yet, it is still a powerful element in human history, and commands the attention even of some occidentals as a means of saving humanity from it present dilemma, as we have already seen in the quotations from Gouilly and Gibb.

Despite the fact that such men are unable fully, to comprehend the Islamic spirit, but confine themselves rather to a review of its practical profit as it now exists, than to an appreciation of its profound spiritual content. For it is difficult for occidentals who have been brought up in the shadow of a deeply rooted materialistic civilization—and such we shall later see that it is to appreciate this subtle spiritual element.

We have already indicated that the first internal disaster which overtook Islam, namely its subjugation by the Umayyads. This was an interlude which neither permanently affected the practical traditions of Islam nor altered its spiritual exhortations and laws.

It did not produce any permanent social principles, any accepted practical traditions, or any rooted practices.

We must now examine quickly the more important developments which befell Islam, and mark their influence through the following centuries. The first of these is to be found in the rise of the Abbasid state, with its reliance on racial elements newly converted to Islam. The attitude of these people to their new religion was never whole-hearted, because of the national loyalties whose roots remained strong within them.

But as time passed on, the Abbasid state deserted these elements on which it had been founded, and which were now beginning to acquire a tincture of Islam, for others whose nucleus was a body of Turks, Circassians, Dailamites and such like. So, this dynasty continued to find its support in elements which were opposed to the spirit of Islam, and to which it gave a favoured position because it relied on them. There was nothing to withstand these racial elements—and hence to withstand the power of the dynasty—except the spirit of Islam, with all the inner force and vitality which it could muster.

Then followed the destructive raids of the Tartars, bursting with savage ferocity on the Islamic world. Without delay Islam turned aside the force of the onslaught, swallowed it up, and assimilated it. Yet, this was not accomplished without causing in the spirit of Islam itself a profound upheaval in which the practices and traditions of this religion were forcibly modified.

Nonetheless in spite of the humiliation of the state by the Tartar onslaught, the Islamic community continued powerful and loyal to its ideals, and constant in the fundamentals of its religion, no matter how far it may have wandered from them in a few purely official aspects.

We must also bear in mind here that the Roman Empire, the building and growth of which had occupied almost a thousand years, was cut off and fell into pieces in a single century, as a result of the incursions of the Huns and Goths; nothing was left of it except a few scattered traces.

However, the Islamic state remained in occupation of a wide territory, although its building had occupied little more than half a century, and though it had to contend with a number of internal struggles between ruling families, as well as the external attacks of the Tartars, and others. Such factors demonstrate the intense vitality of Islam, in that it was able to meet these circumstances.

As we trace the development further, in the West we find the war in Spain, and in the East the disaster of the Crusades. In the first of these Islam was worsted, in the second it was victorious. But from that time to this it has had to contend with ferocious enemies of the same spirit as the Crusaders, enemies both open and hidden.

But the final overthrow of Islam took place only in the present age, when Europe conquered the world, and when the dark shadow of colonization spread over the whole Islamic world. East and West alike. Europe mustered all its forces to extinguish the spirit of Islam, it revived the inheritance of the Crusaders'-hatred, and it employed all the materialistic and intellectual powers at its disposal. With these it sought to break down the internal resistance of the Islamic community and to divorce it gradually over a long period from the teachings and the heritage of its religious faith.

When we speak of the hatred of Islam, born of the Crusading spirit, which is latent in the European mind, we must not let ourselves be deceived by appearances, nor can we let their hypocrisy blind us to the fact that they deny to us any freedom of religion. They say, indeed, that Europe is not as unshakably Christian today as it was at the time of the Crusades and that there is nothing today to warrant hostility to Islam, as there was in those days. This is entirely false and inaccurate. General Alien by was no more than typical of the mind of all Europe, when, entering Jerusalem during the First World War, he said:

"Only now have the Crusades come to an end."

Similarly, the Governor of Sudan was no more than typical of the European mind when he placed all governmental power at the disposal of missionaries in the Southern Sudan, while forbidding any Muslim trader even to enter the country. It happened once that a certain official was stationed for a rather long time in South, and so asked for a transfer to the North; it was not granted. He then bethought himself to try lifting up his voice in the Muslim call to prayer; that single act sufficed to ensure his transfer the following day. And England is, of all the European countries, the most tolerant and patient and skilful in reconciling questions of religion.

People sometimes wonder how this obstinate spirit of resistance to Islam can persist so strongly and to such a pitch in a Europe which has discarded Christianity, and where the exhortations of preacher and monk no longer fill European ears as they did in the age of the Crusades. But this fact ceases to be surprising when we take into account two facts:

> "The enmity which the Crusaders stirred up was not confined to the clangour of arms, but was, before all else and above everything, an intellectual enmity. The European mind was poisoned by the slurs which the Crusaders' leaders cast on Islam as they spoke of it to their ignorant Western compatriots. It was in that age that there grew up in Europe the ridiculous idea that Islam was a religion of unbridled passion and violent sensuality, that it consisted merely of formal observances, and that it had no teaching of purity or of regeneration of heart. And this idea had remained as it started.
>
> "This loathing spread space. The ignorant mass of Crusaders had dependents in many places throughout Europe; and the process was hastened by the Spanish Christians in their war to deliver their country from 'the yoke of the idolaters".

But the downfall of Muslim Spain was to require many centuries before it was completed; when this protracted struggle and the constraint which it involved grew too great, a hostility to Islam started to take root in Europe, and ultimately became permanent.

Finally, it took the form of a complete extirpation of Islam throughout Spain after a conflict which reached a pitch of ferocity and bitterness hitherto unknown. The cries of joy which all over Europe greeted this event were unfortunately uttered in ignorance of the consequences which would arise; for the result was that science and learning were blotted out, and in their place came the ignorance and the barbarity of the Middle Ages.

But before the echoes of these happenings in Spain had died away, there took place a third event of immense significance, which was to hasten the breaking of the ties between the Western world and Islam. This was the fall of Constantinople to the Turks. Europe had always looked to Byzantium as a relic of the glory of ancient Greece and Rome, and had regarded it as the fortress of Europe against Asiatic barbarism. In the centuries which followed, and which were filled with wars, the hostility of Europe to Islam was no longer a question of merely academic importance; it was now a question of political import also. And this fact further increased the violence of that hostility.

In addition to all this, Europe derived great profit from this cleavage. The Renaissance or rebirth of European arts and sciences in the widest sense arose particularly from an Islamic and Arab source; in most cases it can be traced back to material contacts between the East and the West. Europe profited more than did the Muslim world, but it did not acknowledge the gift, because it was blinded by its loathing of Islam. Or, more correctly, the reverse is true, that loathing increased with the passage of time, until it was second nature.

At this point, loathing swamped all understanding whenever the word 'Muslim' was mentioned; it entered into all their thoughts until it came to form a permanent part of the thinking of every European, man or woman. And still stranger than this is the fact that this feeling continued to flourish even after all the movements of intellectual exchange. Then followed the age of the Reformation, during which Europe was divided into various sects, each continually employed in arming itself against every other; yet hostility to Islam was the common feature of all of them.

This in turn was followed by an age when religious feeling started to subside, but the hostility to Islam continued unabated. One of the clearest proofs of this is that French philosopher and poet, Voltaire, was one of the bitterest critics of Christianity and of the Church in the eighteenth century; yet, he was at the same time violently hostile to Islam and to its Messenger. A few score years later came the age in which Western scholars commenced to study foreign learning and to regard it with a measure of sympathy.

All matters connected with Islam the traditional dislike began to creep in under a form of partisan spirit which was not conducive to academic study. Thus, the gulf which history had dug between Europe and the Islamic world remained still unbridged. Dislike of Islam thus became a fundamental part of European thinking; and the fact that the first Orientalists of the modern age were Christian missionaries who were working in Muslim territory meant that the picture which they formed of the teachings and the history of Islam was distorted; for it was founded on an axiomatic conception that Europeans were superior to 'idolaters'.

Despite the fact that Oriental studies have now been liberated from missionary influence, this intellectual bias had persisted, although any mistaken view can no longer claim the excuse of ill-informed religious zeal. Hence, the attacks made by Orientalists upon Islam betray an inherited characteristic, and a peculiarity of nature; they are based on an impression created by the Crusades, and shaped by all the mental influences of these on the early Europeans. But it will immediately be asked:

How does it happen that an ancient antipathy such as this, which was originally religious in its basis, and which in the period of its birth owed its inception to the spiritual mastery of the Christian Church, can persist in Europe in an age when religious convictions are no more than a matter of antiquarian interest?

There is never anything surprising in such a situation; for it is well known to psychology that men may lose all the religious beliefs which they held in their youth, and at the same time retain some of their personal idiosyncrasies, even those which formerly centered upon the very religious beliefs which they have now discarded. It is these idiosyncrasies which provide the intellectual motivation for every act of such men. This is the state which obtains in Europe regarding Islam.

Despite the fact that the religious convictions which gave rise to European hostility to Islam have now lost their power and been replaced by a more materialistic form of life, yet the ancient antipathy itself still remains as a vital element to pour a secret poison into the European mind. So far as the strength of this antipathy is concerned, it undoubtedly varies from one individual to another, but that it exists is indisputable. The spirit of the Crusades, though perhaps in a milder form, still hangs over Europe: and that civilization in its dealings with the Islamic world still occupies a position which bears clear traces of the early Crusader spirit."[8]

European imperial interests can never forget that the spirit of Islam is firmly opposed to the spread of imperialism. Such an opposition must either be crushed or at least diverted. No weight need be attached to the contention of gullible or mercenary writers that religion is of no concern to Europeans, that the source of European power is not religious, and that the only thing about the Muslim world which Europe fears is its material power. Fundamentally, religion is a spiritual power which is always effective for the provision of material powers.

Islam is essentially different from Christianity; it encourages the fostering of material powers, it enjoins self-defence and defensive war, and it warns the weaklings who tamely submit that theirs will be an evil fate in this world and in the next.

> "Prepare for them as much as you can in the way offerees and cavalry, with which you may overcome Allah's enemies and your own."[9]

> "Do not take unbelievers for your friends in preference to Believers."[10]

> "So let those fight in the way of Allah who would exchange the life of this world for that of the next."[11]

> "Do not grow weary or grieve now that you have the upper hand, if you are true Believers..., etc."[12]

Spiritual and Material Powers

Islam is at once a spiritual power and an incentive to material power; it is at once a form of opposition in itself, and an incentive to a still more forcible opposition. Therefore, European imperialism cannot but be hostile to such a religion. The only difference lies in the fact that the form of that hostility varies according to the imperialistic methods of each nation, and according to local conditions. Thus, for example, France declared open war on Islam in the Western Arab world, under the name of "Protecting the Barbars," or some such phrase. But England took a more devious and tortuous road to the same end in Egypt, that of education.

Its aim was to encourage the growth of a general frame of mind which would despise the bases of Islamic life, and even of Eastern life. When this was accomplished there would be a generation educated into this frame of mind, ready to go out into the schools and educational offices to imbue the coming generations with the same ideas.

These would set a fashion in manners and customs which would ultimately lead to the permanent establishment of the desired frame of mind, and would emphasize the difference between the basic elements of Islamic education and the policies of the Education Ministry. Thus, England could dispense with open hostilities as a means of opposition to religious convictions. And this objective was actually ascribed by a large and influential party to a desire to establish a pan-Egyptian mentality. In the Southern Sudan, again, there was no call for such guile; the position there was simply that which we have already described in speaking of the Christian missionaries and the Muslim merchants.

Thus, each imperialist state has proceeded by one means or another to oppose and to throttle Islam since the last century, and even before that. And that they still proceed to do essentially the same thing in concert is obvious from the position taken up by the United Nations on the question of Indonesia and Holland, on that of Kashmir, India and Pakistan, and on that of Hyderabad, India and the Nizam. Finally the same thing is supremely evident in the position of the United Nations on Palestine.

There are those who hold that it is the financial influence of the Jews in the United States and elsewhere which has governed the policy of the West. There are those who say that it is English ambition and Anglo-Saxon guile which are responsible for the present position. And there are those who believe that it is the antipathy between East and West which is responsible. All these opinions overlook one vital element in the question, to which all other elements are subordinate, the Crusader spirit which runs in the blood of all occidentals.

It is this which colours all their thinking, which is responsible for their imperialistic fear of the spirit of Islam, and for their efforts to crush Arab strength. For the instincts and the interests of all occidentals are bound up together in the crushing of that strength. This is the common factor which links together Communist Russia and Plutocratic America.

The truly remarkable thing is that the spirit of Islam has survived all these attacks which have been launched against it from the earliest period of its life right up to the present. It has persisted, in spite of sudden assaults and the effect which these have had on its life; it had lasted out, in spite of the modern conquest by Western civilization with its material and educational weapons, from which some Muslims have borrowed the means of breaking down and destroying Islam at the direction of imperialistic powers.

Despite all these things, the spirit of Islam has remained essentially sound, and its inner force had left clear imprints on the course of human life in the broadest sense. Islam has left its marks on the forms and objectives of civil government throughout fourteenth centuries to the present day. There is no political or military institution in the world that owes something to Islam; and this has been true even in those ages when the Muslim world has been weak and divided, when it has seen its spiritual, social, and economic life disturbed.

But the period of obscurity and weakness is now at an end, and the tide of Islam has commenced to rise. In East and West alike the Arab world is gaining unity, and two great Islamic blocs have made an appearance in Pakistan and Indonesia. These are portents which cannot be overlooked, significant of the underlying vitality of Islam. They are significant also of the massive resources of Islam, sufficient to bring about a complete renewal of Islamic life. Such a renewal need not be based merely on wishful thinking or on good fortune; rather it may be based on actual concrete facts which are apparent to the sight.

I personally, quite apart from the religious faith, have an absolute belief in the possibility of a renewal of Islamic life within the Muslim world. I believe in the soundness of Islam as a worldwide, rather than a local, system for the future. I have no desire to take refuge in vain speculation, but I do believe this to be not only possible, but even easy.

Not that there will not be various and vast difficulties; there will also be great tasks which must be accomplished before the complete renewal of Islamic life can take place with any facility within Muslim society. The assessment of these vast obstacles, and the inspiration to undertake the tasks involved is something which is necessitated by any true understanding of the immensity of the goal at which we are aiming, and of the weight of responsibility awaiting any man who aims at that goal. It is something which is necessitated also by an understanding of the importance of public opinion in such vast undertakings.

But, it is not enough for any one man to issue a ringing call for hope to become actuality, and expectation reality. The results and the consequences must be assessed, and the man who exhorts others must equally offer to them the same vast effort which he demands of them.

In the very nature of the case, the wide divergence between existing political theory and the spirit of Islam, which has arisen over a long period and has hence become deep-seated, will make it a matter of some difficulty to return to a theory which is truly based on that spirit. For the machinery of the state and of society, the foundations of life in all its aspects, the spiritual and intellectual background are all so built up on specific bases that they are difficult to change without the application of vast energy over a long time. And the longer the time, the greater the difficulty, and the greater the need for yet vaster and longer enduring effort.

The time factor is linked up with another consideration in the present age. We do not live only in this world, but we cannot live in isolation from it. Thus, our interests and our needs are interwoven. The with this present world, which is governed by a certain form of civilization, involving an outlook completely contradictory to that of Islam. This we shall see later. In one respect, this fact will slow down our progress along the path of renewing the true Islamic form of life, and in another respect, it will lay additional responsibilities upon us.

The importance of this last consideration is enhanced by the fact that this Western world with which our interests are interwoven is at the present moment stronger than we; we do not have today the control over it, or the strength equal to its strength, that we had in the first age of Islam. At the same time, it is hostile to us, and in particular hostile to our religion. Therefore, it will not permit us to produce a new Islamic system, or to renew a truly Islamic form of life, however great the effort we put forth. This result we could hope for only if we had control of the Western world, if our strength were comparable to its, or if it were honest with us and with our religion to which we seek to return.

But all this does not mean that return to the Islamic system is impossible. All that it means is that this is a great and difficult task, requiring unremitting effort. Above all it demands courage to believe in it, boldness to face the inevitable results, patience to endure the hard work demanded, and faith to believe that this is necessary for Islamic society and for mankind as a whole. It demands the fostering of a new mentality, whose task will not be simply to elevate the existing state of things, but rather to produce a new and perfect state.

This is our task. We have already seen the foundations on which the system must be built; thus, we can now balance the profits which we shall enjoy if we return to it against the labours and sacrifices which we must make in order to realize it. When our faith in these profits reaches the point at which they outweigh the sacrifices, then let us settle the matter, make up our kinds, and leave the result with Allah.

Perhaps one valuable aspect of the present situation might be pointed out here. The great Western civilization has led the world into two global wars within a quarter of a century; after the second of these it has led it to a complete division into two blocs, an eastern and a western, and to the constant threat of a third war.

It has brought about a state of hostility in every quarter, it has produced starvation and destitution and adversity throughout three parts of the world. It should be pointed out also that the social fabric of the whole world today is in that state of insecurity and instability where it must look for new foundations and search for some spiritual means of restoring to man his faith in the principles of humanity.

We must not, however, read more than is legitimate into this readiness of the Western world to accept the foundations of our Islamic civilization; this is another matter. Although it may be, it noted that such a man as Bernard Shaw says that the West had already started to turn in this direction, and even prophesied that it well come to it eventually, in these words:

> "I forecast that the religion of Muhammad will be accepted in Europe in the near future, for it has already started to gain some acceptance. The priests of the Middle Ages insisted on portraying Islam in the darkest colours, either out of ignorance, or from criminal bigotry; but they were led to excess by their hatred of Muhammad and his religion; indeed they held him to be the anti-Christ. For myself I find it preferable to call Muhammad the saviour of mankind, and I believe that if such a man were given authority over the modern world, he would succeed in solving its problems and giving it peace and happiness. And how great is the world's need of these things."

Western Perspective

There were some impartial thinkers in the nineteenth century who discovered how much value there is in the religion of Muhammad. Among them were Carlyle, Goethe, and Gibbon. From this fact, there has arisen a salutary change in the attitude of Europe towards Islam. Thus, Europe has seen a great advance in the past years of the twentieth century, and has even started to respect the faith of Muhammad.

It may be that in the century that lies ahead, Europe will make further progress, and will acknowledge the contribution of this faith towards a solution of its problems. Many among may own nation and among all European nations already belong to the religion of Muhammad, a fact which enables us to say that the conversion of Europe to Islam has already begun.[13]

But so far as we can see Shaw's prophecy is still no more than a prophecy—if, indeed, it is not intended to drug the senses of Muslims and to make them content to wait idly for Europe to embrace their faith. But, however, this may be, we must at least wait until time has proved such a statement, for two principal reasons:

1. There is this deep-seated and inherited hostility to Islam in the very European nature itself. This is at present augmented by the opposition of imperialistic interests to the very existence of our faith, as being an obstacle in their path.

2. European culture is rooted in material foundations, and the influence of intellectual and spiritual interests are very weak; such has been the case from the time of Roman civilization to the present day. This matter requires detailed consideration, and a full treatment, rather than merely a brief mention. So, we must here make an extended study of this important question: Is it possible for Islamic and Western civilizations to work together in partnership? And if so, then what are the limits of that partnership?

We have already asserted at the beginning of this book that Europe was never at any time truly Christian, because by its very nature its people had to fight over their meagre territories. Thus, the tolerant principles of Christianity could gain no footing in such a stubborn ground. In addition to this, Christianity is essentially an asceticism, a refusal to live, or to take an interest in, a practical worldly life. To these two factors we must now add a third, to which we have already made a passing reference.

This factor was the existence of the Roman Empire, and its position to thwart the path of Christianity, together with the permanent influence of that empire on the bases of European civilization even today. And that despite the infusion of Christianity which the Roman Empire received in its last days.

We may quote here some passages from Islam at the Cross-roads, which we find completely satisfactory: The doctrine on which the Roman Empire was founded was to destroy by force, or to exploit other people for the sole benefit of the mother country. In order to indulge this privileged body the Romans saw nothing wrong in their violence and nothing humiliating in their oppression.

The famous Roman justice was a justice for Romans only. It is apparent that such a tendency as this is possible only on the basis of a materialistic ideal, which is wholly devoted to wordly life and civilization—though it may be an ideal promoted and shaped by a philosophical taste.

In any case it was far removed from any appreciation of spiritual values. The Romans did not really understand religion; their traditional Gods were only variant forms of the Greek myths which, as being mere shades, were never believed to have any connection with social affairs, and which were never permitted to interfere in any way with the real business of life. Their duty was to speak in metre through the agency of their attendant priests, when questions were asked of them; but no one ever expected them to enunciate laws for the guidance of mankind. Such was the soil in which modern Western civilization grew up, though during the period of its growth it undoubtedly came under many other influences. Thus, in the very nature of the case, it changed and thereby modified the legacy which it had received from Rome in more than one way. Nevertheless the fact remains that all that is truly great in the modern West, whether of life or nature, owes its origin to Roman civilization. Hence, since, the intellectual and social environment of ancient Rome was always secular rather than religious—and that no exhypothesis, but in actual fact—so the same environment persists in the modern West.

The European mind has neither possible argument against the complete futility of religion nor will it ever admit the need for such an argument. For modern European thinking in general leaves the absolute outside its scheme of practical considerations—although— it does tolerate religion, and even at times may assert that it is a social virtue. Western civilization does not irrevocably disown God, but it can see no place and no significance for Him in its present intellectual system. It has made a virtue out of a philosophical inability on the part of man, that is to say, out of his inability to take a comprehensive view of the whole field of life.

European, modern Europe tends to attach the greatest practical importance to the values deriving from the experimental sciences, or at least from those sciences from which may be expected some perceptible influence of human social relationships. And because the question of the existence of God does not fall into either of these categories, the European mind tends to drop the concept of God out of the sphere of practical considerations. A question emerges here:

> "How is this tendency to be reconciled with Christian thought? Is not Christianity a faith founded on the Absolute, as is Islam? And is it not ostensibly the spiritual background of Western civilization? There is no doubt that all these things are true. But there could not be any greater mistake than to imagine that Western civilization is the outcome of Christianity. The true philosophical basis of the Western system is to be sought in the ancient Roman view of life as a matter of advantage, quite independent of absolute values."

It is a view which can be summarized thus: Because we have no specific knowledge, either in the way of practical experience, or in that of proof, about the fundamentals of human life, or about its destiny after physical death; therefore, it is best for us to confine our powers to those material and mental fields which are accessible to us, rather than let ourselves to be tied down to metaphysical and moral questions arising from claims which can have no intellectual proofs.

Such an argument as this which is characteristic of modern Western civilization, will certainly not find acceptance in Christian thought, as it will not in Islam or in any other religion, simply because it is essentially religious. Thus, to try to establish a casual relationship between Christianity and modern Western civilization, is a gross historical error.

Christianity may indeed have played a very small part in the rise of intellectual materialism which today dominates modern Western civilization, but the truth is that the growth of this spirit had been the product of Europe's prolonged struggle, against the Christian Church, and against its supervision of life. In its general aspect Christianity today is a purely spiritual thing, as was the case with the Roman deities, which were neither permitted nor expected to exert any real influence on society.

No doubt there are in the West individuals who are still prepared to judge and to think on a religious basis, prepared to fight a last ditch action to reconcile their beliefs with the spirit of their civilization; but they cannot be more than isolated cases. To Europe as a whole it is a matter of indifference whether the political system is 'democratic or fascist, plutocratic or bolshevist, technical or intellectual.'

Europe knows but one necessary religion—the worship of material prosperity; the only belief that it holds is that there is but one goal in life—the making of that life easier and easier. It is, as the definition has it in significant terms, an escape from the tyranny of nature.' The shrines of such a culture are huge factories and cinemas, chemical laboratories and dance-halls and power stations. The priests of such a worship are bankers and mathematicians, cinema stars and scientists and aviators.

The inevitable result of this state of affairs is that man strives to gain power a pleasure; this brings into being quarrelsome societies, all armed to the teeth and intent on mutual destruction whenever their conflicting interests come into active opposition.

On the intellectual side, the upshot has been the evolution of a humanism with a moral philosophy confined to purely scientific questions, in which the highest criterion of good or evil is whether or not any given thing represents material progress.

The sum and substance of all this is that the present-day European conscience is not ready to accept the spirit of Islam, or to seek in it a solution of human problems. But even so, it is not impossible that even this may take place after a number of other changes and developments in the West, and after the Islamic world itself has entered upon a clearly defined and independent renewal of Islamic life. In this, the West may find philosophical realities and practical truths which will attract its attention and balance its thinking. But it is my personal belief that many generations must elapse before the West will be able to appreciate the spirit of Islam in any real sense.

Again, the substance of this argument is that the mode of the Muslim doctrine that work must serve moral ends, cannot be reconciled with the mode of the modern Western doctrine that morals must serve some material advantage. We must reckon with this fact, and hence we must work to establish a sound form of Islamic life; this cannot be achieved by the importation of elements borrowed from abroad, since such elements will not fit into the texture of our native beliefs.

The Muslim world will have to admit defeat on the first occasion on which it seeks to renew its own life by borrowing Western ways of thought, life and custom. Such an experiment can only result in the suffocation of that very form of life which it seeks to revive; for from the very first step the Muslim world will be departing from its own true and natural path.

This path involves a belief based on Islam that the moral element is fundamental to the structure of life; it regards work as a means to moral ends, and it will not make material advantage the highest aim of morals. We have already seen in an earlier chapter of this book that Islam satisfies all the highest aims of life, among them the moral consciousness. We have also seen that Islam's supreme virtue is that it preserves the unity of life, and that it makes no distinction between the means and the ends. It will not lend its authority to any idea that there is an opposition between material and spiritual in the substance of life or in the nature of the universe or of mankind; rather it emphasized that the whole of life is a unity which must make an orderly progress towards the highest objectives.

Islam, then, enunciates for men a complete theory of life. This theory is always liable to growth by development or by adaptation; it is not open to change or to adulteration, either in its fundamentals or in its general aims. Therefore, in order that this complete theory may bear its full natural fruits, it is necessary to make a complete application of it. Otherwise, even the slightest change in its fundamentals or its aims will produce a disorder, because it will no longer be in conformity with the Islamic conception of life.

The continual growth of this universal theory by development or by adaptation is a natural product of the nature of Islam; it is encouraged by Islam, the institutions of which are adapted to recognize it. Analogy, interpretation, and the wide powers entrusted to the head of the state—all these are living methods of ensuring growth through development and adaptation, in order to keep pace with life and to meet its needs as they emerge. But there is one thing which must be kept in mind: these developments must not pass out with the roots of the fundamental Islamic theory, nor must they be allowed to serve any foreign aim; they must not betray the spirit of Islam or give allegiance to any other spirit in preference to it.

The criterion by which we may accept or reject any development is first to compare it with the basic theory and the general spirit of Islam. Anything that is in agreement with this theory and this spirit we may accept, and anything which is contrary to these we must reject. Thus, we may profit by all the fruits of human labour within the bounds of our basic philosophy of the universe, man and life; we need raise no barriers between ourselves and human endeavour, nor need we stand in isolation from the continuous business of living.

Above all we must be firmly convinced of the value of faith and enthusiasm; we have a scheme of life greater than any possessed by the followers of any religion or school or civilization which has yet been born. And that is to say the least of it.

No renaissance of Islamic life can be affected purely by law or statute, or by the establishment of a social system on the basis of the Islamic philosophy. Such a step is only one of the two pillars on which Islam must always stand in its construction of life. The other is the production of a state of mind imbued with the Islamic theory of life, to give permanence to external forces leading to this form of life, and to give coherence to all the social, religious and civil legislations.

Social justice is an integral part of this Islamic life. It cannot be realized unless this form of life is first realized, and it cannot have any guaranteed permanence unless this form of life is built up on solid foundations. It is similar in this to all other social systems; it must have the support of public belief and confidence in its merits. Failing this, its foundations will be purely spiritual, and its establishment will depend on the force of religious and social legislation; these are too weak to sustain it, in which case it may easily miscarry.

Hence, Islamic legislation is more akin to ecclesiastical ordinance because it depends on religious belief. Thus, we must always keep in mind the necessity for a renaissance of our religious faith; we must cleanse it of all accretions, such as alterations and interpretations and ambiguities; only thus can it be a support for the necessary social legislation which will establish a sound form of Islamic life. This form of life will depend upon legislation and exhortation, those twin fundamental methods of Islam towards the achievement of all aims.

We must, then, establish our Islamic theory in individuals and societies, at the same time as we set up the Islamic legislation to regulate life. And the natural method of establishing that philosophy is by education.

But how can we possibly induce Islamic theory by education? For educational methods and modes of thought are essentially Western and essentially inimical to the Islamic philosophy itself; first, because they stand on a materialistic basis which is contrary to the Islamic theory of life; and second, because opposition to Islam is a fundamental part of their nature, no matter whether such opposition is manifest or concealed in various forms.

As we have already maintained, we shall advertise our defeat the first time that we adopt a Western theory of life as the means of reviving our Islamic theory. So, primarily, we must avoid the ways of Western thought; rather we must choose the ways of native Islamic thought, in order to ensure pure results.

The import of these words is not that we should adopt a position of isolationism in regard to thought, education, and science; all these are a common heritage of all the peoples of the world, in which we among the foremost have a fundamental part. We shall continue to take our rightful share in the furtherance of these things, even if it should become apparent that we are far removed from the influence which they exert. For the only true and permanent form of cooperation is that between all the nations of the Earth.

Isolation from human life, then, is not our aim; rather what we seek is to build up a characteristically Islamic theory of life, and to renew that form of life now, when it is apparent even to some of the more enlightened occidentals that the philosophy of materialistic Western civilization is a danger to the continued existence of man.

It breeds in human nature a ceaseless anxiety, a perpetual rivalry, a continual strife, and a weakening of human ties to the breaking point. And this is spite of all the triumphs of science which could have tended to human happiness and peace and content, had it not been that the bases of the Western philosophy of life were purely materialistic and hence unsuitable to men along the path to perfection.

As long as our aim is the building up of this Islamic theory along these lines, we must make a distinction between things which we may profitably accept, and those which we may profitably reject, out of Western society. Only thus may we complete the building of an Islamic society out of sound materials which will produce a structure secure against cooperation and opposition alike, against both borrowing and giving.

From another point of view we must ensure to the theory of life which we establish a safeguard in the form of a period of fostering...fostering, that is, in our own minds rather than in its own essence. For Islamic life in itself is a strong and definite thing when in does not stand in awe of any other Western form. Rather, it is we who need to be fostered and nurtured, as we are living on a strange diet hence we must be on our guard while we are engaged in the establishment of our new system.

In the case of the pure sciences and their applied results of all kinds, we must not hesitate to utilize all things in the sphere of material life; our use of them should be unhampered and unconditional, unhesitating and unimpeded.

Similarly, we must be careful to derive the fullest profit from other things also; from philosophy, which is the intellectual treatment of the universe and life; from literature which is the emotional treatment of these things; from history, which is a factual treatment, and from legislation, which is a treatment of the relationships between individuals and societies.

It will do us no harm to make use of the pure sciences in all the spheres of life; but on the other hand, it will do us harm to account these as the sum total of life; for such a view involves a philosophy which is not ours. It tends to establish a conception of the universe and of life which is at variance with the Islamic conception of those things; ultimately, it would led us along a path which is not that of Islam. It is this path which has produced the present ailments of mankind, and which is responsible for their present troubles.

It is sometimes objected that even if this be so, the pure sciences themselves cannot be held responsible, because essentially they cannot be divorced from the method of Western thought. The experimental method rests on the basis of a definite philosophy which is neither intellectual nor spiritual; if this had never established itself in favour, science would never have followed the course which lately it has taken.

In the same way, science can never remain in isolation from philosophy, nor can it be content to be influenced by philosophy without in turn influencing it. For philosophy is benefited by the experimental results of science, and is influenced by it in aim and method.

Thus, a study of pure science involves a study of philosophy, which is influenced by that science, and which in turn exerts an influence on it. All this is over and above the fact that the applied results of science must influence all material life, methods of gaining a living, and the division of wealth. All this will in due time produce new forms of society based on a new philosophy, or at least based on a theory of life which must be influenced by these developments in the course of life.

All this is very true. But what must be there is no possibility of living in isolation from science and its products, though the harm that it does may be greater than the good. There is no such thing in this life as an unmixed blessing or an unalloyed evil. Thus, Islam does not oppose science, or the utilization of science; there is nothing contrary to the spirit of Islam in culling the fruits of science from all the sources of the world.

But while we may acknowledge the universal influences of philosophy and culture, history and law, together with all their consequences in the way of educational methods and modes of thought and logic, we must set all of this in its proper place on a spiritual Islamic foundation. We must hold to the guiding principle that all the results and material consequences of science do not essentially affect our universal philosophy of life and custom.

When we mention educational methods we might well bear in mind here that these are indivisible and inseparable from the general philosophy of the community. Thus, when we borrow Western methods of education, systems of training and curricula, we borrow also a general scheme of philosophy and a mode of thought which underlies these methods and systems and curricula, whether we like it or not.

There is a belief that these are questions of pure 'pedagogy', and therefore universal and identical throughout all countries. This is a naive and shortsighted belief, encouraged by the delusion of the psychologists, who give an undue weight to their own subject; despite the difference between psychology and philosophy, such men believe that they can master their own subject, and through it can answer the philosophical questions of education also.

That claim is one thing, but the actual fact is quite another. Psychology may perhaps be a pure science to be studied in the laboratory. But the treatment of its results and the use to which these are put, such as educational techniques and curricula—all these things are still influenced by the general philosophy of life, still accept the dictation of that philosophy, and still form an integral part of it.

Moreover, the very fact that psychology is ruled by the laboratory is one of the influences exerted by experimental philosophy, or by the experimental method. It is this same method which in later years has governed all materialistic Western thought. The only type of independence which psychology can expect from the philosophy which is its mentor is that superficial independence which cannot influence the final result.

For an example, we may look to the American curriculum, their methods of education and instruction, these are more akin to vocational training than to any system of thorough and systematic study; they have as their objective the promotion of technical skill based on theoretical principles. The reason for this tendency is to be sought in the philosophy of pragmatism, founded by Charles Pierce in 1878 which was advanced by William James and applied by John Dewey, the modern educational philosopher. This school of thought represents a reversal of the accepted terms of thought and study: bare ideas and theoretical principles are abandoned, as is the study of things according to their logical class and nature. According to Pragmatism, all study should be confined to the practical effects and result of objects.

According to Charles Pierce of Pragmatism the idea is no more than a secondary product of some act or activity; it is not in itself a reality. For example, I may have the 'idea' of the horn of an automobile passing in the street; this 'idea' gains no meaning by my study of its nature, its origin, and the method of its production.

It may be a reality or it may be a figment of imagination; it may be produced by the ear and the nervous system, or it may be produced by the horn, whether, the automobile is turning right or left, and whether a path must be cleared for the vehicle and its driver. It means only:

> "I am about to change the direction of my vehicle and to proceed in a different direction. Hence, Pragmatism argues that the idea is secondary to the act, or the product of certain conditioning circumstances. This is the first step along the path of Pragmatism in which all the remaining steps must follow."[14]

It has been the rise of this theory or this method of thought which has produced the educational techniques of America. It has been responsible for a teaching curriculum and a system which will encourage the mind to take this view of things and to rationalize life along this line. Also, it is this which has given American life its most characteristic mark, which has directed it towards technical production, and which has to a large extent diverted it from academic and theoretical education.

Accordingly, we must reckon with this general philosophy of life; if we borrow educational techniques, teaching systems, and curricula, this philosophy underlines all of them. This philosophy shapes and forms them, assisted by the results of pure psychology. Such an influence is inevitable, though this same science in its methods and in its results is itself influenced by that very philosophy.

From the theoretical point of view, then, our method of establishing an independent Islamic scheme of thought is to proceed readily but cautiously in the matter of borrowing such a philosophy along with its concomitants, such as educational techniques, teaching systems and curricula, literature, history and law. But we shall deal now with all these subjects together.

Universe and Mankind

So far as the study of philosophy is concerned, we have already indicated the universal theory of Islam on the universe, life and mankind, this is essentially different from the nature of other universal philosophies which have originated in the West from the days of the Greeks to the present. This is not the place to discuss this difference, and it will suffice to recognize merely that there does exist a radical divergence.[15]

A petition of peculiar importance was once addressed to the Azhar University concerning a matter which was not favourably regarded in this quarter. It requested that study be directed to this universal Islamic theory of life and that a full and clear treatment of it be given in modern terms and applications; also that it be compared with other schools of philosophy. But the Azhar, instead of responding to this petition, continued to teach in its Faculty of Theology what it called the errors of Islamic philosophy, taken from the writings of Ibn-Sina and Ibn-Rushd.

This is, of course, a reversion to Greek philosophy, which has no real connection with the universal philosophy of Islam. Thus, in effect, the petition sent to the governors of the Azhar was neglected, and a spiritual and intellectual defeat was acknowledged in our primary seat of learning, a defeat for the Islamic theory of life.

If, then, we are to establish a sound Islamic theory of the universe, life and mankind, it is essential that Western philosophies and their moral corollaries should not be studied at all in our secondary schools, and that they should be studied in the university only after at least two years in the department of philosophy. And by the very nature of the case they should not be studied in the Azhar colleges until the very end of the course. In every centre of study such Western philosophies should be preceded by a course in pure Islamic thought, as distinct from the so-called "Islamic philosophy," in order to emphasize the true Islamic viewpoint.

Thus, the minds and thoughts of the students will assimilate the native bases of the spirit of Islam, together with its ideas on the universe, life and mankind, good and evil, work and reward, and all the other philosophic aspects of pure Islamic belief. This having been assured, we may in the later years of university study proceed to give some account of the other philosophies; these would include

Greek philosophy and its opposition to Islamic, modern European and American philosophy; these should be compared in every case with Islamic philosophy.

In this way, we can ensure that the student's mind and conscience will not be too much influenced; we can ensure also a minimum influence on student's ideas and thoughts, because by then they will be equipped for critical appreciation. They will have the requisite knowledge to reject all that does not agree with the fundamental modes of thought of a Muslim people. Under these circumstances their new knowledge will not harm, but will rather benefit students; for it will be purely academic knowledge, largely independent of any influence on their conscience or on their conception and understanding of life and its requirements.

We have already given one example of pragmatism in its view of things. But in this example, there was no indication of the dangers inherent in that philosophy or in its method; so we must now follow out this philosophy in its further results, in order to note the dangerous influences of its intellectual system on many a nation which follows such modern of thought.

Most people believe in God. This is an idea which logically may be either false or true. Intellectual theory says:

> "If God really exists, then His existence must be logically demonstrable. Pragmatism on the other hand attacks the problem from a different angle, and lays the emphasis on a different aspect. In its view the truth of the idea of God does not depend on logical necessity; it depends solely on the profit of this idea to our well-ordered life, in our daily activity and on our experiences. If the idea tends to produce a profit in life, then it is sound and therefore true. Hence, God does exist. Apart from this test, pragmatism claims, in the first place we cannot judge this idea; and in the second place we cannot trust our own judgement."[16]

The Islamic line of thought differs to a greater or lesser extent from that of pure intellectual theory, insofar as it does not entrust the whole question to human logic alone, but relies also upon revelation. But it is in complete opposition to pragmatism; for when we follow out its logic to a conclusion we find that the idea of God must disappear if the outward benefits of material life are not forthcoming.

The idea of God loses its existence because it cannot control its instruments and set the machinery in motion. In consequence, material profit becomes the sole criterion, not only of the acceptance or the rejection of things, but also of existence or non-existence. This implies a state of affairs in which man loses all nobility, where he is neither more nor less than an instrument.

Policies in this world cannot be divorced from such philosophies. Thus perhaps, we are not far from the truth when we say that the policy of the United States on the Palestine question and its stand in the United Nations on the question of Egypt were merely the results of its intellectual background of pragmatism—in conjunction, of course, with other factors.

The idea of right and justice had little effective place in materialistic American life; and hence it had little chance of permanent acknowledgement in international policies. This idea is perhaps the most satisfactory comment on these puzzling policies. What we do not want is to establish such an intellectual background as this, in our Islamic society. We must therefore be cautious about the study of Western philosophy until we have first established in adolescent minds a firm, strong, and clear pattern of thought which is founded on the universal Islamic theory.

Similarly, we must be cautious about borrowing educational techniques, curricula, and systems of teaching; for all of these are ruled by the general field of philosophy in their native lands; they subserve the aims which that philosophy assigns to them, whether immediate or remote.

Moral Philosophy

Literature is the emotional response to life. It issues from the same well-spring whence flow in any culture all the philosophies, the religious beliefs, the experiments and the influences. Literature is the most important factor in the establishment of a moral philosophy of life, and in the production of any specific influence on the human mind. Hence, we must exercise care in the choice of Western literature which we make available to our youth, alike in their Arabic and their foreign studies.

It is not necessary to take this as meaning that our youth are to be prohibited from reading European literature; what we have in mind here is simply a process of choice and selection. For in this literature, there are elements, the spirit of which is at one with the spirit of Islam. By this, we do not mean that such books 'encourage goodness and reprobate wickedness' for literature is no preacher to exhort and to direct. Rather, we mean that such books have a view of life which is spiritual and moral, rather than materialistic, and that they acknowledge the spiritual values of life.

This type of literature agrees in spirit with the general teachings of our Islamic theory; it can therefore do no harm to the moral consciousness of our youth, nor can it upset their emotional and mental development at a dangerous stage. This dangerous stage lasts at least until the third year of university work, if not until the time of graduation.

There is no harm, but rather great benefit, in having private reading including all types of the literatures of the world, without restraint or exception. But the prime aim of a process of choice and selection is to safeguard the period of adolescence from being debilitated and led astray.

History is a branch of literature; but it is one which has its own characteristics, and which therefore had also its peculiar dangers. For history is a presentation of the events of life, and it is necessarily influenced by the materialistic background of the West. Even if it is by intellectual theory that it is influenced, it will still ignore the spiritual powers and their effect on the course of events, together with the spiritual explanation of facts. It will give its own interpretations, designed to establish a philosophy of life independent of the spirit and unconnected with moral aims. Here, it is opposed to Islamic theory.

Beyond this, historians, who have been for the most part Europeans, have made the history of Europe the focal point of world history. In view of the nature of man this is excusable, and we have borne it with patience as a characteristically Western and European delusion. Yet, if our youth are to study history in this spirit and by this method, then they will finish with two false beliefs:

1. That spiritual factors have no influence on the course of events in time, or at least that any such influence is very weak.

2. That Europe is the mistress of historical events, and that the influence of the East and of Islam is exiguous.

Both these ideas have harmful and dangerous results; they establish a false general idea of life, of the world, and of events, and they endanger our patriotic pride and our pride in Islam, which is so necessary in face of the sweeping pride of Europe. In order to guard our youth from this evil we must take the two following steps:

1. We must begin by putting general world history, as Islam views it, in perspective, in the form of events and happenings. We must not be concerned solely with the European point of view in this present dangerous fashion. In such a history we must give Europe its rightful place and no more, and we must emphasize the part played in world history by the East in general, and by Islam in particular.

2. We must change the present curriculum of history teaching in our schools and colleges. We must start by teaching primarily the history of Islam throughout the Muslim world, and by expounding it from the Islamic point of view. It is not enough to teach our children the history of Islam as written by Western authors, or as expounded by Western philosophies. When their minds are filled with the history of their own countries, then we can give them the world history as written by ourselves, to form the next stage of study. And when they have completed that,then

we can give them in successive stages the remainder of the developments of history.

The study of law is similarly influenced by the Western point of view, by Western philosophy, history, law, and society. For law is a reflection of society, or is produced by it; and society is the offspring of all these factors.

In order to build up a sound Islamic doctrine, we must teach Islamic law in a broad general way before beginning to teach any specific legal system. The teaching of Islamic law must be firmly in the control of Muslim professors, and the Western point of view must not be allowed to obtrude, except in the later stages. Similarly, the study of law in general must not be opened up till that same later stage.

It is one of the requirements of Islamic life that the religious law shall occupy a paramount position; and that very fact will make necessary such a study of Islamic law as we have indicated. The great necessity which faces our professors of Islamic law in this field is to follow the authoritative path traced out by the Imams and their students at the time of the first growth of Islamic law.

When we have disposed of this theoretical question of the objective, we are still confronted by that of the specific constitutional enactments which will ensure a sound form of Islamic life and which will guarantee social justice to all. In this question, it is not possible to take a stand purely on the form of the original Islamic life; rather we must utilize all possible and permissible means which fall within the general principles and the broad foundations of Islam. Nor must we be afraid to use also all the discoveries which man has made in the way of social legislation and systems, so long as the principles of these do not run counter to the principles of Islam, and so long as they are not opposed to its theory of life and mankind.

We must include these in our legislation so long as they conduce to the true welfare of society, or so long as they ward off any impending evil. In the two principles of 'public interest' and 'blocking of means' we have two clear Islamic principles which give wide powers to the temporal ruler to ensure the general welfare at all times and in all places. Before we go on to deal with the application of these two principles it might be well to quote a short passage in explanation of them.[17]

Public Interest

Any welfare measure which has no specific detailed authority to support it is known as a measure of public interest. The question of whether or not it is a root of jurisprudence is a matter of dispute among the jurisconsults. Al-Qarafi has argued that all the jurisconsults have used it or have admitted it as a proof at one time or another, even though in lecturing most of them deny it the status of a root. He says in regard to this point:

> "Other people loudly deny the validity of public interest. But when the case is closely examined, they are found to refer to the word in its absolute sense. They do not trouble to take any account of the evidence offered by the reference of the term in its synonyms and contexts; they hold that it means merely convenience, and that such is the sole meaning of the phrase, public interest."[18]

No matter whether this claim is true or false, it is certain that the validity of any measure of welfare which lacks a specific validating authority is a matter on which the ulema may well disagree. And even if public interest is not one of the accepted roots of jurisprudence, at least it had the status of a custom, as Al-Qarafi indicates. The opinions of the ulema in this matter can be divided into four main views, as follows:[19]

1. The Shafi'ites and those who share their opinions do not believe in any form of public interest whose validity is unsupported by legal evidence; for they only admit legal precedents and the treatment of these by analogy, based on the existence of a solid connection between the root and its derivatives, that is to say, between a case governed by a precedent and another analogous to it. If we follow Al-Qarafi we must admit that it is strange that they should deny public interest while they admit analogy.

2. The Hanafites and others of similar opinions maintain the principles of preference and analogy, but their interpretation of preference is sometimes almost indistinguishable from public interest. A fair estimate would say that in their system they make a greater use of interest than do the Shafi'ites, But even so, the extent to which they do use it is negligible, and hence we cannot say that this principle is one of the roots of their system; not, at least, on any grounds of the use which they make of it in itself.
3. There are those who attach an excessive importance to public interest, even to the point of making it stronger than precedent in their dealings with cases; they regard it as a form of precedent, or rather, as a form of consensus. Thus where the ulema are agreed on a point turning on precedent, but some aspect of that point runs counter to public interest, then the validity of the latter is the stronger. This applies also to specific cases, as Al-Tufi has maintained.
4. There are those who hold a middle course, which is the soundest of all. Here, validity is granted to public interest, but it is not derived from precedent, which is held to be entirely different. To this view most of the Malikite rites adhere.

Malik held that public interest was an independent root of the system of jurisprudence, but that it was a derived, rather than an original root; and that so, for the following reasons:

1. The Companions of Allah's Messenger found that questions arose after his death which had not been apparent during his lifetime. Thus, they collected the noble Qur'an in book form. This had not been done in the time of the Messenger, but now such a collection was in the public interest; for they feared that the Qur'an might be forgotten because of the deaths of those who had memorized it. Umar saw such men dying in numbers during the Wars of Apostasy, and, fearing that through their death the Qur'an might pass from memory, he advised Abu-Bakr to have it collected in book form to this the Companions gladly assented.

2. After the death of Allah's Messenger his Companions agreed that the punishment for wine-drinking should be eighty lashes. Their reason for this was the public interest or general inference; for they saw that drinking tended to produce lying and the slandering of chaste women because of the wild talk in which drinkers indulged.

3. The orthodox Caliphs agreed upon imposing conscription on craftsmen, although the root principle was that the exercise of their craft was a matter of good faith. But it was found that unless they were conscripted they would neglect the care of the people's belongings and wealth. There was great need of craftsmen, and therefore, it was in the public interest to conscript them, that they might perform the duties which they had. Thus Ali, when he prescribed the conscription, said: 'The people's interests cannot be served otherwise.'

4. Umar ibn-al-Khattab used to claim half of the wealth of those governor whom he suspected of having increased their resources by extortion. This also was a form of public interest, because to his mind it was in the interests of the governors to prevent them capitalizing on their power to amass money and heap up illegal plunder.

5. It is told of Ali that he poured out on the ground milk which had been adulterated with water, as a lesson to the man who had done it. This act also was akin to public interest, to show that people were not to adulterate goods.

6. There is tradition that Umar put a whole community to death for the murder of one man, for which they had been jointly responsible. This he did because the public interest demanded it. There was no precedent for the case, but the public interest demanded that the case be considered as one of premeditated murder of a sacrosanct individual. To let the murder pass unavenged would have been to deny the root principle of 'an eye for an eye', while to choose one out of the many who had a hand in the business would have made the whole matter ridiculous. For the man chosen would know that in his case it was not a case

> of retaliation. Or if it were said that this was an anonymous murder, a killing without a killer, on the grounds that every single individual could not be said to be the murderer, then the guilty party was the community itself. The whole of a community can commit a murder in exactly the same way as an individual criminal. And murder can be charged against a community just as it can against a single person, and the members of the community stand in the same relation to the act of murder as does an individual. Hence, the community furthers the public interest when it prevents bloodshed and guards communal life."

Role of the Imams

Another general aspect of public interest is the power which is granted to the Imam to levy upon the rich whatever toll he thinks that the circumstance warrants. This he can do when the public treasury is empty, or when the army has extraordinary needs, while there are no funds to meet those needs. Toll may be levied until the treasury is replenished, or until the needs are sufficiently met.

Further, the Imam has the duty of instituting this levy at times of bountiful harvest and plentiful crops, so that the rich will not be overburdened by the fact that it is they alone who pay it. The public interest here lies in the fact that if a just Imam did not do this, his power would be in vain, and wealthy establishments would provide an incentive to civil war, and to attacks by envious persons. It is sometimes said that the Imam, instead of enforcing the provisions of the levy, borrows money for the public treasury. To this Al-Shatibi retorted that:

> "Borrowing in times of need is allowed only when the treasury has the prospect of more revenue. Otherwise, or alternatively when the revenue is too small to be sufficient, then recourse must be had to the principle of a levy."

A means is that which leads to an end, and to 'block the means' is to remove it. The sense of the phrase is that anything which conduces to a forbidden end is itself forbidden, while anything conducive to a desirable end is itself desirable. Thus, for example, adultery is forbidden, and, therefore, to admire the charms of a strange woman is also forbidden, as being a means towards adultery.

On the other side, attendance at prayers is compulsory, and therefore an effort to attend prayers is also compulsory, as is leaving one's business to make that effort. To make the pilgrimage is compulsory; therefore an effort to visit the Sacred House and to perform the other rites of pilgrimage is also compulsory.

The fundamental reason for the validity of 'blocking the means' is a realization of the repercussions and final results of all actions. If they are conducive to those public interests which constitute the aims and objectives of the dealings of man with man, then they are as desirable as those aims themselves. But if they are not equally desirable, or if their results might be evil, then they are forbidden just as evil is forbidden, even though the means may be somewhat less objectionable.

In considering the results of actions, the matter of interest is not the purpose or the objective of the agent; rather, it is the result and outcome of his action. The individual will be rewarded or punished for his intention in the next world; but in this world, it is according to its result and outcome that an action is good or bad, desirable or undesirable. For this world must take its stand on the welfare of mankind, on judgement and justice, and these things require a scrutiny of results and outcomes rather than of estimable aims and worthy intentions. A man who out of a sincere love for the worthy intentions and for the worship of Allah reviles idols has gained the approval of Allah by the formulation of his purpose; and yet, he has forbidden such reviling in cases where it would result in the rage of the idolaters, who would then revile Allah the Great, Himself. So, His exalted words run:

> "And do not revile those who invoke deities other than Allah, lest in response they revile Allah without knowledge."[20]

In this noble prohibition, regard it had to be the actual consequences, rather than to the commendable religious aim.

Hence, it appears that in cases which tend towards crime or evil, the veto is directed not towards the aim itself, which is sincere, but towards the consequences which will arise; thus an act may be forbidden because of its consequences, even though Allah may be aware that the intention underlying it is sincere.

Sometimes also a man may seek an evil end through a legal act, in which case he is guilty in his own conscience and in the sight of Allah. But no man may take measures against him, nor may any legal penalties be invoked upon him. Such is the case of man who cuts the price of his goods in order to injure a business rival. This is undoubtedly a legal act; yet, it is a means towards a crime, that on injuring another.

This crime is the man's object, but in spite of that his action cannot be punished by the power of the law, nor does it fall under any penalty which the law of the land can impose. His action, from the point of view of intention, is a means to evil, but externally it is a means to public and private benefit. Undoubtedly the seller benefits by selling, by the circulation of his goods, and by the goodwill which he gains; equally certainly the public benefits by the cut in price, by which a general lowering of prices is encouraged.

The principle of blocking the means had regard not only to individual aims and intentions, as we have seen, but also to the encouragement of public welfare and to the prevention of public evil. Thus, it must take account of the consequences along with the intention, or even of the consequences alone.

The principle of 'means' is firmly established in the Qur'an and the Sunna. In the former, there is the verse: "And do not revile those who invoke Gods other than Allah, lest in response they revile Allah without knowledge." Of this it is related that the idolaters said that they were content to have their Gods reviled if they in turn could revile Muhammad's God. Thus again: "O you who believe, do not say Ra'ina; say Unzurna and hearken. This was because the Muslims used the former word with good intention, but the Jews took it as implying a derogatory sense to the Prophet."[21]

In the Sunna there are many stories of the Prophet and many decisions of his Companions. Among them is that of his refusal to kill the hypocrites, lest the unbelievers should have a pretext for saying that Muhammad killed his Companions.

There is also the story that the Prophet forbade a man who had loaned money to accept a gift from the debtor, unless the gift was counted as part repayment of the loan. The reason was simply that the gift was a means of postponing payment, and was therefore a form of interest. For the lender would get his money back and extra also in the form of the gift. We have also the account of the Prophet's having forbidden that men's hands should be cut off in time of war; the purpose was to stop this practice leading to an illegal treatment of fighting men which would inevitably ensue.

Similarly, laws should not be intermitted in times of war, lest freedom become licence; the two are closely related. And there is the account of the earliest Believers, both Emigrants and Helpers, having on their death-beds appointed their divorced wives as their heirs; this they did because there was a suspicion of a plot to debar such wives from inheriting. It was not even certain that such a plot existed, but divorce was a 'means' which might have produced injustices.

Again, the Prophet forbade monopolies, saying: 'Only sinners hold monopolies.' For a monopoly is a means to oppress the people in all things which are considered to be essential. But there is no law against a monopoly in any article which cannot injure the people by being withheld, such as cosmetics and the life; for these things do not come under the heading of necessities.

The Prophet also forbade any man who had given alms to buy them back, even though, he might see them displayed for sale in the market. Thus, he sought to check the means to recover what had been given to Allah, even by purchase. Thus, anyone who gives alms is forbidden to repossess them by purchase, and is yet more stringently forbidden to repossess them by other means. To permit repossession by purchase might be a means of cheating the poor; the rich out of his wealth would give alms to the poor, and might then buy them back from him at less than their value. The poor man, on the other hand, would see some profit to himself, and thus his conscience would not oppose the sale.

Thus, there are many indications of this principle, deriving from the Messenger and his Companions. Ibn-Qiyam has collected some ninety such examples from actual occurrences, in all of which the principle of blocking the means is clearly illustrated.

> "Means are counted to be half of the legal principles of Islam."

These two principles, that of public interest and that of blocking the means, both run back to a common root, that of ensuring the welfare of society. They are integrally connected with the established laws of Islam and with its general purposes. It is these two principles which can guide us towards the legislation necessary to ensure a sound form of Islamic life and to include in its scope a comprehensive social justice.

This principle must be our concern in a general work dealing with social justice in Islam; yet, it is desirable to mention some of the things which Islam is able to ensure in this sphere for the present and the future. We must also deal with the legislation necessary to produce these things, so that it may be used as a pattern for analogous treatment in other cases. We cannot deal with all possible developments but these may be safely left to the dictation of circumstances times and conditions.

Governing Laws

This tax was a compulsory duty in Islam, levied on all possessions according to a sliding scale of one-tenth, one-twentieth, and one-fortieth. In all cases, it represented a very small fraction, and hence, it is but natural that the question should arise: How could such a small sum be of assistance to all the Muslim poor? To answer this question we must consider the following facts:

1. The small amount of capital on which the tax had to be paid made the greater part of the community liable to it. The exemption value for the poor-tax was fixed at six pounds, which meant that practically all the population

had to pay the tax; thus the income from it was relatively great.

2. Disbursements from the tax money were confined to specifically limited classes of people. For their livelihood the great majority had to rely on work, which has always been reckoned by Islam to be the primary source of a living.

3. Most important of all, the livelihood of the very poor did not depend solely upon this source of income. There were also the vast sums acquired as booty during the war days, sums which lasted for more than half a century. In this booty all the fighting men shared, and most of them were of the poor classes. They received four-fifths of the booty, while the other fifth was turned into a charitable foundation for the benefit of all classes of necessitous persons, relatives, orphans, the destitute, and the wayfarer. And when Umar resolved not to take the booty away from the conquered countries, but to leave it for the benefit of the native peoples, he instituted the land-tax in its place, as this later on was sufficient to provide for all the poor.

Today, the last primary source of revenue is no longer available, and the poor-tax in itself is not sufficient. Therefore, we must consider alternative sources to take the place of booty and plunder, in order to provide an ample living for the generality of men.

Before we consider new sources we must first exhaust the poor-tax as a source in itself. It is a compulsory duty, and it must be paid if the community is justifiably to be described as Islamic. For the payment of the poor-tax is a spiritual duty as well as financial one. Again, we must consider the source of the poor-tax as including all types of property, some of which are not at present included because they were not familiar in the early days of Islam.

That is to say, we must bear in mind those forms of wealth which are liable to the poor-tax but which are not mentioned in the Qur'an except generally in the verse:

"O you who have believed, expend of the goods which you have acquired, and of that which We have provided for you from the Earth. And do not propose any evil in thus expending it; for you got it yourselves only by connivance."[22]

The fact that the poor-tax was prescribed as a duty only upon such types of property as were familiar in the time of the Prophet does not prevent its being prescribed today as a duty on all that is known as Property or wealth, and on all that produces an income. It may not be of difference that such things may not be the kind on which the tax was originally imposed.

Similarly, we can control the outlets for the tax money, just as Umar exercised the same control when he stopped payments designed to convert unbelievers. It must not be given in any form of money to those who are eligible for it; rather it must be given to them in the basic form of goods or services, or it must be used to buy for them some part of their basic necessities. The source of their livelihood must be fixed and unconnected with any kind of temporary or haphazard charity; for these things are not in accord with the needs of modern life.

But in any case such detailed considerations have no place in this book. The scope of our thinking here is the broad field of the promotion of social justice and equity, as the Muslim world gives its attention to a renaissance of the true Islamic life.

Mutual Responsibility of Society

The Prophet said: "Any household which suffers a man to remain hungry among them is outside the protection of Allah, the Blessed and the Exalted." In this brief sentence, he emphasized the principle of mutual responsibility in society, a principle which most of us must recognize from the precedents and the examples provided by our study of the Qur'an. This principle was authoritatively imposed on both the individual and the social conscience. Today the law must again enforce it as an essential root of Islam. This means that the law can enforce that which Umar intended to enforce:

> "If I had known earlier what I now know, I would have taken the excess of their wealth from the rich and given it to the poor."

Thus, the law can impose taxes, the only limit of which is the establishment of equality in the social sphere, the removal of crime and oppression from the community in general, and the ample provision of food and drink, clothing and housing, medical treatment and skill for every single individual in the country. It does not matter how much tax is placed upon capital so long as the latter is not thereby made incapable of work and of reasonable increase; this condition must be observed because the steady turning of the wheels of labour brings other benefits which cannot be overlooked.

Thus, the law can put into the hands of the poor with perfect justification a stretch of funded property which they may use without paying any basic rent, or at a nominal rent, that they may from it obtain a means of life. For this constitutes a source of livelihood and is the only means of work within their power. By this act the law will fulfil the Messenger's words:"

> "Anyone of you may permit to his brother the use of his land as gift, without exacting for it any agreed rent."

The law may also with justification fix the wage of the factory or the farm worker at a stipulated proportion of the production or of the harvest. The lowest limit of this wage must be a competence to cover food and drink and clothing, and medicine and medical care to a certain extent. The standard is to be taken as that of a moderate living, determined by the proportion of the inhabitants of the country to its general wealth.

General Taxation

Every individual in the Muslim community has the duty of taking a share in the general expenses of the state according to his ability. We have already noticed the opinion of the Imam Malik on what may be done when the treasury is empty, or when the needs of the army are increased; the law has the power according to need to levy a toll on the wealth of the rich. Similar to the needs of the army are the other needs of the state, such as improvements in public services, irrigation of waste lands. the education of the people, and the medical treatment of the sick.

All these things are communal duties which must be met and satisfied just as much as the needs of the army; they must be preserved as strongly as frontiers and defence posts must be guarded. This is particularly true today when wars make demands on all the resources and services of the belligerent nations. In modern war, everyone may be said to be in the army, and thus should be capable of taking responsibility in time of peace.

Public Resources

Monopolies on the necessities of life are forbidden by Islam. A monopoly on food is forbidden, for example, since Islam has always asserted the communal ownership of water, pasturage, and fire, as being the primary needs of life. But the needs of life are not unchangeable, varying as they do from age to age. Consequently, the preservation of this general Islamic principle demands what is known today as the nationalization of natural resources.

It is essential not to have in the hands of private individuals or companies the resources of water, light, heat, electricity, coal and oil, or the resources of public transport and public food supplying, and other such things. For private ownership gives the power of monopoly, imposes upon the general public he will of the monopolists, and permits them to indulge in that disgraceful exploitation which we witness today.

The head of the state has the power to make all these things state-owned, and to fix prices and costs of them so that they can get it at equitable rates without excessive prices. By these means the Islamic aims for the checking of monopolies can be realized.

Public Interest and Blocking of Means

Everything which tends to advance the public welfare or to retard oppression of the public is a duty laid upon the law, and everything which tends towards a prohibited end is itself prohibited. The application of these established principles of Islam lays on the law today following duties:

1. The taking of excessive wealth out of the hands of bloated capitalists. The fact that such excessive wealth is in their possession tends towards a number of crimes. In the first place, it tends to produce that luxury which is forbidden by Islam. Luxury is a relative matter, which can be defined only in terms of the general condition in each age and country. The permanent rule is that luxury shall not increase beyond the mean struck by the national wealth in proportion to the population. One result of luxury is the iniquitous rise in prices which springs from the fact that one section of the populace has an unlimited power to buy, while the goods available for sale are not equal to the demand. Another result is the rise of social vices, springing from the fact that some people possess more money than they need; to dispose this, they look for illegal outlets and seek sensual and corrupt pleasures; through these, their morals and their standards are degraded, and on the other hand their victims are the needy men and women who always exist in an unbalanced society.

2 The removal of extreme, poverty, because it results in the way of crime and evil. These results include a great number of social evils which can only exist in surroundings of privation and destitution, theft, infamy, and moral degradation, a general atmosphere of corruption. This is over and above the vast differences which are set between those who have and those who have not, the hatreds and the social disturbances which the law must prevent before they occur by removing their causes. If it be asked how this extreme poverty is to be removed, it is by the ample provision of work for every able-bodied man, and by the provision of an adequate wage, by social security for all who are disabled, and by speedy relief. This is the method in general outline; the specific applications are easy once the general aim is established.

3. The struggle against disease and ignorance: Because of their evil effect on the individual and the community these weaken the general strength of the community and afford a footing to its enemies. This condition is forbidden, as is any factor which leads to it. Nothing can oppose disease and ignorance successfully except a rise in living standards and in general wealth; but the laws of charity and such other things are only a palliative to soothe the sore, not to heal it. The real treatment is that every individual should be possessed of private means for medical and educational purposes. Or alternatively that medical care and education should be provided free to every individual in the country on a common basis and to a common level. The rich must not be able, by money, to get more than the poor in schools or hospitals.

Legacies

When there are present at the division of the estate relatives, orphans and poor people, give them a provision out of it and speak to them fair.[23] Thus runs the Qur'anic precept. It clearly means that out of every estate there must be a share for relatives, orphans and the poor. The law has the power of disposal according to the nature of the case; it may change the beneficiaries, or it may leave them unchanged. So, Umar did in the case of paying out money to convert others to Islam. The law also has the power to apply the regulations according to the needs of the estate or according to those of the community.

We must remember that the meaning of being 'present' can legitimately be extended to cover virtual presence, 'that is to say, existence. In every community, there are orphans and poor, and there is no necessity for them to be present fn person when an estate is being divided; they are already present in time and space. So by the power of the law all duties must be enforced which are not enforced by the power of conscience.

Mutual Help and Usury

Islam rooted out usury, and fought it in all its forms and

appearances; hence, it is impossible for any form of Islamic life to exist on an economic basis which includes the principles of usury. We have already discussed the causes which made Islam unable to countenance usury, but they may be summed up by saying that it is the negation of the spirit of mutual help and friendliness. If usury obtains, then it is to the benefit of the capitalist who can thus increase his wealth without working and without the risk of loss.

The national economy must be set on a basis of mutual help rather than of usury. All the faults which can be alleged against the later system have been summed up to justify its rejection by Maulana Muhammad Ali in his book, *Islam and the New World Order*, from which we may quote the following passage:

> "It is objected that to forbid interest on money will hinder business and commercial transactions, and will hinder the accomplishment of important domestic projects. We may grant the truth of this, but on the other side we have the far greater advantage that to proscribe interest will prevent world wars, which can only end in misery, and which are kindled and inflamed only by loans and debts governed by interest. And if we examine the facts of the case, we shall find that from the very first, trade followed its natural course and spread over more and more widely! Wider limits were brought within the Islamic sphere. So that today the Islamic states are still among the greatest of the old-established countries of the civilized world."

This prohibition of usury cannot in any sense be reconciled with the conditions of the new world which materialistic Western civilization is bringing into being. The social system most required is that practical system which Islam today has in mind, which was successfully applied in practice by, at its inception, centuries ago.The As for the capital sums, without which business cannot be carried on, there was little difference between the gains which they made under the Islamic system and those which they made by ordinary lending; for the Islamic system was in effect of partnership between capital and labour. Such a partnership is not impossible, for the Islamic system holds that capital and labour should share together in all profit and loss; whereas the result of paying a steady rate of interest is that, capital makes a continual profit, even when labour had to work at a loss.

It is sometimes objected that the partnership of capital and labour in both profits and losses is not practicable, because it means that regular accounts have to be kept, since this is one of the necessities of trade; and further, because trading records have to be available for the assessing of taxes which have to be paid. But all the share-issuing companies which take part in trading on a large scale have to keep accounts.

Indeed this partnership system is more to the public advantage than that of giving all the dividends to capital; for it is the latter system which produces most of the evils of capitalism, and which is the source of the oppression of the workers. And the loans which are floated by governments or companies to carry out immense projects such as railroads or canals or such things have done no more than prove this point.

But since the system of state banking depends on the principle of mutual help, which is approved by the Islamic social system, it must be of great benefit to mankind.

This is a general statement, the particular details of which are too lengthy for a book dealing with general ideas. At the same time, there can be no harm in giving an example as a guide to the general objective which we have in mind. Suppose, the state decrees the abolition of interest on funds in banks, companies, public enterprises, and private loans, what will happen then?

What will happen will be that capitalists will find themselves unable to increase their wealth except by two general methods. First, they may put it to some profitable use themselves in manufacture or trade or agriculture. Or second, they may put it to a profitable and helpful use by investing it in share-issuing companies, where the share values may rise or fall. Both these methods are sanctioned by Islam, and neither of them will work the slightest injury to economic life.

It is sometimes feared that the rich will refrain from depositing their money in the banks, which generally finance the large public projects. This is an imaginary danger which gains currency among us because we are familiar only with European methods of using money.

In Europe, the primary natural impulse is to make money increase; this can be accomplished only by using it for some means of exploitation, and so, this natural impulse is a guarantee that money will not be kept out of circulation. But when he desired to take in handsome large project to justify what is known as the great ear of production, we have the power to create legislation covering various kinds of industry; this legislation enacts that no new enterprise may be set up except on the basis of capital over such and such a sum. On that capital sums flow in to take up shares and to become liable to profit and loss on the market.

Thus, there is no more need for banks, except for the issuing of currency. If other banks wish to make a profit, then they must only with permission-in some profit seeking enterprise, where the shares are liable to fluctuation in the open market. But the system will not stop the flow of capital, either domestic or foreign; for the greater proportion of capital wealth is not deposited in banks, but is put out to profit in enterprises.

At for insurance companies, it may be that their basis is Islamic, inasmuch as the funds which are deposited with them are liable to profit and loss, to fall or rise. Funds deposited in these companies are put to work in profit-seeking enterprises, subject to fluctuation. Everytime a beneficiary receives more than he has paid in, the amount of the company's loss is deducted from the remainder of the depositors in proportion to the funds which they have invested. Thus insurance companies' members form a body united for mutual help; in effect they pay out of their own pockets to support any unfortunate one of their number, when need arises.

They have a form of security from which they can benefit in time, of hardship or need. This can be applied also to savings banks and similar institutions, all of which rest on the basis of mutual help in one way or another, and from which funds are employed in profit- seeking enterprises, always liable to fluctuation. Such institutions have no fixed rate of interest, and hence our economic system here can be free from the taint of usury; hence also all capital is compelled to work as the only method of achieving profit and increase.

Sources

1. The Holy Quar'an, Sura, 5:48. Cf, supra, p. 10.
2. A/atwa is the decision of a Mufti, based on the Islamic law.—Trans.
3. The Qarmatians, thus named from Qarmat, the dwarf, which was the nickname of the original leader, were Islam 'ills' who raised a dangerous rebellion in Iraq and Syria during the reign of Al-Muktafi. They were defeated in the province in 901 A.D. [288 A.HL but their Fierce risings continued to trouble the Abbasids for at least fifty years.—Trans.
4. Alphonse Gouilly, L'lslam devant le Monde Moderne. -Trans.
5. H.A.R. Gibb: Whither Islamf p. 379,-Trans.
6. From Prof. Hasan Habashi: The First Crusade.
7. This takes place through equating the form Mahomed an^tW form "Mohound." "Ma" whichis the first person possessive pronoun, my, and 'hound' from the German "hand' ' a dog. This is a play on words betweenthe forms "Mahumad" and "Mahund"—From Leopold Weiss: Islam at the Crossroads. This work was originally written by Muhammad Asad, and published by Ashraf, 1937, Lahore. It was translated into English in 1938 by Weiss, and thence retranslated into Arabic by Umar Farrukj.—Trans.
8. Ibid.
9. Sura, 8:62.
10. Sura, 4:143.
11. Sura, 4:76.
12. Sura, 3:133.
13. Quoted from Haikal's 'Life of Muhammad', where he quotes from an article in the magazine .iVura/-/5/am. No. 40, p. 5720, dated 1934 A.D. [1353 A.H].
14. Jacob Fahm, Pragmatism, or the Philosophy of Means.
15. The present author hopes in the near future to produce for the Arab reader a complete study on The Islamic Doctrine of the Universe. Life, and Mankind.

16. Jacob Fahm, op. cit.
17. Quoted from The Iman Malik by Prof. Muhammad Abu Zuhra Professor of the Shari's in the Faculty of Law in the Fu'ad al-Awwal University.
18. Public interest" is an arbitrary but convenient translation for a phrase which means literally a measure of welfare for society which lacks a precedent in the primary authorities—Trans.
19. Reference is made here to three of the four schools into which Muslim jurisprudence is divided; these are the Shafite, the Hanafite, the Malikite, and the Hanbalite schools. The roots by which the system of jurisprudence is governed, being also mentioned here, may be said to include: nass or precedent, drawn from the Qur 'an or the Swna; these two authorities are in theory-the sole root of jurisprudence {fiqh); Ijma ' or concensus of opinion; qiyas or analogy. Other principles in use but more dubious of acceptance are ray, or independent critical opinion and, istihsan or preference. Vd. Lammens; Islam p. 82ff.-Trans.
20. Sura, 6:108-Trans.
21. Sura, 2: 98. Baidawi in his commentary on this verse gives the explanation that the Jews of Arabia took the form ra'ina, look at us, or better, pay attention to us, as connected with a similar word meaning 'evil'. Muhammad, therefore, disliking their ridicule, prescribed the use of the word, which was to be replaced by another which did not lend itself to such paranomasis. Vd. Jeffery, Foreign Vocabulary of the Qur'an 136, and Palmer: Koran, 13. —Trans.
22. Sura, 2:269-270.
23. Tradition No. 2541 in Prof. Ahmad Muhammad Shakir: Musnad, iv, published by Dar al-Ma 'arif. (The isnad, or chain of transmit ting authorities, which has been omitted in the body of the trans lated text, follows tradition. It runs as follows: Related by Ahmad on the authority ofAffan, from Humad ibn-Zaid on the authority ofAmr ibn Dinar, who quoted it from Tawus, who had it from Abdullah Ibn Abbas.- Trans.

NINE

Conferred Security Covers

Islam's gift to its followers, is exemplary. Out of the fundamental rights conferred by it on its citizens, we shall take up, to begin with, those rights which are equally enjoyed by all the citizens as human beings without distinction of creed. Later on we shall take stock of the exclusive rights of Muslims and non-Muslims.

Human Life, Saved

Islam regards human life extremely sacred, and maintaining murder of one man as the murder of entire humanity, has stressed the security of human life. A parallel is not to be found any where in the world in the religious, moral or legal literature. God says:

> If any one slew a person... unless it be for murder or for spreading mischief in the land ...it would be as if he slew the whole people. And if any one saved a life, it would be as if he saved the life of the whole people.
>
> Al Quran V 32.

At another place it has been said:

> Nor take life...which God has made sacred...except for just cause.
>
> Al Quran XVIL33

Islam has limited taking of life for just cause to the following situations:

(a) Qisas (or life for life) for a deliberate murder.

(b) In Jehad against those resisting the advancement of the True Faith.

(c) As a punishment to those trying to overthrow the Islamic order.

(d) As a punishment to a married man or woman for adultery or fornication.

(e) As a punishment for apostasy.

(f) As a punishment for highway robbery.

Barring these six exemptions the violation of the sanctity of human life can never be allowed.

Such instructions have been repeated in the Quran so often—VI: 152, 11:178-179 and XXV: 68. Taking of human life is such a serious and heinous crime in the sight of God that its perpetrator even after being executed under the Islamic Law is to be consigned to Hell-fire after death, and is the target of Divine wrath and eternal damnation (except those who repent sincerely before execution are forgiven. Tr.):

> If a man kills a believer intentionally, his recompense is Hell, to abide (there in) (for ever): and the wrath and curse of God are upon him, and a dreadful penalty is prepared for him.
>
> Quran IV: 93

The Quran also forbids talking the life of one's own offspring for fear of hunger and poverty:

> Kill not your children on a plea of want;
>
> We provide sustenance for you and for them;
>
> Al Quran VI: 151

And the same instruction has been repeated in Surah XVII: 31 and VI: 140 also. The Arabs during the days of Jahiliyah so often buried their daughters alive—(this heinous practice was partly due to poverty and partly due to false notions of honour—the daughters were not a source of strength but were taken away by the enemies in case of attack by a rival tribe for mere plunder if not blood-fend. Tr.) Pointing to the severe punishment in the life Hereafter, God says in an extremely wrathful tone (without so much as addressing the culprit directly. Tr.):

> When the female (infant), buried alive is questioned for what crime she was killed;
>
> Al Quran LXXXI 7-8

God has not only forbidden taking the life of others but not to take one's own life either. And in the way the path of suicide has been barred:

> And do not kill or destroy yourselves: Al Quran IV 29

And after these very definite Quranic injunctions relating to the sanctity of human life, now we shall take up some sayings of the Prophet on this theme and some incidents of his period.

In his harangue on the occasion of the last Hajj, the Prophet said:

> O ye people; your blood, goods and honour dignity have been declared totally sacred, one's for the other. Their sanctity is eternal as the sanctity of this day and of this month of Zul Hajjah in this town (of Makkah). Beware! Lest you should take to beheading each other after I am gone, and be 'associated with the group of unbelievers.
>
> Bukhari, Abu Da'ood, Nasai and Musnad Abroad.

Later, presenting the first example of putting this instructions into practice he says:

> All the blood-fends are being ended herewith. The first vendetta which I end here and now is connected with my own family... the blood of the suckling baby, the son of Rabi'a bin-al-Harith, who had been murdered by Bani Huzail. I now forgive them for it.
>
> Bukhari, Abu Da'ood, Nasai, Musnad-e-Ahmad

Once the Prophet said:

> In comparison to the murder of a believer, the degradation of the whole world has no value in the sight of God.
>
> Muslim

And it is not the blood of a "Muslim" alone that is sacred but it is true for every servant of God. If an innocent zimmi is killed by a Muslim, the latter's entry to heaven is barred:

> Whoever murdered a zimmi. God closed the doors of heaven upon him.
>
> Nasai

> One who killed a zimmi, would be denied even the fragrance of heaven.
>
> Bukhari.

Once it happened that some children of the unbelievers were accidentally killed in a skirmish against the registers of the faith. The Prophet was very much grieved. The companions said, "They were only children of the polytheists." The Prophet said in reply:

> The children though polytheists are better than you. Beware! Never kill the children. Every living thing has been created on the nature conferred on it by God.
>
> Musnad-e-Ahmad

Ibn-e-Abbas reports that during the period of the Prophet, a dead body was found, but the murderer could not be traced. The Prophet, very much irritated said in his harangue:

> O ye people! How is this that a person is murdered while I am here amongst you, and his murderer is untraced. If the entire creation in the heaven and the earth concurs on the murder of one person, God will not let any one of them go unpunished.
>
> Tabrani

In a certain skirmish, a woman got killed. The Prophet on seeing her dead body, said:

> Oh! What have you done? She was not among the combatants. Go and tell Khalid not to kill women, children and the disabled, old, infirm and cripples not combat-fit. Tr.

A correct idea of the sanctity of human life and the attitude of the Islamic state in this behalf can be had from the general amnesty granted on the occasion of the conquest of Makkah. So long as the unbelievers were in the position of aggressors and were after wiping out the Islamic state of Madinah, they were treated as combatants of an aggressive country. As against the opinion of Abu Bakr that the prisoners of war of Badr be freed against payment of ransom, the suggestion of Umar that they must all be put to sword received Divine approbations and the following verse was revealed:

> It is not fitting for an Apostle that he should have prisoners of war until he had thoroughly subdued the land, Ye look for the temporal goods of this world; but God look to the Hereafter and God is exalted in might, wise. Had it not been for a previous from God, a severe penalty would have reached you for the (ransom) you took.
>
> Al Quran VIII: 67-68

Now that the situation had changed after the conquest of Makkah, their state had been liquidated and with it its aggressive character and the position of the unbelievers as aggressors, they, as the citizens of the conquered territory came under the authority of the Islamic state, became its citizens. And according to the Divine Will they became "subdued" (brought low):

> Until they pay the jizya with willing submission and feel themselves subdued.
>
> Al Quran IX:29

Therefore, the Prophet, who had been given the glad tidings of the conquest of Makkah by God, as head of the Islamic state, before the stage of the conquest could attain completion, while the war had not yet laid down its spoils took extraordinary care to save the lives of the new citizens of his state.

Makkah was the stronghold of the blood-thirsty enemies of the Prophet and deadly antagonists of Islam. Here lived those who had strewn the paths of the Prophet with thorns, brought great afflictions to him and his companions, kept him confined to Sha' b-e-Abi Talib, (a narrow gorge between the mountains in Makkah), plotted and made attempts on his life. And when he had migrated to Madinah, they did not allow him to live in peace either. Made repeated surprise attacks on Madinah with murder and pillage. In the battles of Badr, Uhad and the battle of Clans, thrust on Madinah, they killed many of his faithful and trustworthy friends and wounded him also. Those of his companions who had migrated from Makkah to Yemen, Syria, and Abyssinia were not left undisturbed there either. At the time of the conquest of Makkah, Wahshi, the murderer of the Prophet's uncle Hamzah, Hindah who had tried to chew the liver of Hamzah, and Ikramah b. Abu Jehal, Safwan b. Umayyah, Ka'b b. Zubair and many such other enemies of Islam were in Makkah. The Prophet was now in a position to settle old scores with them. But he, in spite of the power to avenge himself, issued to his army the following orders to save their (his enemies) lives:

1. He who discards arms should be spared.
2. Whoever enters Ka'bah should not be killed.
3. Whoever takes shelter in the house of Abu Sufyan should be left alone.
4. Whoever takes shelter in his own house, should be spared.
5. One who betakes himself to the house of Hakeem ibn-e Hizam should not be killed.
6. One who takes to his heels should not be pursued.
7. No wounded person should be killed

After the conquest of Makkah when people gathered before the Ka'bah, the Prophet addressing them said:

> Do you know, What I am going to do with you to day?

There arose a response from the crowd:

> You are a noble brother and the son of a noble brother.

The Prophet said in reply:

> This day let no repreach be cast on you. Go you are all at liberty.

The great example of magnanimity and forgiveness set by the Prophet became an important chapter of the Law pertaining to war. And during the period of the rightly guided caliphs on all the occasions of the conquests of Syria, Iraq, Egypt, Iran and the Roman territories abstention from blood-shed was the rule after the enemy had been subdued. A glance at the orders issued by Abu Bakr, 'Umar, 'Uthman and Ali to their military commanders and the governors shows clearly that they had on them a deep impression of the general amnesty of the conquest of Makkah.

An important question in connection with the security of life is when it becomes applicable. All the laws in the world commonly regard the right of the security of life applicable only after the birth. But the Divine Law makes it applicable from the time of initiation of pregnancy. We find that the Prophet abstained from immediately pronouncing the punishment of stoning to death on Ghamidiyah even after her clear confession of fornication, since she had also stated in her confession that she was pregnant. She was meted out this punishment after the birth of the child and the termination of period of suckling the child. If this punishment had been immediately enforced, an innocent life (of the unborn child) would have been lost. The legists have determined the applicability of the right of security of life from 120 days after conception, since during this period the embryo starts taking shape from an agglomerate of rapidly multiplying cells, and then the term "human entity" is applicable to it. This opinion of our legists after centuries has now been recognized by the modern medical science. The American Supreme Court in a case Reo versus Wade have pronounced the decision with reference to the findings of modern embryology that the "human entity" in the mother's womb would be recognized three months after conception.

Security of Property

In the Islamic state all such private properties as have been legally acquired and from which all the rights and' obligations such as Zakah, Sadaqah (charities), the expenses of the upkeep of the parents, wife and children, brothers and sisters and those under purchase and sale and other maintenances and obligations have been paid, and the regular and temporary taxes levied for defence, administrative needs, public welfare or to meet the emergency needs like war, famine, flood, earthquake and epidemics have also been paid, and also that they are not being surrendered on illegal and unapproved pursuits (of lusts) or business of this nature, shall be immune against the interference of the state, and the owner shall be entitled to the following rights relating to the properties :

(a) The right of their utilization, management and control (change, sale, gifting, donation etc. Tr.)

(b) The right to invest them in business to earn profits.

(c) The right to transfer them.

(d) The right to protect them. There is a definite Quranic injuction:

> And do not eat up your property among yourselves for vanities.
>
> Al Quran II; 188

If the government has to acquire some body's private property in public interest, it will do so with the consent of the owner after paying compensation at the market rate.

The piece of land that the Prophet selected as the site for the mosque belonged to two orphans. They offered it as a free gift, but the Prophet had its value estimated, and purchased it at the market rate of that time.

On the occasion of the battle of Ummah the Prophet asked Sefwan bin-e-Umayyah for some armours. And when he said, "O Muhammad, are you taking them from me without payment," the Prophet said in reply, " We are taking them temporarily for use and all those damaged or lost shall be paid for." Qazi Abu Yusuf says in his *Kitab-al-Khiraj*:

The Imam (government) has no right to take any thing from the (rightful) possession of an individual without a proved legal right (of the government to that item.)

In the harangue of his pilgrimage to Makkah what the Prophet said about the sanctity of property along with that of life, has already been mentioned. The security of proprietary rights can be had from the following tradition:

> Whoever is killed in the protection of his property is a martyr.
>
> Bukhari

Security of Honour and Dignity

An important right of every citizen of the Islamic state shall be that his dignity and honour be protected. The Prophet in his harangue of the last pilgrimage included the sanctity of the dignity and honour also along with life and property. God says in the Quran:

> O ye who believe! Let not some men among you laugh at others:
>
> It may be that the (latter) are better than the (former): nor let some women langh at others: it may be that the (latter) are better than the (former): nor call each other by offensive niknames:
>
> Al Quran XLIX : 11
>
> And do not speak ill of each other behind their backs.
>
> Al Quran XLIX: 12

Further, it occurs in the same verse:

> Avoid suspicion as much (as possible): for suspicion in some cases is a sin:
>
> Al Quran XLIX 12

Use of harash and abusive language has also been strictly prohibited in mutual conversation:

> God loveth not that the evil should be noised abroad in public speech, except where injustice hath been done:
>
> Al Quran 148

In this verse where it forbids man to use abusive language, he has been permitted to raise his voice against the oppressor with full force.

> Say to the believing men that they should lower their gaze and guard their modesty:
>
> Al Quran XXIV: 30

> And say to the believing women that they should lower their gaze and guard their modesty:
>
> Al Quran XXIV: 31

In these verses the believers have not been addressed directly but these instructions have been conveyed through the Prophet means that while the Muslims are to practise them individually in their lives, the Islamic state has also to keep an eye on that they are being practised. And where their violation is noticed it should be effectively stopped. In other words, it is the obligation of the state that it should make efficient arrangements for the protection of the honour and dignity of the people and stop spread of immodest practices.

The Prophet, in many of his sayings, has forbidden beating people and insulting and bringing them to disgrace. Once he said:

> The back of a Muslim is sacred (he cannot be beaten), except when he comes to deserve it through guilt. Whoever beats a Muslim will have to face Divine wrath.
>
> Tabrani

> If a person does not help a Muslim where he is being disgraced and his honour is at stake God will not help such a person where he is most in need of His Help and implores Him for it. And if a person helps a Muslim in a situation where he is being disgraced and his honour is at stake, God helps him in situation where he needs God's help most and prays to Him for it.
>
> Abu Da'ood

In another tradition the Prophet has said:

> Whoever has insulted another person or disgraced him or has wronged him in any other way should have it forgiven today (in this life), before the Day when there will neither be money nor other goods of this world, save his own good deeds which will be taken away from

> him and given to those wronged by him in this world according to the measure of his crimes. And if all his good deeds fail to compensate for his wrongs, the evil deeds of the wronged victims will be cast upon him.
>
> Bukhari

The Prophet has termed disgrace of a person the worst oppression.

> The worst oppression is unjustified attack on some body's honour.
>
> Abu Da'ood

Umar, when giving a send-off to his executive officials, used to give them the following instructions:

I am not sending you out as tyrants and oppressors, but as leaders and guides. Take heed! Do not disgrace and debase Muslims by beating them.

Defamation Cases

In cases of defamation the Islamic principle is that every member of the society is honourable no matter what his position, rank and financial status, which is the same as to say when some body is filing a suit of defamation against any one he need not prove that he is honourable, and by the action of the defendant he has really been disgraced. It was on the basis of this principle of equality that 'Umar, the second caliph, got Muhammad b. Umar the son of Umar b 'As, the governor of Egypt, beaten by an Egyptian since he had beaten him (the Egyptian) for his only fault that his horse had beaten all others in a race and (Muhammad) had said. "Take these stripes of the lash, I am the son of the noble." Umar called both the father and the son to Madinah and handing over the lash to the Egyptian, said, "Beat the son of the noble." And after he had been thrashed, 'Umar said to the Egyptian, "Now a few stripes for Umar bin-al-'As too, for, by God, the son dared beat thee on the strength of the father's authority and power.

It was in connection with protection of honour that two murders were committed during the caliphate of Umar but he dropped Qisas against both murderers. In one of the incidents a member of Bani Hazail tribe criminally assaulted his host's daughter, who threw a stone at him fatally damaging his liver. Umar pronounced his decision, "He has been murdered by Divine arrangement, no blood money can be allowed in this case."

The other incident is this that two young men fraternised with each other. One of them went out for Jihad and deputed the other to look after his family. One night he saw a Jew in a compromising position with his brother's wife and slew him. He threw his naked dead body out on the road. In the morning the Jews brought up a complaint to the court of Caliph 'Umar, who, on hearing the statement of the young man, said to him, "God bless thy hands," and the murder of the Jew was declared unworthy of any legal action.

'Umar, the second caliph, sentenced the three persons, who had brought accusation of fornication (for adultery) against Mughira bin-e-Sha'bah, the governor of Basrah, to eighty stripes each of the lash for false accusation in support of which they could not produce requisite evidence.

Abu Musa Ash'ari had a person flogged (twenty stripes of lash), for demanding greater share from the spoils of war, and got his head shaved. He went straight to Madinah and complained to 'Umar about the insults heaped on him. Umar sent Abu Musa a written order. "If you have disgraced him publicly, in herewith bind you by an avowal to God to allow him to avenge himself on you publicly. And in case it was in privacy let the revenge be taken in privacy." People tried to make him to forgive the offender but he did not agree. At last Abu Musa offered himself in public to receive chastisement at the hands of the wronged person, who at this stage, raised his eyes towards the heavens and said, "O God! Be Thou witness to it, I forgive him."

An idea of temperament of Islam in the matter of security of honour and dignity can be had from the Quranic verses (XXIV: 11-19), in which censuring those accusing 'Aisha, God testified to her chastity and modesty and severely warned Muslims against inventing lies and bringing false accusations against innocent people:

> Those who brought forward the lie are a body among yourselves: Think it not to be an evil to you; on the contrary it is good for you; to every man among them (will come the punishment) of the sin that he earned, and to him who took on himself the lead among them, will be a penalty grievous. Why did not the Believers.—men and women, when ye heard of the affair,—put the best construction on it in their own minds and say, "This (charge) is an obvious lie?" Why did they not bring four witnesses to prove it? When they have not brought the witnesses, such men, in the sight of God, (stand forth) themselves as liars! Were it not for the grace and mercy of God on you in this world and the Hereafter, a grievous penalty would have seized you in that ye rushed glibly into this affair. Behold, 'ye recieved it on your tongues, and said out of your mouths things of which ye had no knowledge; and ye thought it to be a light matter, while it was most serious in the sight of God. And why did ye not, when ye heard it, say —It is not right of us to speak of this: Glory to God! this is a most serious slander! God doth admonish you, that ye may never repeat such (conduct), if you are (true) believers. And God makes the Signs plain to you: for God is full of knowledge and wisdom. Those who love (to see) scandal published broadcast among the Believers, will have a grievous Penalty in this life and in the Hereafter: God knows and ye know not.
>
> AI Quran XXIV: 1-19

The Quran stresses, in general, the security of honour and dignity of every individual, but special emphasis has been laid where security of women's honour is concerned, and God has seriously admonished those violating it:

> Those who slander chaste woman, indiscreet but believing, are cursed in this life and in the Hereafter: for them is a grievous Penalty ...on the Day when their tongues, their hands, and their feet will bear witness against them as to their actions. On that Day God will

> pay them back (all) their just dues, and they will realize that God is the (very) Truth that makes all things manifest.
>
> Al Quran XXIV:23-25

It was due to these instructions that in the numerous stories of oppression and tyranny and coercion and violence during the history of the Muslims, there is not a single instance where a ruler to bring down their enemies to their knees might have violated the chastity of their women folk.

Security of the Private Life

Perfect security of the private life has been provided to the citizens of the Islamic state, and the enclosure of a private residence has been given the position of a citadel, where nobody has a right to pry. The Quran says:

> O ye who believe! Enter not houses other than your own, until ye have asked permission and saluted those in them: That is best for you, in order that ye may heed (what is seemly). If ye find no one in the house, enter not until permission is given to you: if you are asked to go back, go back: that makes for greater purity.
>
> Al Quran XXIV : 27-28

The Prophet has instructed the believers not to enter even their own houses unannounced, so that there may be no chance for them to look at their own women folk in an embarrassing position which is deemed immoral.

> Only those buildings are exempted from these restrictions which are not residential:
>
> It is no fault on your part to enter houses not used for living in, which serve some (other) use for you.
>
> Al Quran XXIV : 29

Under this category fall offices, public buildings, hotels, inns, guest houses, shops, schools and other places like them. Along with instructions not to enter houses without permission, the Muslims have also been told not to meddle into the private lives of other people. The permission granted by the owner to enter his house, does not mean that the visitor should stay there longer than necessary and not allow the owner of the house to pass his time even in his own house according to his will and programme:

> O ye who believe! Enter not the Prophet's houses,—until leave is given you, for a meal, (and then) not (so early as) to wait for ita preparation: but when ye are invited, enter; and when ye have taken your meal, disperse, without seeking familiar talk....
>
> Al Quran XXXII: 53

In connection for entry to a house and to stay there only as long as barely necessary, it was also said that if one has to take some thing at the door, he must ask for it from before the door screen:

> And when ye ask (his ladies) for any thing ye want, ask them from before a screen.
>
> Al Quran XXXIII; 53

Similarly, peeping into other people's houses has been strictly forbidden. The Prophet said that if somebody catches any one peeping into his house and blinds him by sticking it. He has also forbidden to look into somebody else's letter or even cast a side glance at the letter somebody is reading.

Along with provision of security to a citizen's house from outside interference, the Quran has also impressed it on Muslims that they should strictly abstain from prying into each other's secrets, and spying on each other:

> And spy not on each other, nor speak ill of each other behind their backs: Would any of you like to eat the flesh of his dead brother? Nay, ye would abhor it.
>
> Al Quran XLIX 12.

Man through spying on others comes to learn some of their secret faults and infirmities and then takes a morbid pleasure in disclosing them to others, and thus becomes the means of their defamation and disrepute. The Quran strictly forbids both spying and back-biting.

The Prophet once said:

> If you are bent upon learning the secrets of other peoples,, you will corrupt them or at least make their approach to corruption certain.
>
> Abu Da'ood

In another tradition he says:

> Whoever noticed sombody's fault and kept it to himself (abstained from exposure,), he, as it were, quickened a living corpse.
>
> Abu Da'ood, Nasai

The Prophet has specifically prohibited the rulers from spying on their people:

> When a ruler comes to search for reasons behind mere suspicions, he is sure to corrupt them.
>
> Abu Da'ood

In this connection an incident of the period of 'Umar gives us an idea of the limits to which the Amir of the Islamic state can go in the matter of interference in the life of a citizen, and how strong a defence he has been provided against such meddling. Once he ('Umar) heard (on one of his nightly vigilance rounds) somebody singing in his house. Suspecting dirty game, he scaled the wall and entered the house, to find that there was not only wine there but a woman also. 'Umar called out to him saying.

> O enemy of God! Art thou under the (erroneous) impression that thou will be allowed to go on with thy transgression against God and He will not expose thee. In reply he said, O Amir-al-Muminin Don't be hasty. If I am guilty of one sin you have committed three. Allah forbade you to spy on people and you have spied on me. Allah commands you to enter houses through their gates and you have scaled the wall to my house. Allah has ordained that permission is necessary for entry to the houses of other people, and here you are without my permission. Hearing this Umar confessed his fault and

took no action against him, but made him promise that he would take to the path of righteousness.

Tafheem-al-Quran, Vol. V, p 89, with reference to Makarim-al-Akhlaq

Another incident of the period of 'Umar in which a girl to escape the limit set by God, tried to commit sucide with the help of a knife but could not succeed in her attempt. And then she repented for her sin. A certain person who was ignorant of her former guilt proposed to her. The guardian of the girl asked 'Umar, "Shall I enlighten the would be groom the tragic event in her life? 'Umar said in reply, "Will you reveal what God has kept concealed? By God, if you let a breath of it pass to any body I will make you an admonitory example for people. Marry her off as chaste virgins are married."

This is how Islam protects private life and maintains its sanctity. How can the government, that is committed to these commandments and instructions of the Shariah, justify it, conduct in weaving a network of espionage, set a spy or informer in pursuit of every citizen, dug people's private apartments and offices, tap their telephones, censor their letters and keep their photostat copies for record, photographing people's private apartments, and resort to other measures of black-mailing their (political) opponents?

Security of Personal Freedom

In the Islamic state no citizen can be imprisoned without proving his guilt in an open court. Arresting people on mere suspicion and incarcerating them without proper trial in a court of law is not permissible under the Islamic order. Whatever is being done under the name of "Preventive Detention" in the "interest of the state", there is no room for it in the Islamic Law. There is a definite injunction of the Quran that the freedom conferred by God on his servants, not to speak of a common ruler, even the Prophet of God cannot take away:

It is not (possible) that a man, to whom is given the Book, and wisdom, and the Prophetic office, should say to people: "Be ye my worshippers rather than God": On the contrary (He would say):

Be ye worshippers of Him who is truly the cherisher of all: for ye have taught the book and ye have studied it earnestly."

Al Quran III; 79

Say: "Shall I seek for judge other than God? When He it is who hath sent unto you the Book, explained in details."

Al Quran VI: 114

What! Have they partners (in goodhead), who have established for them some religion without the permission of God?

Al Quran XLII:21

The Islamic attitude in this behalf is that as far as possible punishment should be avoided, and reasons and evidence should be sought, not for punishment, but for acquittal the Prophet says:

As far as possible spare Muslims (citizens) from punishment. If you can find any excuse for that, acquit them. It is better for the Imam (ruler) to err on the side of acquittal than in the matter of punishment.

Tirmizi

So long as you can find a way for it, spare people from punishment.

Ibn-e-Majah

A remarkable instance of this attitude of the Prophet is reflected by the incident connected with Ma'iz bin-e-Malik. He became involved in fornication. He came to the Prophet and said, "O Prophet of God! I am guilty of fornication be so good as to cleanse me of this filth." Now it is remarkable the way the Prophet sought ways to avoid meting out punishment to him. To begin with he turned his face away from him, and said to him, "Go and repent and ask forgiveness of God." But he (Ma'iz) came before the Prophet and repeated his request. The Prophet once again turned his face. He came before him for the third time and made the same request, and the Prophet once again turned his face away from him. Abu Bakr warned Ma'iz that if he confessed his guilt for the fourth time, the Prophet would have him stoned to death. But he was adamant, and repeated his request for the fourth time. Now the Prophet became attentive and asked him, "Perhaps you indulged in kissing and hugging, or indulged in preliminaries or looked at her with lust." He replied," "No". The Prophet asked him, "Were you in the same bed with her?" He said, "Yes". The Prophet again asked him, "Did you cohabit with her?" And he said. "Yes". He was again asked. "Did you copulate with her?" And he said, "Yes". Similarly to the further three (very definite) question of the Prophet he replied in the affirmative. Finally, he asked him, "Do you know what is fornication?" He said, "Yes, I did to her illegally what a husband does with his wife lawfully." Prophet asked him, "Are you married?" And he said "Yes" The Prophet asked him, "You are not drunk, I hope?" He said, "No". Then the Prophet asked his neighbours about his sanity, and they testified that they had never witnessed any thing in his wits to the contrary. The Prophet said to Hazzali bin-e-Na'im, who bad brought up Ma'iz, and had advised him to request the Prophet to seek forgiveness of God on his behalf: "It would have been better for you to keep his guilt concealed". And then he gave the decision to have Ma'iz stoned to death. He was taken out of the town and stoned to death. When he was being stoned, he tried to run away and said, "O people take me to the Prophet. My tribesmen have brought me to this end. They deceived me that the Prophet would not have me executed". But those entrusted with stoning him, did their job and killed him. When the Prophet was told of it, he said, "Why did you people not let him go? If you had brought him to me, it was possible he would have repented and God would have forgiven him"

Tafheem-al-Quran, Vol.111, p.335-336.

In this incident every question of the Prophet put to Ma'iz makes it evident that he was doing all that was possible to save Ma'iz, and was trying to find a flaw in his own statement or the evidence of the neighbour that could provide cause for doubt, and through benefit of that doubt his life can be saved. He also sought for the doubts arising from drunkenness and witnesses. But when there was no plea left for his defence he gave the decision. And then he was sorry for the sentence being executed. This incident also reveals to what extent thorough investigations are necessary to get to the true facts of the case before pronouncing a decision, especially when passing a sentence.

Numerous incidents of the period of the Prophet and those of the rightly guided caliphs that in the Islamic state no citizen be incarcerated without trial and proving his guilt.

> Once the Prophet was delivering a haraugue in the mosque. A certain person stood up and said, "O Prophet of Allah! For what crime have my neighbours been arrested". The Prophet made no reply and he again put the same question to him. The Prophet continued his harangue and made no reply even then. When he rose for the third time and repeated his question, the Prophet ordered the release of his neighbours.
>
> Abu Da'ood, Kitab-al Quzat

Why the Prophet kept quiet twice was due to the fact that the Police Officer was present in the gathering in the mosque, and if there had been any justifiable excuse for their arrest he would have spoken out. But when he kept mum the Prophet concluded that then arrests were unjustified and therefore he ordered the release.

During the period of 'Umar's caliphate a certain person came from Iraq and approaching the caliph said, 'Amir-al-Mu'minin, I have come to you in connection, with a certain affair which is very complicated, revealing neither head nor tail." 'Umar asked him, "What is that?" He said, "The nefarious practice of false evidence has started in our country", 'Umar said. "Has it"? He said, "Yes". 'Umar said, "Don't you worry on that score. By God, no body can be incarcerated without justice being against him."

Mo'atta, Chapter on the conditions for Witness :

The Incident of 'Umar's period in which he called Umro-bin-al-'As, the Governor of Egypt and his son Muhammad bin-e-'Umro, heard the case of the Egyptian against them and had Muhammad bin-e-Umro flogged by the wronged Egyptian has been mentioned earlier. 'Umar allowed him to give some stripes of the lash to' Umro-bin-al-'As also, whose gubernatorial authority and powers had most probably encouraged his son to disgrace a citizen. But plaintiff said, "O Amir-al-Muminin, I have avenged myself. I am satisfied that I have beaten the person who had beaten me." At this juncture 'Umar addressing Umro-bin-al-'As, made the historic remark, "O 'Umro! Since when you have made men your slaves; their mothers had delivered them as free individuals."

From these precedents it is evident that under the Islamic order, the Islamic state can neither inflict any punishment on a citizen nor depriving him of his freedom, can imprison him. The Quran announces in clear terms:

> And when ye judge between man and man, then ye judge with justice:
>
> Al Quran IV: 58

Along with this general order for the believers, the first ever head of the Islamic state of Madinah, the Prophet, had been particularly ordered to do justice:

> And I am commanded to judge justly between you.

The words of the first verse clearly indicate that justice is not an arbitrary decision. It has a norm of its own, a well known concept, a firm regulation and as such the decision must of necessity be according to due process of Law, meeting all its conditions. In this matter, the course of the judicial process of the Islamic state is made evident by a decision pronounced by the Prophet himself:

It happened a little before the conquest of Makkah, while the Prophet had been making preparations for his march towards Makkah, and the success of his plan of action depended on strict secrecy so that the Makkans may not be forewarned. A certain companion of the Prophet, Hatib-bin-e-Abi Balta'ah, for consideration of the safety of his family, sent a letter of warning to the Quraish through an old woman going that way. The Prophet learnt of it in time and sent Ali and Zubair in hot pursuit of the woman bearing that (dangerous Tr.) letter. They obtained that letter and came back with it. When it was opened and read out, it was found to contain the information that the Quraish were to be shortly attacked. When Hatib was called to explain his conduct in an open court he remorsefully said,' 'O Prophet of God, I am neither an apostate nor an unbeliever. I didn't do it as' a traitor to the cause of the Islamic state. My family is in Makkah. There is no tribe there on whose support I could count. I had written this letter with a view to oblige the Quraish so that they may not harm my wife and children. Apparently, it was a case of high treason. If this letter had found its way to the Quraish, the entire plan of war prepared by the Muslims would have gone topsyturvy. In face of the gravity of the crime, 'Umar got up and said, "O Prophet of God, permit me to behead this traitor." But the Prophet who had been commissioned by God as a Mercy to the peoples, said very gently, "Hatib is one of Badr-fame, and the plea he has put forward in his defence is according to the fact." 'Umar was so overwhelmed with passion (righteous anger Tr.) that he began to weep, and sat down saying, "Allah and His Apostle know best."

This acquittal of Hatib is an unparalleled example of the sanctity of human life, hearing of the most serious case in open court and giving the accused the chance of defence. No other government in the world would have brought the perpetrator of a crime of this nature to an open court for trial. Nor any court would have sentenced the culprit, with solid documentary evidence against him, and his own confession, to anything less than capital punishment. But the Prophet in view of the past life of Hatib, his services in the battle of Badr and his most honest and sincere statement, not to speak of death penalty, acquitted him honourably, considering the lowering of his prestige for the time being among the believers enough punishment for him. This incident has come for mention in the Quran (LX:1). (For greater detail of the incident see *Tafheem-al-Quran* Vol.V, P. 422).

The behaviour of the Kharijites during the period of Ali has come for mention earlier. He never put any member of this group behind the bars for their antigonism to him. He was all patience upto the last, adhering to the principle that so long as they do not rise in an armed rebellion against the state, the caliph cannot take any step against them.

'Adi bin-e-Artatah, an executive of the government headed by 'Umar bin-e-Abdul Aziz, wrote to him (the caliph) that the people of the territory under his charge were such as did not pay the revenues due from them unless they were tormented in some degree, and solicited permission to adopt that measure. In reply 'Umar bin-e-Abdul Aziz wrote back:

> I am amazed to find that you seek permission to torment people which amounts to saying that I shall be able to save you from the Divine wrath and His torment, or my approval of your actions will stand between you and the Divine torment. On receiving my letter make it a rule to realize the dues only from those who willingly pay them to you; and those who do not pay, take an oath from them and let them go. By God! I would much rather have people going before God (on the Day of Reckoning) with the burden of their own crimes, than that I should be brought before Him with the crime of tormenting them.

Qazi Abu Yusuf, the Chief Justice of the Abbasid period, has written about Detention:

It is neither allowed nor is there any room for such allowance that a person should be detained in the custody of police or jail just because some body has accused him of some crime. If such a situation arises, both the plaintiff and defendant should be summoned. If the plaintiff has proof of the crime, decision in his favour should be given, failing which the defendant should be released against security. If later the plaintiff brings forward proof of the crime, suitable action will be taken against the defendant strictly according to law, otherwise he will be let alone.

These Islamic laws are not dependent on the existing conditions at any particular time or place. They cannot be held in abeyance by proclaiming a state of emergency. They will remain enforceable under any circumstances whatsoever. Therefore, in the Islamic state, the citizens shall enjoy perfect protection against unjustifiable detention.

Immunity against the Responsibility of other People's Actions

A citizen in an Islamic state shall also have the right not be held responsible for other people's actions. The Quran has determined the following rule in this behalf:

> Every soul draws the meed of its acts on none but itself: no bearer of burdens can bear the burdens of another.
>
> Al Quran VI: 164

The same thing has been repeated in Surah Fatir (XXXV:18). In such Baqarah (11:193) it has been clearly stated:

> Let there be no hostility except against wrong doers.
>
> Al Quran II: 193.

In the presence of these commandments his father, sons, mother, sisters or other relatives cannot be arrested in place of the accused. Such examples are to be met with in the highly developed so-called democracies of the twentieth century. The entire Muslim history before the period of western colonization is free from such incidents. Hajjaj bin-e-Yusuf is notorious for his tyranny and murders. But with all his ferociousness, he was not found guilty of beheading the relatives of his opponents. A well known incident of his period is that he got arrested a person named Qatari bin-e-Faqa'at and told him that he would have him murdered. Qatari asked him the reason for this drastic action, and Hajjaj said in reply, "Because your brother has brought an attack against us." Qatari said, "I have a letter from the Amir-al Mominin to the effect that should not be implicated for my brother's crime." Hajjaj asked him to produce that letter and show it to him. Qatari said in reply:

> I have a letter more worthy of compliance. God says:
>
> No bearer of burdens can bear the burden of another.
>
> Al Quran VI: 164

Hajjaj was pleased with the answer, smiled and released him.

TEN

Exclusive Rights in Exercise

Right of Protest against Tyranny

Islam has conferred on the citizens of the Islamic state the right that in case of tyranny they can raise their voice against it, are not to be cowed down by the tyranny and not to take his tyranny lying down. Allah says:

> God loveth not that evil should be noised abroad in public speech, except where injustice has been done.
>
> Al Quran IV: 148

What is meant here is that speaking ill of others, however disagreeable, when, tyranny has crossed all limits and patience is tried, and the oppressed speaks ill of the tyrant in a passion over which he has no control, in spite of the highest moral teachings, such ill speech on the part of the oppressed is forgivable in the sight of God. The oppressed has a right to complain and in so doing if his passion forces him to lose sight of regard for a civil tongue, he is not blame-worthy. A well known tradition runs like this:

> The most superior type of Jehad is to openly declare the Truth (or justice) before a tyrant (a despot).
>
> Abu Da'ood, Tirmizi, Ibn-e-Majah, Nasai, Musnad-e-Ahmad

> When people see a tyrant (oppressing people) and do not hold his hand, it is not unlikely that a general visitation from God may overtake them.
>
> Abu Da'ood, Tirmizi

> Help your brother whether he is an oppressor or oppressed. The companions (wonderingly) asked him, "We shall certainly help our oppressed brother, but how to help him in case he is the oppressor?" The Prophet replied, "Hold his hand to stop his tyranny."
>
> Bukhari

The Prophet was an embodiment of mercy, and never oppressed any one in the least. But if any one had any complaint against him, he gave him a chance to put his grievance before him, and presented himself for his revenge.

Once he was getting the spoils of war distributed. A certain person in the crowd came forward in haste and fell on him face forward. The Prophet had a thin stick in his hand and tried to stop him with that stick. By chance the end of the stick came against his face and bruised it. The Prophet said to him:

> You may avenge yourself on me for it. He said, O Prophet of God, I have forgiven you.
>
> Abu Da'ood

On the occasion of the Battle of Badr, the Prophet was straightening the rows of the Mujahidin (the fighter in the way of Allah). Sawad bin-e-Ghazyah was standing a little ahead of others in the row. The Prophet with a gentle poke of the arrow said to him, "Fall in line." Sawad said, "O Prophet of God! You have caused me injury, when God has commissioned you to do justice and restoring (usurped) rights to the people. So kindly allow me to avenge myself on you." The Prophet exposed his abdomen and said, "Sawad, avenge yourself." Sawad kissed the exposed abdomen.

A certain person came to the Prophet and demanded repayment of the loan taken by him. He used harsh language in that company. The companions were annoyed by his aggressive style of address and some of them got up to give him a good thrashing. The Prophet said:

> Let him say, let him say what he likes. He who has a claim on somebody can say things like that.
>
> Bukhari

The harangues of Abu Bakr and 'Umar have been quoted earlier in which they had asked people to take notice and action wherever they witnessed tyranny and oppression. The incident of complaint against Abu Musa has earlier come for mention under the heading security of honour, in which he had a person gagged and his head shaved. He collected the shaven hair and went to Madinah with them. As soon as he approached 'Umar he threw his locks of hair at his chest and said in a very rude manner, "Here, by God, it is Fire." 'Umar said, "Yes, by God, it is Fire." He said, "O Amir-al-Mominin, I am a person with a high pitched voice and exert heavy pressure on the enemy. I have received twenty stripes of the lash and my head has been shaved. Umar instead of getting into a rage at this rude behaviour of his, paid tribute lo him thus:

> By God! If all men were high-minded and resolute like him, I would have liked it more than all the spoils of war God has given us so far.

Islam has not only conferred on men the right of protest against tyranny, but also that of refusing to obey the tyrant and removing him from his office, if their voice raised in protest against tyranny falls on deaf ears, since the first and foremost responsibility of the high position of emirate is crushing tyranny and the establishment of justice. Justice is an essential condition for the emirate. The Quran says:

> (And when God said Ibrahim). I will make thee an Imam to the Nations. He pleaded: And also (Imams) from my offspring! He answered: But my promise is not within the reach of evil-doers.
>
> Al Quran II: 124

The Muslims have been commanded:

> And follow not the bidding of those who are extravagant (not respecting the limits set by God)
>
> Al Quran XXVI: 151

Several Quranic verses and traditions on this theme have been quoted under 'The Limits of Obedience', which clearly bring out the fact that tyrants cannot be tolerated in the Islamic state, and raising one's voice against their tyranny is not only a right but an obligation for any shortcomings in it shall be liable to accountability before the Sovereign.

Freedom of Self-expression

The citizens of the Islamic state do not only enjoy the right to open their mouths when oppressed but also to freely express their opinion about the affairs of the state and problems confronting the country. These traits of the believers have been mentioned in the Quran:

> They enjoin what is right and forbid what is wrong.
>
> Al Quran III: 110

This quality can never develop without freedom of self expression. This verse does not only ensure this freedom but determines the direction of its use also. A Muslim can use it only for promoting what is right but not for spreading an evil, since it is the trait of the character of a hypocrite about whom the Quran says:

> They enjoin evil and forbid what is just.
>
> Al Quran IX: 67

The Quran points it out as one of the reasons behind the degeneration of the Israelites:

> Nor did they (usually) forbid one another the iniquities which they committed.
>
> Al Quran V: 79

Warning the Muslims against this negligence it was said:

> And if ye distort (justice) or decline to do justice, verily God is well acquainted with all that ye do.
>
> Al Quran IV: 13 5

What the Quranic verse is intended to convey is this that if you lapse in proclaiming the truth, or under any pressure, threat or avarice, adopt the hypocritic attitude by mincing matters and speaking ambiguously, you may save your skin in this world, but can never escape the punishment of this crime (of concealing the truth) in Hereafter. The Prophet says:

> There are going to be some rulers after me. One who supports them in their falsehood and helps them in their tyranny, he is not from me and I am not from him (God and His faith, Islam, and His Prophet have nothing to do with those who aid and abet tyranny and falsehood. Tr.)
>
> Nasai, Kitab-al-Bai

It was customary with the Prophet to consult his companions in various matters and encourage them in the expression of their opinions. Several examples of it have been given in this book earlier. On the occasion of the battle of Uhad, the Prophet and his high-ranking companions with seniority in age and advantage of experience were of the opinion that they should meet the enemy in the town of Madinah; but Hamzah and the young men among his companions were in favour of confronting the enemy in the open, outside Madinah. Seeing that the majority was in favour of facing the foe out of the town, he decided in favour of the young men and went into his room to get in battle array. During this period (in the absence of the Prophet) the elderly men raised an accusing finger at the young men that they did not respect the opinion of the Prophet and put him to some trouble in taking decision. This moved the young men to revise there opinion and they gathered outside the Prophet's room to apologise. The Prophet came out and hearing apologetic revision of their opinion said to them, "It does hot become a Prophet of God to disarm himself before achieving the objective. We shall now engage the enemy in the open outside Madinah.

Once, while the Prophet was distributing the spoils of war, somebody remarked "The booty has been distributed against the Divine Will (or Justice)." It was a serious matter, but he forgave the offender. Another voice was heard, "You have not done justice." He said in reply, "If I do not do justice, who will." But he did not take him to task. A certain case of dispute between Zubair and an Ansari came up before the Prophet and he decided it in favour of Zubair. The Ansari in a rage taunted. "You have favoured your cousin!" The Prophet took no notice of his rude remark and did not say a word.

In a certain skirmish against the unbelievers, the Prophet instructed the Muslims to put up tents for sojourn at a certain place. A certain companion asked him, "Is that through revelation from God or your own opinion?" The Prophet said, "It is my personal opinion." The companion then said to him, "This place is not suitable for sojourn; such and such place will be suitable for it." So the place suggested by him was approved for sojourn.

Abu Bakr in his managerial harangue actually invited people to express their opinions. When 'Umar came to occupy the seat of authority vacated through Abu Bakr's death, Abu Ubaidah and Ma'az bin-e-Jabal jointly addressed a letter to him, in which they had invited his attention to the responsibilities of the caliphate and accountability of the Hereafter. They had written in their letter.

We seek refuge in Allah that this letter of ours may not be given by you the importance it really deserves. We have written it in a spirit of well-wishing and sincerity.

'Umar thanking both of them in a long letter wrote to them:

Your joint letter is full of truth. I need such letters (of advice) so remember me in this behalf from time to time.

Sa'd bin-e-'Ubadah Ansari neither took an oath of fealty at the hand of Abu Bakr nor at 'Umars. He neither attended congregations led by them in the mosque, nor the weekly Friday congregation, nor performed Hajj pilgrimage led by them. Ibn-e-Qutaibah has written about him:

If he had found some supporters he would have attacked the persons in authority. And in case some people had sworn loyalty to him, He would have risen in revolt against them. He was adamant in his attitude. When Abu Bakr died and 'Umar succeeded him, he went to Syria and died there.

In spite of this attitude of Sa'd bin-e-'Ubadah, neither Abu Bakr, nor 'Umar ever had any thing to do with him, since, in spite of his abstention from taking an oath of fealty and adopting an 'attitude of rebellion against them he never indulged in any mischievous activity.

During the period of 'Umar freedom of self-expression had reached a stage that any person could stop him on the way or interrupt him during a largely attended harangue and question him or put up a complaint before him, or take him to task. And to keep this spirit of self-expression alive he paid full attention to the complaint, and if any one else tried to interfere or stop him he was annoyed and allowed him (complainant) full freedom to say what he had to say, encouraged him and took immediate action in connection with his complaint. He heard complaints against governors like 'Umar-bin-al-As, Mughira bin-e-Sha'bah and Abu Musa'Ash'ari, publicly, and took action against them. Explained how he came to have two sheets while all ethers had one, in a big gathering, withdrew his suggestion of limiting the dower of women also in public, and thanked the woman who had brought well sustained objection against such limiting, for showing him the right path. And when a person got up in a public gathering and told him that they would bring bin', to the right path with the sword if he deviated from it, he thanked God that there were such individuals among his people who could stop him from going astray. The entire period of his caliphate is replete with incidents of encouragement of self expression. The most important aspect of these incidents is that never any questioner, reckoner or complainant was silenced. Neither he ever took exception to the tone and language which were very often uncivil, even rude and insulting. Here are some instances of this attitude of his:

A certain person addressed him on the public road and said to him, "O 'Umar fear God." He repeated this sentence several times. At this stage some body tried to stop him saying, "Keep quiet! You have said enough to the Amir-al-Muminin." Umar immediately intervened and said, "Do not stop him. What use are they if they stop saying such things to us. And if we do not accept these things from them we should be shorn of all good, and it would be no wonder if this remark (being shorn of all good) came to stick to the person making it."

A person came to 'Umar and said' "O Amir-al-Muminin! Would it be better for me to openly criticise every evil that I witness and never care for any reproach I have to face in the way of Allah, or devote myself throughout my life to cleaning my own innerself? 'Umar replied:

"An individual in any degree made responsible for the collective affairs of Muslims, should never mind any reproach in the way of Allah. But one free of any such responsibility should care for the reform of his own self and be a well wisher of his ruler."

A lady on a public road burst out on 'Umar saying "O 'Umar I deplore the condition you are in; I am witness to the period when you were called 'Umar, and with a stick in hand, went about grazing flocks of goats in 'Ukaz. Then I witnessed that period also when you became 'Umar. And now this phase of your life is also before me when you go about as the Amir of the Believers. Fear God in the matter of the people entrusted to your care, and keep in mind that whoever is in constant dread of the promised retribution of God and shall always imagine the apparently far off Here-after, very close to himself, shall fear death and shall always be occupied with the thought that the respite granted by God may not be wasted."

Jarud 'Abadi who was in the company of' Umar at the time, said, "You have been harsh and most unkind to the Amir al-Muminin." 'Umar reproached him for that intervention and said, "Let her say whatever she wants to. Probably you don't know that she is Khaula bint-e-Hakeem, whom Allah heard from beyond the seven skies. How dare poor 'Umar refuse to listen to her."

In his journey to Syria when' Umar explained the reasons behind the deposition of Khalid bin-e-Waleed in a huge gathering, a certain person got up and said, "O 'Umar! By God, you have not been just to him you have dismissed an office bearer appointed by the Prophet. You have consigned to the scabbard a drawn sword of the Prophet. You have severed ties of kinship. You have been jealous of your cousin." 'Umar listened to what he said in silence. And when he had finished his reproach 'Umar gently said, "You are in a passion in support of your brother."

It was a general proclamation from him

"Whoever is in need of any thing or he is oppressed or is offended by any thing that I have said or done should let me know of it. After all, I am one of you.

I stand between you and Allah. There is no one between Him and myself. Allah has devolved on me the responsibility of hearing the complaints of those who call on me (for their redressal). So bring your complaints to me. If some of you find it difficult to come to me, take your complaints to those who can put them up before me. We promise to restore the right unsurped from him without any trouble to him."

'Uthman allowed so much freedom of expression of political differences, that he preferred to lay down his own life instead of crushing his opponents or even silencing them. Neither 'Ali crushed those at variance with him with use of force against them. Rather, he allowed them full freedom of opposition. Whatever was due to them from the Bait-al-Mal was paid to them regularly. No body's property was confiscated and no allowance was stopped. What he had written to the Kharijites in his message to them clearly said: "You have freedom to live wherever you like. However, there is an agreement between you and us that you shall not shed any body's blood unlawfully and abstain from breach of peace, and not oppress any one either. If you are found guilty of any of these offences I shall declare war against you."

This freedom of speech was not limited of the period of the rightly guided caliphate alone. A glimpse of it can be had throughout the Muslim history. Undoubtedly the later day rulers didn't have that spirit of putting up with difference of opinion we found in the days of the rightly guided caliphate. But in spite of degeneration in this matter, the examples of the courage of conviction and respect for difference of opinion that we find in our history are proof enough of the fact that the Muslims have never been totally deprived of their right of freedom of speech.

Hajjaj bin Yusuf was the worst tyrant of the Ummayyid dynasty once asked a certain person, "Do you happen to know Muhammad bin-e-Yusuf?" He replied "Yes, why not?" Hajjaj said to him, "Tell me something about his character." He said in reply, "He is very bad person, unparalleled in transgression against God and his commandments." Hajjaj became red in face with rage and said in a harsh tone, "You rascal, don't you know that he is my brother." He replied very coolly, "Yes I know it well enough, but dost thou not know that Allah is my Lord and Cherisher, and my God, He is much dearer to me and sought after than thy brother is to thee."

Once Haroon Rasheed went on Hajj pilgrimage. While circumambulating the Ka'bah, Abdullah 'Umri happened to look at him, and called out to him, "O Haroon!" Haroon came forward and said in reply, 'Respected uncle! this servant of yours is here before you." Abdullah 'Umri asked him, "Can you tell me the number of people who have come here for Hajj pilgrimage?" Haroon said, "A very large number, and God alone knows the real count." Abdullah 'Umri said, "Man! do not forget the fact that every one in this huge crowd is responsible to God for his own deeds, alone, while you are answerable for all of them. Just think what will happen to you at the time of reckoning." Haroon on hearing this much from him began to weep but said nothing to Abdullah 'Umri.

The advice tendered by Qazi Abu Yusuf in the preface of his *Kitab-al-Khiraj* to this same Haroon Rasheed, is a masterpiece of courage in the matter of freedom of the expression of opinion.

Haroon was once delivering a harangue to his audience when somebody stood up and said, "By God, you neither maintained equality nor justice and equity in the distribution of the spoils of war. Instead you were guilty of such and such inequities. "Haroon ordered his arrest. After the prayer was over, Qazi Abu Yusuf was called to his presence. Haroon told him that the person in question had said things never said by any one before that. He was in a rage at the moment and the (outspoken) person was standing guarded on both sides by the executioners. The Qazi putting forth the beautiful pattern of the Prophet's conduct and the precedents of the rightly guided caliphate, said to him taking courage in both hands. "You cannot punish him." Reference to the pattern of the Prophet cooled down Haroon's anger and he ordered immediate release of the (outspoken) person.

Sultan Sanjar, son of Malik Shah Saljuqi, was the ruler of Khorasan. Imam Ghazali saw him, and said to him "It is a pity that the neck of the Muslims are being broken by adversity and misery, and the neck, of your horses with heavy collars of gold."

Shaikh-al-Islam 'Izzuddin bin-e-Abdus Salam was advised by some body to kiss the hand of the king to end his differences with him, after which he would be reinstated with promotion. The Shaikh said in reply:

"You simpleton! I cannot allow the king to kiss my hand, not to speak of my kissing his hand. O ye people! You are living in a world different from mine. And I cannot thank God enough that I am free from what holds you in its grip."

It was the same Shaikh Izzuddin who, when celebrations were in full swing and people were presenting their offerings on their knees to the king, called him out in the crowded durbar (court) and said, "O Ayyub! What will be your plea to God's query whether you had been given the rule of Egypt that you may let the people alone to drink freely." The king asked him "Is this a fact?" The Shaikh said, loudly "Yes, at such and such bar liquor is being sold, and other acts too heinous to be named, are going on freely. And here you are enjoying yourself." The king immediately ordered the closure of that public house.

Islamic history abounds in such incidents where Truth was proclaimed with great courage, in a very strange tone and in crowded gatherings and durbars. Even the despots heard them with patience and did not punish those who admonished them.

How many rulers elected by the popular vote are there in this age of democracy, who would allow people to adopt this style of address and present themselves for such impartial reckoning of themselves?

Determining the limits of the freedom of expressing one's opinion in Islam, Allama Shaukani writes:

> The Islamic Shariah does not allow killing of those who believe in revolting against the Imam (ruler), so long as they do not rise in sums to give a practical shape to their

> convidious, or at least make preparations for an upsurge, since the Prophet has said that they should be put to sword only when they rise in revolt.

If a group of people show signs of nursing ideas of a rebellious nature the way the kharijites did, it would not justify their execution. Their murder would be justified only in the event of their number multiplying and arming themselves menacing the lives and properties of people.

These limits clearly indicate that on the basis of mere suspicion even the openly expressed most serious differences of opinion or even opposition, no punishment can be meted out to the opponents so long there is no practical demonstration of rebellious activities. In the Islamic state no government can put a ban or even restrictions on the free expression of opinion, since it will be tantamount to usurp a right given to people by God and as such a rebellion against the Sovereign on the part of the rulers.

Freedom of Conscience and Belief

The Islamic state confers freedom of conscience and belief on every body. The Quran proclaims decisively:

> Let there be no compulsion in religion: Truth stands out clear from error.
>
> Al Quran 11.256

What the verse is intended to convey is that the right course is the one to which Islam calls, and it has also sorted out the wrong and misleading ideas from the Truth, so that there is a clear line of demarcation between them. Now the will and pleasure of God, and the striving of the Muslims is that the mankind should accept the Islamic message of Truth. But there should be no compulsion in this business. Whoever wants may accept it on the basis of sound reasoning. But those who are not prepared to do so shall not be compelled to accept it. The Quran addresses the Prophet thus:

> If it had been thy Lords Will, they would all have believed, all who are on earth! With thou then compel mankind, against their will to believe. Al Quran X 99

At another place detailing the responsibilities of the Prophet in connection with the call to the Truth, it has been said:

> Thou art not one to admonish. Thou art one to manage (Men's) affairs (a warder over them).
>
> Al Quran LXXXVIII 21-22

The same thing has been repeated over and over again— L:45, X:108, XVII:29, VI: 107, XXIX:46, XXXIX:41.

The only responsibility of all the Prophets commissioned by God, was to convey the Message of Truth without any amendments. They themselves said about their mission:

> And our duty is only to proclaim the clear Message.
>
> Al Quran XXXVI 17

Similarly, it has been said to the Prophet:

> But if they turn away, thy duty is only to preach the clear Message.
>
> Al Quran 'XVI 82

In Surah Shura (XLII), the Prophet has been instructed to tell the unbelievers and polytheists rejecting and falsifying the faith:

> God is our Lord and your Lord: for us (is the responsibility for) our deeds, and for you for your deeds. There is no contention between us and you.
>
> Al Quran XLII 15

The same theme runs in Surah CIX from the first to the last verse:

> Say: O ye that reject Faith! I worship not that which ye worship. Nor will ye worship that which I worship. And I will not worship that which ye have been won't to worship, nor will ye worship that which I worship. To you be your way and to me mine.
>
> Al Quran CIX: 1-6

In this matter, the best example of tolerance is the incident of Wasaq Rumi, the slave of 'Umar. He himself relates that "I was slave of 'Umar and he used to say to accept Islam. If you become a believer, I shall give you some responsibiliy of the affairs of Muslims, since it is not permissible for me to appoint unbelievers to jobs of the trust of the believers." But I did not accept Islam. And he used to say, "There is no compulsion in faith." And when his death was approaching, he freed me and said, "Go where you like."

These incidents relating to Said bin-e-'Uvadah Ansari have been mentioned earlier. He adhered to his opinion regarding caliphate, but neither Abu Bakr nor 'Umar compelled him to take a vow of fealty from him. The freedom of the difference of opinion on minor issues ever continued among the Muslims. During the period of the rightly guided caliphate, many people differed in opinion from the decision of the Amir in advisory council. To the extent of the opinion they adhered to their own but complied with the decisions of the Amir. A good example of it is served by the incident of Uthman not shortening his prayers at Mina. Many people violently disagreed with him, but when it came to prayer led by him, they joined it and finished it according to his manner. This difference continues to this day.

'Umar prayed in a corner of the Christian church of Bait-al-Maqdis. Then it occured to him that the Muslims might adopt his praying there as a plea for ousting the Christians from this church (and convert it into a mosque Tr.). So he wrote out an edict and entrusted it to the charge of the bishop according to which the church was made an exclusive place of worship for the Christians, and one and only one Muslim could enter the church at any given time.

In the matter of freedom of creed, Islam not only commanded that there should be no compulsion in religion but also forbade injuring the feelings of any one professing a different faith, through disrespect to his deities. God says in the Quran:

> Revile ye not those whom they call upon besides God.
>
> Al Quran VI: 108

In religious debates it happens so often that people lose sight of regard for the feelings of others and make the belief of the opponent the target of taunts and revilement, and along with their objects of worship they go on to speak ill of their reverend religious leaders. But the Muslims have been srictly forbidden from indulging in any irreverential behavior

> And dispute ye not with the People of the Book, except with means better (than mere disputation).
>
> Al Quran XXIX, 45

In this one word Ahsan (better) are included all the fine qualities like gentleness and good manners, patience and tolerance. This commandment is not exclusive to the People of the Book but the followers of all religions.

Right of Equality

The Quran regards all men as human beings, equal in rank:

> O mankind! We created you from a single pair of a male and a female, and made you into nations and tribes, that ye may know each other (not that ye may despise each other).
>
> Al Quran XLIX.-13.

The same thing was said by the Prophet in his harangue of the last Hajj pilgrimage to Makkah, in these words:

No Arabian has any superiority over a non-Arabian nor non-Arabian over an Arabian. No person of white compexion has any superiority over a black one, nor a black person over a white one, save for Taqwa or piety.

> You are all the offspring of Adam, and Adam was fashioned out of clay.
>
> Bukhari and Muslim

In the words of the Quran and those of the Prophet all persons living within boundaries of the Islamic state, shall be equal in status in the sight of law. Even in the social sphere of life there shall be no other norm among them for distinction save superiority in Taqwa (Piety). Islam has made the entire human race as a brotherhood on the basis of kinship (blood relationship due to common parentage). And the basis, of belief and Faith has made the Muslims brothers, and as such perfect equality of status exists among them.

> The believers are but a single Brotherhood.
>
> Al Quran XL1X: 10

The Prophet has called not only Muslims but the entire humanity a brotherhood:

> I bear witness that all men are brothers among themselves.
>
> Abu Da'ood, Kitab-al-Salat

During the period of the Prophet, that of the rightly guided caliphate and in later periods too, we come across many instances in which master and slave, the rulers and the common citizen, the rich and the poor and Muslim and non-Muslim have been treated with perfect equality in the dispensation of justice. The Prophet kept himself at the same level with others in the matter of rights and dealings. A certain woman of the Quraish, Fatima, committed theft (a young companion and very close to the Prophet Tr.) Usamah pleaded with the Prophet that she should be forgiven. The Prophet replied strictly:

> O Usamah! Dare you interfere in the punishment under the limit set by God, with your intercession? Take heed! Never repeat that mistake again.

Then he ordered Bilal to call the Muslims to the mosque. When they gathered in the mosque, he addressed them thus:

> The Ummahs preceding you met their ruin for the reason that they discriminated among criminals on the basis of their status. They let those lower in status be punished according to the Law, but allowed the high placed ones to go scot free. By God, in whose hand is my life, if Fatima, the daughter of Muhammad had been involved in a case like this, I would have amputated her hand.
>
> Bukhari and Muslim

The Muslims have been commanded this:

> O ye who believe! Stand out firmly for God, as witness

> to fair dealing, and let not the hatred of other to you make you swerve to wrong and depart from justice. Be just: that is next to piety: and fear God. For God is well acquainted with all that ye do.
>
> Al Quran V:8

The Prophet never oppressed any body, yet he was so anxious and careful in the enforcement of the Divine injunctions that he used to invite people to avenge themselves on him if they had even been injured by him. So we find many instances in his life when he offered himself for being avenged upon. Sawad bin-e-'Umar says that he once went to see the Prophet with gaudy clothes on. The Prophet on seeing him said, " change them, change them" and gently poked him with the stick (he had in hand at the moment). I said to him:

> O Prophet of God! I shall avenge myself upon you. And he (the Prophet) at once exposed his abdomen before me.

Similarly, he had offered himself to Sawad bin-e-Ghaziyah on the occasion of the battle of Badr, Usaid bin-e-Hazair while talking to him and a certain companion during the distribution of the spoils of war, for their revenge on him because he had gently poked them with his stick.

Referring to these examples established by the Prophet, Dinar, the second caliph had said in reply to the query of Umar-bin-al-'As,the governor of Egypt, whether he would punish the governor of a province for the chastisement of some body (Meaning an ordinary citizen)Tr.)

By God in Whose hand is my life, I shall bring him (the governor) even for revenge, since I have seen the Prophet present himself for revenge.

So we find him strictly adhering to this principle during his ten years term of caliphate. Jabala bin-e-Adham Ghassani to escape revenge for slapping a beduin, had put forth the plea:

> O Amir-al-Muminin! How can you do it? He is a common citizen and I am a king.

To which 'Umar replied:

> Islam has established fraternity and equality between you two. You can excel him in Taqwa, but not in any other way.

Umar by issuing orders of punishment to Abu Musa Ashari, Umar bin-al-'As, his son Abdullah, Abdullah bin-e-Fart, the governor of Hams and Qudam-al-bin-e-Mazoon, the governor of Bahrain, and execution of the limit set by God on his own son Abdullah bin-e-'Umar had established unparalleld precedents.

'Umar's attendance of the court of Zaid-bin-e- Thabit as a defendant, showing displeasure at his paying respect to him ('Umar) saying "It is your initial injustice in this case," sitting by the side of Ubai bin-e-Ka'b, the plaintiff and consenting to make statement on oath in the absence of a witness that he could produce, and angrily reproving Zaid bin-e-Thabit on his suggestion to Ubai bin-e-Ka'b for sparing the Amir taking an oath, saying, "Zaid! Unless a common citizen and 'Umar are equal in your sight you are not fit for the responsible post of a judge," is a bright example of equality of men in the sight of law.

Another example of this nature had been furnished by 'Ali in his period of caliphate. In the case of the theft of the armour, he presented himself at the court of Qazi Shuraih when summoned. The defendant was a Zimmi in this case. Qazi Shuraih addressed Ali saying:

> "Abu Tureb! Sit by the side of the opponent."

The Qazi realized that Ali had felt his remark, and said, "Abu Tureb! Perhaps you took my remark ill, but it is the demand of equality in the sight of law and judicial process under Islam, that you have to sit by the side of the opposite party."

'Ali replied "I don't feel it that you directed me to sit beside my opponent. What I took to heart was your discrimination of calling me by the title, (Abu Turab or the father of dust), which was honouring me in comparison to my opponent and as such a manifest injustice."

> 'Umar had forbidden men to go about with women. He witnessed a certain person praying with women, and flogged him. He said, "By. God, if I was doing a good deed you have been harsh to me. And if I did something evil, you had not informed me of it."

Umar said, "Were you not present when I got it proclaimed?" He replied "No".

Umar threw the lash he had in his hand, before him and said "Take thy revenge on me."

He said, "Not today (some other time)."

Umar said "Well, if you do not avenge yourself on me, forgive me then."

He said, "No, I would not forgive you either." And they parted. Next day when 'Umar met that person, he found, Umar's face a little pale. He said, "Amir-al-Mominin! Perhaps you have taken my words to heart?"

Umar said, "Yes".

He said, "God be my witness, I have forgiven you."

One of the evil traits of character to which Pharoah had degraded himself mentioned in the Quran was that he bad divided his people into high and low and noble and ignoble. And one of these two classes he depressed and degraded. The Quran says:

> Truly Pharoah elated himself in the land and broke up his people into sections, depressing a small group among them. Al Quran XXVIII 4

As against this, Islam has it to its credit that bringing the high a little low and elevating the low a little, it created a balance in the society and equality among people. When 'Umar was told by Nafi bin-al-Harith, the governor of Makkah that he had left the freed slave Ibn-al-Bara as his officiating deputy, he ('Umar) inquired about his qualities and was much pleased and said:

"Why not, our Prophet had said that God would elate some with this Book (Quran) and some he would degrade."

Right to Seek Justice

The very aim and object of the existence of the Islamic State is establishment of justice. God commands the Prophet to proclaim:

> And I am commanded to judge justly between you.
>
> Al Quran XLII:15

> Say: My Lord hath commanded justice;
>
> Al Quran VI 1: 29

God says the purpose of commissioning the prophets in the world, revelation of the Scriptures or inspired Books, and the political and fighting force of the Muslims is the establishment of justice in human society:

> We sent afore time our apostles with Clear signs and sent down with them the Book and the Balance (of Right and Wrong), that may stand forth in justice; and we sent down Iron, in which is (material for) mighty war, as well as many benefits for mankind, that God may test who is that will help unseen. Him and His apostle: for God is Full of Strength, Exalted in Might (and able to enforce His will).
>
> Al Quran LVII: 25

The justice for which the Prophet and after him, the Muslim Ummah as a whole, were commissioned, its norm was also given in great detail so that it may be easy to determine the meaning of this' "Justice" and there may be no ambiguity in the proper understanding of God's will and pleasure:

> O ye who believe! Be ye staunch in justice, witnesses for Allah, even though it may be against yourselves or (your) parents-or (your) kindered, whether (the case be of) a rich man or a poor man, for Allah is nearer unto both (than ye are). So follow not passion lest ye lapse (from truth) and if ye lapse or fall away, then Lo! Allah is ever informed what ye do.
>
> Al Quran IV: 135

In this verse not only the meaning of justice has been explained, but all the conditions of the establishment of justice have been put forth. If even one of them is dropped and neglected, justice shall no more be justice but shall become injustice. These conditions are:

1. Do not only establish justice but hold its banner aloft. And where you find it suppressed, do all in your power for its uplift.
2. Bearing of witness should not be for the success or failure of either party but to seek the countenance of Allah, since justice cannot be established without true evidence. Never for a moment be anxious whose interests it affects adversely your own, your parents or your kindred's interests.
3. When testifying in a case not only disregard your relationship with the parties concerned but also be unmindful of their social or economic status, since you can never be a greater well wisher of any body than Allah. Discrimination in evidence is not benevolence but manifest injustice and malevolence.
4. State the facts of the case in your knowledge as they are without any admixture of your own wishes. Wishes pervert the facts, and the person hearing the evidence fails to get to the bottom of the facts, which becomes a hindrance to just decisions.
5. If you state the facts of the evidence vaguely, concealing some and interposing others of your own creation, with a view to save a party, or get one punished, shirking true and impartial evidence, and becoming a means of tyranny and injustice, know it well that your state of mind shall not be hidden from God, and you will not be able to save yourselves from the evil consequences of your doings.

It was in view of this verse of the Quran that 'Umar had written in a letter to Qazi Shraih:

> In the Majlis-e-Qaza (the court of law) neither try to weigh people, nor wrangle with any body, nor indulge in purchase and sale, nor ever pronounce judgement in a quarrel between two people when you are in a rage.

In short, it is essential for the quality of being just that the person dispensing justice should be free from all such internal and external motivations which can influence a just decision. God says that when you come to sit in judgement, do full justice to it:

> And if ye judge between mankind, that ye judge justly.
>
> Al Quran IV: 58

> Whenever ye speak, speak Justly, even if a near relative is concerned.
>
> Al Quran VI: 152

In connection with justice, the Quran has also laid down the following principles:

> Life for life, eye for eye, nose for nose, ear for ear, tooth for tooth, and wounds equal for equal.
>
> Al Quran V:45.

And the same rule has been stated at another place in these words:

> The recompense for an injury is an injury equal there to (in degree): but if a person forgives and makes reconciliation, his rewards is due from God: for (God) loveth not those who do wrong. But indeed if any do help and defend themselves after a wrong (done) to them, against such there is no cause to blame. The blame is only against those who oppress men with wrong doing and insolently transgress beyond bounds through the land, defying right and justice: for such there will be a penalty grievous. But indeed if any show patience and forgive, that would truly be an exercise of courageous will and resolution in the conduct of affairs.
>
> Quran XLII: 40-43

In this verse along with presenting the principle of fit for let in connection with justice, the oppressed person has been directed to restrain himself from oppression in retaliation and persuaded to forgive the oppressor. In other words, he may avenge himself on equal basis if he likes, which will be justice indeed. In case he oversteps in retaliation it will be injustice. And Allah does not love the wrong-doers. But if the oppressed person resorts to forgiveness it will be an act of high mindedness and magnanimity and appreciated by God.

> God commands justice, the doing of good, and liberality to kith and kin, and He forbids all shameful deeds, and injustice and rebellion:
>
> Al Quran XVI: 90

But "Ehsan" or doing of good, is an individual act. The judiciary of the Islamic state is bound to pronounce judgement according to the dictates of justice when a complaint is made to them. However, the oppressed complainant has all the time the right to withdraw the case against the defendant, and be rewarded for this act of kindness by God. As for the judiciary, it is bound by the commandment:

> If any do fail to judge by (the light of) what God hath revealed, they are (no than) unbelievers..........they are (no better than) wrong.

According to this commandment, it may be an individual, an arbiter, a panchayat, or a regular court of law that judges, must do it by the light of the Book of God and Sunnah of the Prophet. The prophet says:

> One day of a just Imam (leader) is better than sixty years of devotional service.

He also said:

> Among the people He has created, God loves most a just Imam. And the one most detestable person in His sight, arousing His wrath, is the Imam who judges unjustly.
>
> Musnad-e-Ahmad

How the Prophet and the rightly guided caliphs, coming after him, put these commandments into practice, some examples have been mentioned earlier. The Prophet presented himself before people so that they may avenge themselves upon him. 'Umar and 'Ali in their periods of caliphate presented themselves in the courts of law (in the capacity of a common citizen as defendants). 'Umar executed the punishment, prescribed by the limit set by God, in case of his own son, presented himself for being avenged upon by the people who fall offended, chastised his governors in connection with the complaints lodged by common citizens, and removing all the obstacles standing in the way of seeking justice, he made redressal of grievances and deliverance from oppression very easy.

Abu Bakr, appointing 'Umar the Qazi of the Islamic state with its centre at Madinah, made judiciary independent of the executive. Umar on coming in authority gave it the shape of an institution, and presenting himself at the court as a defandant, practically demonstrated the superiority of the judiciary over the executive. After him, throughout the Muslim history this system was kept alive. The most important characterstic of this system is that people secured justice free of cost. There were no such things as court fee and the fees of the pleaders. In the Indian subcontinent this system was in practice till the Britishers took over. And the countries that escaped the subjugation of colonialism, this system exists to this day. For example, in Saudi Arabia justice is available for the rich and the poor alike free of cost. Truth to tell, there is no other system of justice in the world that, has not made the high sounding claims of "Equality in the sight of Law" and "Justice for all alike", meaningless by making justice a saleable commodity. How many people are there who can pay the fees that have to be paid to the High Courts and the Supreme Court and the fabulous fees of the advocate pleading their cases at these courts? And if they cannot afford to pay these costs, is it not tantamount to closing the doors of these superior courts of the country upon all such people. And thus deprived of the facilities of getting justice have not all such people been automatically deprived of the protection of law and its support against those who are in possession of the needful resources.

The judicial system of the Islamic state is entirely free from this commercial outlook. Here all the expenses of the establishment of justice are borne by the state. All that is required of distressed person is to knock at the door of the court. And in case he is not satisfied with the judgement of the lower court, he is at liberty to go to the High Court and the Supreme Court. He will not be burdened with any expenses any where. Such a burden on him shall be injustice repeated twice over, that he, coming with the complaint of wrong done to him, may be involved in further financial troubles to get justice.

Moreover, this financial burden in going to the courts discourages poor and indigent people, and establishing the superiority of those in possession of resources further encourages them in their tyranny and oppression.

Islam conferring equality on the rich and the poor, the high and the low, influential and the fundamental, in the sight of the judiciary has made the principle of equality in the sight of law, enforceable in its true spirit, and has brought the fundamental right of seeking justice within easy reach of every citizen.

Right of Economic Security

After 'Fatihah (or the opening surah of the Quran when we start reciting Surah Baqrah (II), in the verses in the very beginning, the following qualities of the Quran and those believing in it, have been mentioned:

> A.L.M. This is the Book; in it is guidance sure, without doubt to those who fear God: who believe in the Unseen, are steadfast in (establish Tr.) prayer, and spend out of what We have provided for them:
>
> Al Quran II 1-3

Pondering over these verses it becomes a manifest that belief in the Book of God and the unseen facts stated therein, such as the Entity of God, decrees of God, relating to us men and the rest of the creation, the creation of the universe, creation of Adam, Heaven and Hell, the life Hereafter, and the geni and the angels, two obligations devolve on man. In the sphere of the relationship of God and man, the first and foremost obligation is that he should bow down his forehead before God, and establishing the system of Prayers, he must repeat his covenant with God alleging his own sub-service and God's worshipfulness five times a day.

Immediately after the prayer, the first and foremost obligation devolving on man in the context of relations between man and man, is spending in the way of Allah, or help and support of the needy and the indigent out of that with which God has endowed him. This order of the rights of God and man is not exclusive to this verse, but every where in the Quran we find that Zakat immediately follows Prayer or devotional service to God. Nay, at places the Quran declares the prayers of a person wasted where this worshipping person adopts a miserly attitude in meeting the needs of a needy servant of God. God says in the Quran:

> Seest thou one who denies the judgement (to come)? Then such is the man who repulses the orphan (with harshness), and encourages not the feeding of the indigent. So woe to the worshippers who are neglectful of their Prayers, those who (want but) to be seen (of men), but refuse (to supply even neighbourly needs).
>
> Al Quran CV1I: 1-7

The first verse of this Surah now brings before us the fact stated in Surah Baqarah (II) from a different angle. One who does not believe in the unseen or the reward and punishment of the Hereafter, can neither fulfil his obligation to God (Prayers), nor fulfil that of helping his needy brothers through Infaq or spending in the way of Allah. When praying he will manifest lack of earnestness and would like to be seen of men, and the bounty of God he will hoard, neither spending on himself nor on others in need of it. He will kick out the orphan and not only refuse food to the indigent but not persuade others to feed him either. And he will also flatly refuse those asking for loan of very ordinary things of use in daily life. Those adopting this attitude are being warned that such prayers will not at all avail them, but will be thrown back into their faces, and will fail to protect them from the ruination awaiting them for their unfulfilled obligations to the needy and indigent servants, of God.

This is the importance of "the economic problem of men in Islam, and the nature of the injunctions from the Sovereign to the Believers to solve this problem. At more than thirty places in the Quran the payment of Zakat has come up for mention along with the establishment of the system of Prayer, and at more than seventy places Infaq or spending in the way of Allah has been stressed. Unfortunately, the Muslims themselves have assigned Zakat the fifth position in the order of the Pillars of Islam, God only knows for what reason, when the fact is that the Quran has assigned it a position immediately after belief and Prayer, and Fasting and Hajj in order of their importance come after Zakat.

After this preliminary talk on the importance of the economic problem in Islam, let us now see how much stress has been laid on spending in the way of Allah to provide economic protection to man in the Religion of God. What are those measures, adopted to achieve this end, and what the responsibilities devolving on the Islamic state in this behalf. Let us study some of the Quranic verses relating to the injunctions regarding Infaq and inducement to it:

> And those in whose wealth is a recognized right for the needy who asks and him who is prevented (for some reason from asking,);
>
> Al Quran LXX:24-25

> And in their wealth and possessions (was remembered) the right of the (needy), him who asked, and his who (for some reason) was prevented (from asking).
>
> Al Quran LI: 19

> And establish regular prayer and pay Zakat regularly, and loan to God a beautiful loan.
>
> Al Quran LXXII: 20

In Surah Baqarah (II) after saying "It is not righteousness that ye turn your faces East or West," God goes on to say:

> (Righteousness in this that) you spend of your substance, out of love for Him, for your kin, for orphans, for the needy for the wayfarer, for those who ask, and for the random of slaves; to establish regular prayer and pay Zakat regularly.
>
> Al Quran 11:177

The order of injunctions in this verse is worthy of note. Among the conditions of belief enumerated herein spending one's cherished goods has come up even before the establishment of prayer. In the same Surah, it occurs again:

They ask thee what they should spend in the way of Allah Say:

> Whatever you spend that is good, is . for parents, kindered and orphans and those in want and for way-farers.
>
> Al Quran 11:215

> They ask thee how much they are to spend; Say: What is beyond your needs.
>
> Al Quran II: 219

Explaining undue stress on Infaq the Quran says:

> In order that it (Wealth) may not (merely) make a circuit between the wealth among you.
>
> Al Quran L1X: 7

And then, to ease man's mind in connection with the dread of diminishing one's good and coming to poverty through Infaq, it was said:

> Whatever goods you spend in the way of Allah benefits your own souls, and ye shall do so seeking the countenance of God. What ever goods you spend in the way of Allah, shall be rendered back to you, and shall not be dealt with unjustly.
>
> Al Quran 11:272

And further on it has been said:

> (Those who spend of their goods in the way of Allah, by night and by day, in secret and in public, have their reward with their Lord:) On them shall be no fear, nor shall they grieve.
>
> Al Quran II: 274

The Quran tells us that spending one's goods in the way of Allah does not diminish it but there is an increase in it. This is a dealing altogether profitable and not one of loss. This is not an obligation to the receiver of the goods, but to the person who spends, since it will return to him with manifold profit. And then in the Hereafter, becoming the means of the pleasure of God on his own honour, shall make him deserving of that great reward of the eternal peace and satisfaction which is the real goal of a Muslim's life contrarily, if the goods of this world is hoarded, it will become a means of ruination in this world and in the Hereafter. Below are given some Quranic verses on this theme:

> And they feed, for the love of God, the indigent, the orphan, and the captive—(Saying), we feed you for the sake of God alone: no reward do we desire from you, nor thanks. We only fear a day of distressful Wrath from the side of our Lord. But God will deliver them from the evil of that Day, and will shed over them a light of Beauty and a (blissful) Joy.
>
> Al Quran LXXVI: 8-11

> The parable of those who spend their substance in the way of God is that of a grain of corn; it groweth seven ears, and each ear hath a hundred grains. God giveth manifold increase to whom he pleaseth: and God careth for all and He knoweth all things.
>
> Al Quran 11:261

> And the likeness of those who spend their substance seeking to please God and to strengthen their souls, is as a garden high and fertile heavy rain falls on it but makes it yield on double increase of harvest, and if it receives not heavy rain, light moisture sufficeth it. God seeth well whatever ye do.
>
> Al Quran II: 265

> Who is he that will loan to God a beautiful loan, which God will double unto his credit and multiply many times? It is God that giveth (you) want or plenty, and to Him shall by your return.
>
> Al Quran 11:245

> And there are those who hoard gold and silver and spend it not in the Way of God: announce unto them a most grievous Penalty—On the Day when heat will be produced out of that (wealth) in the fire of Hell, and with it will be branded their forehead, their flanks, and

> their backs....This is the (treasure) which ye hoarded for yourselves: taste ye, then, the (treasurer, ye hoarded!
>
> Al Quran IX: 34-35

> And let not those who covetously withhold of the gifts which God hath given them of His Grace, think that it is good for them; nay, it will be the worse for them: soon shall the things, which they covetously withheld, be tied to their necks like a twisted collar, on the Day of Judgement.
>
> Al Quran III: 180

> Who pileth up wealth and layeth it by thinking that his wealth would make him last for ever! By no means! He will be sure to be thrown into that which Breaks to Pieces.
>
> Al Quran CIV: 2.4

Along with extraordinary emphasis on Infaq and instructions to keep away from miserliness. God has also determined for the Muslims the moderate course of spending also, so that they may be spared from excess either way:

> O Children of Adam; Wear your beautiful apparel at every time and place of prayer: eat and drink: but waste not by excess, for God loveth not the wasters.
>
> Al Quran VII: 31

Here adornment or wearing one's beautiful apparel means proper dress which not only covers the nackedness but is also neat and clean. And the natural urge of food and drink must also be satisfied. However, there should be no wastage due to excess in the matter of dress, food and other needs of man's life. For wastage of the bounties, conferred on man by God, is most detestable in the sight of God. And in the immediately following verses, the negative attitudes of asceticism and Monasticism have been discouraged:

> Say: Who hath forbidden the beautiful (gifts) of God, which He hath produced for His servants, and the things clean and pure, " which He hath provided for

sustenance? Say: They are, in the life of this world, for those who believe, and purely for them on the Day of Judgement.

Al Quran VI 32

Along with the general commandments and instructions, the practical measures adopted for the economic security and prosperity of the individuals of the society are briefly these:

1. Every man has been instructed to take part in the economic struggle, so that he may not be a burden to others.

2. That man can have nothing but what he strives.

   Al Quran LIII 39

3. Determining the limits of approved and forbidden and proper and improper the sphere of striving and action was defined. By imposing restrictions on the sources of income such as interests, liquor, gambling, bribery, shameful pursuits and maintaining houses of ill-repute, purchase and sale of prohibited articles, adulteration, giving short measure or weight, black-marketing, hoarding and such other fraudulent practices, plundering of the society was eradicated, and economic exploitation was stopped.

4. Through prohibition of spending the earned income in ways not allowed by the Shurah. Squandering and immoderation, luxuriousness and show of pump and pelf, and destruction of goods, the drain of wealth into the wrong channels was stopped, and burning its now in the right direction towards the really deserving individuals, they were saved from deprivation of their rights.

5. By determining the rights of other individuals in the earnings of every individual, is and has been enlisted for the collective system of maintenance of the Islamic state. According to the Islamic Shariah the individual's responsibilities are the following:

   (a) The obligatory maintenances or the responsibility of the support of the parents, wife and children, grandfathers, grandmothers, both paternal and maternal, grandchildren (offspring of both sons and the daughters), brothers, sisters, aunts (father's sisters), nieces, and other blood relations.

(b) Zakat which is to be spent on the maintenance of the general run of the needy which have been defined in the Quran. The income from this source shall go towards the support of the needy who ask, and those who don't and also those deputed for the realization of Zakat. Also a part of it will go to encourage and to win the hearts of the fresh converts to Islam, and for the freedom of the slaves and the Muslims in the clutches of the enemies, for the paying the debts of the indigent or the deceased persons, also for maintenance of those fighting in the wayof Allah, the students and other people engaged in the cause of Allah (in such a way that they don't find time to earn their livelihood Tr.) and to help the travellers who have been stranded and have no place to stay and maintain themselves during sojourn.

(c) Additional spending of one's goods or that even after providing for maintenance of family and blood relations, and paying of Zakat, it is incumbent on the individuals with plentiful resources, to go on spending on the support of the, indigent and the needy in the charities. The Prophet says:

> There is a share of the deserving in your goods besides the regular payment of Zakat.
>
> Musnad-e-Darima, Tiremizi, Muslim

The reporter of the tradition, Fatima, bin-e-Qais, also adds that the Prophet quoted those verses of the Surah Baqara (Al Quran 11-177) in which it has been said that "It is not righteousness that you turn your faces towards the East or the West, but true righteousness lies in spending one's cherished goods and possessions in the cause of Allah."

In this behalf there is a definite Quranic injunction that

whatever one has beyond one's own needs (within the approved limits) should be given over to other needy persons:

> (They ask thee how much they are to spend;) Say: "What is beyond your needs.
>
> Al Quran II: 219

Under additional Infaq (spending in the way of Allah), three categories of persons have priority, even obligatory rights: The travellers who asked "for food, the needy who asks and one under conditions of emergency, a ravenously hungry or a very thirsty or a naked person, one in need of shelter from heat, cold or rain or in need of medication in case of being ill.

The Quran has granted this right to a disabled or a hungry person:

> It is no fault in the blind, nor in one born lame, nor in one afflicted with illness, nor in yourselves, that ye should eat in your own houses, or those of your father, or your mothers, or your brothers, or your sisters, or your father's brothers, or your father's sisters, or your mother's brother's or your mother's sisters, or in houses of which the keys are in your possession, or in a house of a sincere friend of yours:
>
> Al Quran XXIV:61

According to this Quranic verse to every blind, cripple, ailing and every such person who is incapable of earning his livelihood, every Muslim's house is open where he asks for food. To a common citizen too, not one but many doors are open where he may eat. Besides his own house, he can eat at his parents, grandparents brother's and sisters', uncles', aunts' or a friend's and at the house of those people who have given him keys of their houses, as freely as at his own house. So that it can be said that in the Muslim society it is not possible for any person to go hungry, naked or remain deprived of shelter and medication.

(d) Loan and allowing temporary use of the articles of daily use:

The wealthy persons have also been instructed by Islam to give loans to the needy freely and not to refuse temporary use of ordinary articles of daily use by those in need of them:

> It is not proper for a servant of Allah to disappoint his brother coming to him for a loan, if he is in a position to do so. Kanz-al-'ummal, Vol. Ill, Tradition No. 3581 To give a loan is an act of charity.
>
> Tabrani, Al-Mojim-al-Sagheer, p. 89

Surah Ma'oon (CVI1) has been quoted earlier in which even those who are regular in their prayer but refuse temporary loans of articles of daily use to the people in need of them, have been warned with total ruination.

(e) Inheritance, will and alimony to wife and children in case of divorce, and other things. The legacy of a person after his death shall go to meet the requirements of inheritance, will, power and alimony to the wife and children for an appointed term in case he has divorced the wife, according to the law of the Shari'ah. And from the one third of his bequest that he willed, as permitted by the Shariah, will go to those named in his will.

The number of persons benefited by an individual's earning including those directly under his support, those related by blood the indigent and the needy of the society and the inheritors approaches thousands. And in this way the earnings of an individual in the Islamic Society became a source of beneficence for countless individuals. And he himself in turn must be benefited by such other fountains of benevolence.

Where there exists an economic system in which every individual is looking after the support of dozens of people and they themselves are supporting one another, how many people can remain deprived of board, lodge, clothing and medication in such a society.

The collective support and maintenance in Islam is not that the government taking over all the resources and the properties of the people entirely under its control, and reducing every individual of the nation to the position of a salaried servant, and depriving them of all freedoms, put them to work as it is pleased to do, and in return for this slaving or forced labour, provided them with food, clothes and shelter. As against this, collective maintenance or social justice here takes a different form altogether. Every individual is required to earn as much as he can within the limits of the Shariah, spend the barest minimum to meet his own needs, and what remains after that must go to the comparatively backward and indigent people to help them rise above poverty and indigence, so that gradually the economic disparities may come to an end, and moderation and equilibrium may be established in the society. The Prophet has termed this type of economic striving equivalent to Jehad. He says:

> Striving for charities to sees the countenance of Allah is like Jehad (armed struggle) in the way of Allah.

Before taking up the responsibilities of the state relating to economic security, a detailed discussion of the individual efforts and responsibilities was necessary since in Islam like other rights, this right too is not limited to the sphere of the mutual relation of the individual and the state, but right from an individual the families brotherhoods, small and big organizations and the government, this obligation devolves on every one according to the resources and powers at one's command.

Now let us take stock of the responsibilities of the state in this matter:

The first and foremost responsibilities of the state is to completely close the doors on the illegal earnings in the society, open up the avenues of earnings and through its economic and educational schemes provided for every individual the necessary education and training for earning honest livelihood so that he may be capable of striving in the economic field.

The second responsibility of the state is that it must help in the fulfilment of all those rights determined by Allah. If a son refuses to support his father it must bring him to comply with the Divine injunction. If a husband denies his wife and children their maintenance charges, it must force him to pay their dues. In short, whatever is due to any one from any body else it must make its payment certain.

The third responsibility of the state is this that it must establish the system of Zakat and realizing the dues of the deserving from those who owe it to them. Take it to them or spend it collectively for their well-being.

The fourth responsibility of the state is that it must support those who have no other people to support them. The Prophet has said:

> One who has no guardian or supporter can look to Allah and His Prophet for his support.
>
> Tirmizi

Similarly, the Prophet prescribed the responsibility of the state to pay the debts of the deceased and the support of those left behind by him.

> The Muslim who dies leaving behind debts, their payment is my responsibility and the assets left by him shall go to his inheritors. Bukhari, Muslim, Abu Da'ood, Nasai. One who leaves behind goods, is for his dependents, and he who leaves them without support, their support is my responsibility.
>
> Tirmizi, Abu Da'ood.

When sending out Ma'az bin-e-Jabal to Yemen (as the governor), the Prophet stated the following principle in connection with the economic responsibilities of the Islamic state:

> Tell them that Allah has imposed on their goods, Sadqah (Zakat) which will be realized from their haves and distributed among their have-nots.
>
> Bukhari, Mo'atta, Masliq, Abu Da'ood, Nasai, Tirmizi.

This economic security is not limited to the Muslims alone but the non-Muslim subjects of the Islamic state have an equal right to it. When 'Umar found a Jew begging, he took him to his own house.gave him something to meet his immediate needs and then calling the treasurer of the Bait-al-Mal and instructing him to dole out to him and all others in his position, their daily needs, he said:

> By God! It is far from justice and fair play that we realize from them Jizya when they are young (capable of earning) and leave them to fend for themselves when they get old and infirm.

'Umar, during his period of caliphate, has imposed on the Islamic state the provision of the following needs in connection with the economic rights of the citizens:

(a) The necessities relating to food (b) Clothes for the winter and summer seasons, (c) Conveyance for normal movements and Hajj and Jehad.

So during his ('Umar's) period, stipends were given to the common citizens, even the new born babies, from the public treasury (Bait-al-Mal), and they were totally rid of their economic needs. This use of the Bait-al-Mal continued during the periods of 'Uthman and 'Ali too.

The Islamic state of today, can, on the basis of this principle, keeping in view its, own resources and the minimum needs of the citizens, determine their economic rights. Islam has also empowered the state to make additional provisions by further taxation if the normal revenues of the state fail to meet its responsibilities in connection with the collective welfare and social justice in the economic field.

The temperament and the character and the sense of responsibility of the Islamic state relating to the economic security can be judged from a speech of 'Umar the second caliph and from the correspondence of 'Umar bin-e-Abd-al-Aziz. 'Umar said in connection with his responsibility relating to the distribution of the resources:

> By God! If I live long enough, a herds man looking after his cattle on a hill in Sur'a (in far off Yemen Tr.) shall get his share out of the goods coming to us (Bait-al-Mal) at his own place, without reddening his face (running about so much that his face gets flushed before he can have his due).

And we come across the following correspondence between 'Umar bin-e-Abd-al-Aziz and the governor of Iraq province relating to the economic rights of the common people to the Bait-al-Mal:

> 'Umar bin-e-Abd-al-Aziz wrote to the governor of Iraq, Abdul Hameed bin-e-Abd-al-Rehman: Give the people their stipends.

Abdul Hameed wrote back in reply:

> I have already paid the stipends of the people and still there is enough left as balance in the Bait-al-Mal.

At this, 'Umar bin-e-Abd-al-Aziz wrote the following reply:

> Now look for those who are indebted, and if they have not taken these loans for extravagance and dissipation, pay up their debts from the balance in hand at the Bait-al-Mal.

Abdul Hameed once again wrote to him:

> I have paid such debts, but still there is a balance with us at the Bait-al-Mal.

Umar bin-e- Abd-al-Aziz wrote the following reply to this:

> Now look for such unmarried people who are poor and would also like that you get them married. Get them married then, and pay the dowers from them to their wives.

Abd-al-Hameed said in his written reply:

> I have got married all such unmarried men whom I could find and yet there is a surplus reserve at the Bait-al- Mal.

Umar bin-e-Abd-al-Aziz then wrote to him:

> Now look for all those that have to pay Jizya and they are unable to manage their lands (for want of funds for the inputs). Give all such zimmis enough to enable them to manage their lands, since we don't have to deal with them temporarily for a year or two.

Right to Abstain from Sin

Islam has granted every citizen living within its boundaries to refuse to obey any laws involving transgression and sin. Such refusal to obedience is no crime in the sight of the Islamic law. Rather, obedience to such orders shall be deemed aiding in the crime, since the authority issuing such order shall itself be liable to prosecution for the violation of the commandments of the Sovereign. Recourse to legal action in a court of law against such orders is permitted, which will not only provide legal protection to the person refusing to obey sinful orders, but shall also mete out appropriate punishment to those issuing such orders. In this connection the Quranic verses and the saying of the Prophet have been profusely quoted under elucidation of the heading "Limits of Obedience". They have been summed up in the following two traditions:

> No obedience to the created beings where transgression against the creator comes in.
>
> Kanz-a-Ummal, Tradition No. 294

> Obedience to the Amir's, is obligatory so long as they do not order things involving transgression against God and disobedience to His Prophet. But when it comes to orders in contravention of loyalty and obedience to God and His Prophet, one is neither bound to hear nor obey.
>
> Bukhari

Freedom of Organisation and Assembly

The citizens in the Islamic state shall have the right of organization and assembly, conditional to the basic condition of enjoining good and forbidding evils. The aim of the existence of the Muslims has been fully explained in the following verse of the Quran:

> Ye are the best of People, evolved for mankind, enjoining what is right, forbidding what is wrong', and believing in God.
>
> Al Quran 111:110

This is the mission assigned to the Muslim Ummah as a whole. But if all the Muslims are not devoted whole-heartedly to this mission and lacking in sympathy and an internal urge to strive for this cause, even then there must remain a powerful and duly conscious group among them which remains devoted to it. The Quran says:

> Let there arise out of you a band of people inviting to all that is good, enjoining what is right, and forbidding what is wrong:
>
> Al Quran 111: 104

So if some people in the Islamic state wish to organize themselves into a party to discharge the duty of enjoining what is right and forbidding what is wrong, and for this purpose they want to assemble for organizational needs or contact people, they shall be entitled to do so. This principle shall also apply to the organization established for the protection of their lawful rights, redressal of grievances and solution of problems, and it shall also apply to the meeting of such an organization, provided the establishment of the organization audits gathering are for the purpose of enjoining good and suppressing evil.

Right to Participate in the Political Life

Since, according to Islam, the vicegerency on earth, has been conferred on the Muslim Ummah as a whole and not any particular individual, group, family, race or a party, every Muslim as a vicegerent has a right to participate in the affairs of the state. It is for this reason that to run the administration of the Islamic state the Quran has laid down the following principle:

> Who (conduct) their affairs by mutual condition.
>
> Al Quran XXII:38

Even the Prophet, who, being guided at every step by revelation, needed no consultation, was commanded:

> And consult them in affairs (of moment).
>
> Al Quran 111:159

In this sense of Shura are included the following political principles of the Islamic state:

1. The Amir and his advisory body be elected by the free will of the people.
2. The people and their representatives should be free in the matter of criticism, contention and expression of opinion.
3. A true picture of the circumstances and problems confronting the country must be presented to the people so that they may have a correct idea of and opine correctly on them.
4. The people should have the right that only the person enjoining their confidence should rule and one who loses that confidence must be deposed.

Freedom of Movement and Residence

Every citizen of the Islamic state shall have freedom to reside anywhere in the country he likes and move about within the country, and under normal conditions, anywhere in the world outside his own country. The Quran has declared it a crime to oust people from their homes. Commenting on the betrayal of trust on the part of the Israelites and other crimes committed by them, it was said:

> ....And banish a party of you from their homes; supporting one another against them by sin and transgression—and if they come to you as captives, ye ransom them, though their expulsion itself was unlawful for you.
>
> Al Quran]I:85

Similarly, freedom of migration and moving about has also been conferred by God on His servants:

> Was not the earth of God spacious enough for you to move yourself away (from evil).
>
> Al Quran IV: 97.

> He who forsakes bis home in the cause of God, finds in the earth many a refuge, wide and spacious:
>
> Al Quran IV: 100.

> Islam has prescribed banishment for mischief-makers and rebels only. The citizens in general cannot be punished in this way. In Surah Alma'ida (V), along with execution crucification and the cutting off hands and feet from the opposite sides, this punishment was also prescribed for waging war against God and His Apostle, and striving with might and main for mischief through the land: Or exile from land:
>
> Al Quran V:33

During the period of Ali's caliphate, the headstrongness, mischief- making, creating tumult had crossed all limits. But All gave them the right of moving about freely in the land and living where they liked. And in his message, giving them assurance of this right he said:

> You are free to move about where you like. However, there is a covenant between you and us that you will not shed anybody's blood unlawfully, not create breach of peace and not oppress anyone. If I find you guilty of any these crimes I shall declare and wage a war against you.

Right to Wages and Compensation

The workers, peasants and other toilers shall have the right that they should not be made to work as slaves (forced Labour, not paid any wages for the work done by them) in the Islamic state. They should be adequately paid for the labour they put in. Compensation should be paid for monetary loss or physical injury. They should not be burdened with harder or greater amount of work than they are physically capable of. And they should be treated benevolently.

Along with this, the Quran has imposed the obligation on the persons receiving the remuneration for service (workdone) that they must put in the best service in return for the wages mutually agreed upon, put in all the energy they can in their work and whatever material, they are given to work with, they should treat it as a trust and should not waste it through misappropriation, unlawful use or in any other form. In connection with a good servant the Quran says:

Truly the best of men for thee to employ is the (man) who is strong and trusty.

^l Quran XXVJ1l-.26

Sho'aib, (the father in law of Moses), after offering Moses the conditions of service, gave him assurance about his own responsibilities in the capacity of his employer:

......But I intend not to place thee in difficulty: Thou will find me indeed if God wills, one of the righteous.

Al Qu ran XXV1I1:27

What he meant to say was that he on his part would abide by the terms agreed upon between them and would not demand more work from him, and pay in full the remuneration settled. And that he would find him (Shoaib) a true a righteous person.

The first right ot the workers among those determined by the Prophet, is that they should not only be paid full wages for the work done, but should also be paid with due haste. He said:

The wages of a worker should be paid before the sweat of his brow dries up.

Baihiqi, Ibn-e-Majah.

In another tradition he said:

God says that he would be the enemy of three persons. One of them would be the person who made a promise in my name and then went back upon his plighted word. The other person would be the one who sold free man or woman (as slave) and consumed the price he got for it. And the third person would be the employer who took full benefit of the labour of a worker and denied him his wages.

Bukhari

Anas says,

The Prophet never underpaid a worker. Bukhari

The Prophet has also directed:

Do not employ a worker without first setting the wages for the work to be done. Baihiji, Kitab-ai-Iyarah

What he meant to say was that so long as the worker is satisfied with the offer of wages for his work and accepts the terms gladly, he should not be put to work forcibly.

The Prophet has also instructed us to pay the worker a share out of the profit we make through his labour:

> Let the worker have his share out of the profit gained through his labour for God's agent is not to be deprived.
>
> Musnad-e-Ahmad

Hidayah, the well-known book on Muslim jurisprudence, explaining the reason for the share of the worker in a business, says:

> The capitalist is entitled to the profit for the capital he invests in the business and to his working partner, the worker, it accrues because of the labour put 'in by him in that business.
>
> Hidayah, Kitab-al-Mazaribah

For determination of the wages and conditions of working, the Prophet gave us the following rule:

> The workers should be provided proper food and clothing according to the existing standards at a particular time and they should be burdened with only as much work as they can easily cope with (without totally exhausting him or affecting his health adversely).
>
> Mo'atta Imam Malik

What the Prophet meant to bring home to the employer is that the worker should be paid wages at the rate appropriate to the existing conditions at any particular time or place and the wage earner may be able to provide himself and his dependents with food, clothing, a place to live in, medication, education and other basic needs with what he gets for his work. It is the same as to say that the employer is responsible for the complete support and maintenance of the workers employed by him. And along with that he imposed this condition on the employer that in return for this total support of worker, he should not burden his workers and salaried staff with more work than they can easily put up with. Mawardi stating the responsibilities of the state in this behalf says:

The Muhtasib should, in case of the men and women workers or salaried staff being harassed by the employer, take him to task, and order them not to take work from them harder than they can endure. Similarly, if they do not provide adequate food for the working animals or put them to work harder than their normal capacity they should take proper action against them.

> It was customary with 'Umar to go to the hamlets around midnight on Saturdays, and if he noticed any body burdened with work heavier than his capacaty, he managed to lighten the burden on him.
>
> Mo'atta Imam Malik

The incident relating to the Abbasi caliph Mansur has already come for mention under accountability through the judiciary, in which Mansur had been summoned by Muhammad bin-e-Imran, the Qazi of Madinah, all the way from Baghdad and compelled to pay the camel owners the freight for the transport of luggage, during the Hajj season, agreed upon mutually, but not paid.

Similarly, a peasant complained to 'Umar bin-e-Abd-al-Aziz that he had sown his field, but the Syrian armies passing that way trampled and ruined it. The peasant was paid ten thousand dirhams by him from the Bait-al Mal.

In connection with the compensation for the acquired properties, it has already come for mention under the right of ownership, that the state cannot acquire the lawfully gained properties of an individual without paying due compensation for them. It can certainly acquire them against his will, in public interest, but cannot deprive the owner of his right to compensation.

Rights Exclusive to the Muslims

The fundamental rights that have come for mention so far are enjoyed by the citizens irrespective of belief and faith. Now we are going to take up the rights exclusive to the Muslims. We have thrown ample light on the causes of this distinction in the chapter dealing with the "Islamic Concept of the Fundamental Rights."

According to the concept of the Fudamental Rights given to us by Islam, all the rights determined by the Quran and the Sunnah shall be deemed fundamental rights for the Muslims. They include the rights of inheritance, ownership, alimony, dower, Nikah (Wedlock), divorce, Khula or obtaining of divorce by the woman, sale and purchase and all those rights relating to other affairs of human life determined by the Shariah externally, and which are inviolable in as much they cannot be amended or cancelled through Legislation.

Besides, these rights, where in the matter of civil rights all the citizens enjoy equal status, in that political rights there shall be distinction between the Muslims and the non-Muslims. Since the non-Muslims not believing in the Quran and the Sunnah, do not fulfil the condition of allegiance to the principle on which is based the entire system of government, nor are they committed to any covenant with the Sovereign for the practical enforcement of these principles. It is for this reason that Islam does not approve of their heading the Islamic state or appointment to the key posts which are concerned with the shaping of policies. They can however be appointed to high ranking posts where the machinery responsible for the execution of these policies is concerned. In this connection defining the position of the Zimmis, Mawadi has written:

> A Zimmi may become a minister of enforcement, but not a minister with executive and judicial powers. The way these two posts differ in their powers, the condition pertaining to them are also different. This difference is apparent in these four aspects. The first difference is that a minister with executive and judicial powers can himself issue orders and can judge criminal cases but a minister with only the powers of enforcement does not have these powers. Secondly the minister with executive powers can appoint government servants, but not so the minister with powers of enforcement only. Thirdly the minister with the executive powers can take administrative steps in matters pertaining to the army and warfare, while the minister with the powers of enforcement only cannot. Fourthly, the minister with

executive powers can realize the dues of the state and pay whatever is due from the state, but the minister with powers of enforcement alone cannot do that. Besides these four conditions there is no other thing barring Zimmi from being appointed to this (key) position.

Dr. Hasan Ibrahim Hasan also concerning with Mawadi writes:

A Zimmi cannot be appointed to the post of a minister with executive and judicial powers or that of the Prime Minster, since for these posts the condition pertaining "Imamat" (Leadership of the Islamic State) are essential. bn-e-Taimiyah, Nizam-al-Mulk and other Muslim political thinkers have also expressed the same opinion concurrently. Under this principle the Muslims shall have the following political rights:

1. The President and the Prime Minister must be Muslim.
2. They shall be elected by the Muslim votes, and the voting right shall also be limited to the Muslims in their election.
3. Since the Quran has laid down the condition for "those in authority" of being from "among you", all the key posts shall go to the Believers, so that they may frame the guiding principles of their policies according to the dictates of the Quran and the Sunnah, and in the capacity of those in authority may enforce them with the cooperation of the Muslims. So under this principle the Chief Justice, Judicial Minister, Commander-in-Chief, Defence Minister, Finance Minister (Nazim-e-Bait-al-Mal) and other officers having similar importance shall be appointed from among the Muslims.
4. Since the Quran has imposed the condition of "mutual" (consultation) for Shura or the advisory council, (Who conduct their affairs by mutual consultation Al-Quran XLII 38), the members of the advisory council or those of the parliament shall also be elected from among the Believers. This is the Central

and most important policy-making institution of the Islamic state. All the affairs of the state shall be conducted in the light of the Quran and the Sunnah. So in this institution only those can do justice to counselling, who not only believe in the Quran and the Sunnah, but have an insight into their teachings, and have also been endowed with the capability to solve problems with reference to them. Besides these rights there are no others in which any distinction is permissible between the Muslims and the non-Muslims.

Special Privileges for Non-Muslims

In connection with the rights of the Zimmis, non-Muslims subjects in an Islamic state first of all it must be clarified that the way the Islamic state is committed in connection with the enforcement of and respect for the rights of the Muslims determined by the Quran and the Sunnah, so also it is bound by the limits prescribed by them relating to the rights of the Zimmis. That is to say that the rights of the Zimmis too are inalienable. The Muslims have no power to amend or cancel them. The Islamic state cannot curtail the rights determined by the Shariah. However, it can grant them additional rights provided such additions are not in contravention of the Islamic principles. It comes to this then, that as regards the determination and protection of the rights, the position of the Muslims and the Zimmis is the same in the Islamic state. The rights of both have been guaranteed by the Quran and the Sunnah. The constitutional and legal safeguards enjoyed by the Muslims are also enjoyed by the Zimmis. Rather, from this point of view of safeguards, they are better placed than the Muslims. The Islamic state, in view of the exigencies and the demands of times, can levy additional taxes on Muslims and can acquire their properties in public interest. But it can not put any additional burden on the Zimmis beyond the conditions of the agreement. If the Islamic state fails to protect the lives and properties of the Muslims, and in case of a foreign aggression, are unable to make proper defence of them, it is not bound to return the taxes received from them. But under the similar conditions, they will have to return the amount of jizya realised from the Zimmis. Abu Ubaidah, the Muslim general, had returned the amount of jizya realised from the Zimmis of Hams and Damascus on the occasion of the battle of Yarmuk, since he was not sure they would be able to fulfil their responsibilities of their defence, (engaged as they were in an all-out war against the Christian world Tr.).

Islam has divided the Zimmis into three categories according to their position:

1. Party to a treaty or covenant: Those who agree to live as Zimmis in the Islamic state under a treaty or agreement, during a war or even without it. They are called Muahids or those who are a party to a treaty.

2. The subdued Zimmis: Those who have been fighting up to the last and defeated in a battle might have come under the domination of the Islamic state as subjects. In the terminology of the Islamic Fiqh (jurisprudence) it is also known as All-al-Janwah (those taken by force).

3. Zimmis who have come to be citizens of the Islamic state in some way other than through a peace treaty or during a war, like non-Muslim citizens of Pakistan who opted for Pakistan on partition of the Indian subcontinent. The basic law of the Shariah relating to the Zimmis under an agreement, is this that they shall be treated according to the terms of the agreement, which shall be strictly adhered to, and shall not change with the change in the government of Islamic state. Their position is eternal, save where the contracting party itself requests certain changes and they are mutually agreed upon. The Islamic state shall not have the power to make alteration in the contract as they please. The Prophet says:

> Take heed! Whoever oppresses a Muahid, or a zimmi covered by an agreement or curtails his rights or burdens him with a heavier burden than he can bear, or acquires something from him against his will, I

> shall stand up against him as a complaint on the Day of Reckoning.
>
> Abu Da'ood, Kitab'-al-Jehad

Similarly, he has said in another tradition:

> If you happen to fight against a people and vanish it in a combat, and they agree to pay you tribute to save their own lives and those of their children (in another tradition it was said They enter an agreement with you), do not demand later, a grain more than agreed upon, since it will be unlawful for you to do so.
>
> Abu Da ood, Kitab-al-Jehad

Qazi Abu Yusuf explaining the Islamic law in this behalf, says:

> They shall pay only what has been mutually agreed upon to the treaty. The terms of the treaty shall be fulfilled and no enhancement made in the amount of the tribute.

The vanquished non-Muslim subjects of the Islamic state shall have the following rights:

1. Once they agree to pay Jizya, the Islamic state shall become committed to provide them protection (both internally and against outside aggression). Their lives and properties shall be sacred. Neither their properties and possessions can be confiscated nor they can be enslaved.

2. The Zimmis shall have proprietary rights over their properties and they shall be transferred to their inheritors. They shall have perfect authority to sell, gift or mortgage them as they please. The Islamic state shall have no right to oust them.

3. The amount of Jizya shall be determined according to the state of the person concerned—more from the wealthy, less from the middle class and a minimum from the poor. Those having no source of income of their own and dependent on others for their livelihood, shall be exempt from Jizya.

4. Jizya shall be imposed only on the combatants. It shall not

be realized from women, children, old and infirm individuals, disabled persons, monks, those engaged in the service of the houses of worship, those permanently ailing and the slaves.

5. The places of worship of the Zimmis shall be allowed, to remain untouched. During the period of 'Umar's caliphate not a single church or synagogue was touched. Qazi Abu Yusuf writes:

   They (the churches and the snagogues) were left alone. They were neither demolished nor tampered with in any other way."

During the period of the Prophet and that of the rightly guided caliphs, the Muslims unexceptionally gave assurance of the protection of their places of worship in all their treaties with the Zimmis, and the later day governments also remained committed to this practice. Besides these special rights of those under a treaty or conquered people, all the three types of Zimmis shall also have the following rights:

1. The Penal Laws of Islam are, generally speaking, the same for the Zimmis and the Muslims. But the Zimmis are exempt in the matter of wine and drinking. According to Imam Malik they are exempt in the matter of fornication and adultery also. He argues from the decision of 'Umar and 'Ali that if a Zimmi is found guilty of fornication, his case should be left to his own millat (people).

2. The civil laws too are the same for the Zimmis and the Muslims. In the matter of proprietary rights and restrictions relating to their possessions. The methods and trade and commerce prohibited for the Muslims are also prohibited for the Zimmis. The dealing involving interests are also equally prohibited for the Muslims and the Zimmis. However drinking and eating of pork is an exception in the case of the latter. The Zimmis have the right to prepare alcohol, drink and sell it also in their own community. They also have the right to breed pigs, eat its flesh and sell it to their own people. If a Muslim destroys the liquor or a

pig belonging to a Zimmi, he will be forced to pay compensation for it.

3. The contract with the Zimmis is eternally binding on the Muslims. Once entering it, they can never walk out on it. But the Zimmis have a right to break this tie whenever they like. However great the crime of a Zimmi against the Muslims their commitment of protection to the Zimmis remains intact. Even if they stop paying Jizya, under a Muslim, make disrespectful remarks about or indulge in destructive criticism of the Prophet, are guilty of molestation of a Muslim women, the tie does not snap. The criminal shall certainly be punished according to the law but shall not be excluded from the protection of the state. Only in the exceptional cases of a Zimmi's joining hands with the enemy of the Islamic state and openly rebelling against it creating mischief and resorting to sedition will make him liable to be dropped out of the contract.

4. The personal affairs of the Zimmis shall be decided according to their own Personal Law. For example, if their Personal Law allows Nikah or marriage contract without witnesses, marriage without dower, second marriage within the period of Iddat or waiting (after divorce or death of the husband), or incest marriage with the eternally prohibited ones, all these shall be deemed allowed for their sake. To a query of Umar bin-e-Abd-al Aziz, Khowajah Hasan Bash had issued the following edict:

   They have agreed to pay Jizya only after the freedom to live according to their belief and faith. Your business is to follow the usage of old and not invent anything new for yourself.

5. The Zimmis shall be perfectly free to observe their religious ceremonies and national symbols in their own localities and towns. However, they shall not be allowed to openly observe their religious symbols in the Muslim localities. In their own places of worship they shall any way be perfectly

free to do as they please. The government shall not interfere with it in the least.

The places whose land belongs to the Muslims and they have specified those places for the observance of their religious symbols, if any old standing places of worship of the Zimmis exist in such exclusive Muslim lands, they shall not be tampered with. If they get demolished, the Zimmis shall have the right to rebuild them. At other places which are not exclusive to Muslim's religious observances, the Zimmis can even build new places of worship.

6. The Zimmis shall have perfect freedom to make arrangements for the religious education of their children, building and running schools for them and preaching and teaching of their own religions among their own community. They shall also be free to state the merits of their religions. However, they shall not be allowed to attack Islam in an antagonistic way (levelling destructive criticism against it and reviling the religious leaders Tr).

An important problem in connection with the Zimmi is how to accommodate them in the Islamic state of today. Where local bodies are concerned they can be allowed all the rights of representation in them. However, their representation in the central and provincial advisory councils or assemblies is an intricate problem. Two courses can be adopted for this purpose.

1. On the basis of separate elections, the Zimmis should be allowed proportional representation. But in the Parliament they would have to remain committed to the legislation according to the dictates of the Quran and the Sunnah. However, in those matters where Quran has itself allowed freedom to exercise their right to act, in such situations they would be perfectly at liberty to express their opinions and put up their suggestions.
2. A separate representative institution be created for the Zimmis where they can solve their own problem as they please and the government should aid them in giving

> their recommendations as practical shapes. They should have the authority to legislate and amend the current laws to the extent of their own personal affairs, and their suggestions and recommendations may become enforceable after the approval of the head of the state. They may present their suggestions, complaints and objections concerning administrative affairs and the decisions of the Parliament and the government may consider them sympathetically under the demands of justice and remove the complaints as far as possible.

In this behalf we have no fixed and accepted principle before us. Any appropriate course can be adopted to meet the situation. What Islam aims at and has at heart is that the non-Muslim subjects of an Islamic state should not interfere with the way Islam likes to be demonstrated as a way of life. At no stage in its working and rule in an Islamic state the non-Muslim subjects should become a strongly resistant force. Islam stresses benevolent treatment of them, safeguards their rights more indulgently than those of the Muslims, offers them the shade of its blessings and makes them a partner in its fruits and blessings, but cannot allow them to become a stumbling block for itself.

Reference-I

Ahd-e-Nabvi men Nizam-e-Hukmrani: Dr. Muhammad Hamidullah, Maktaba-e-Ibrahimiyah, Hyderabad Dacan.

Abu Bakr: Muhammad Husain, Haikal, Translation by Seikh Muhammad Ahmad Panipati, Meri Library, Lahore, 1973.

Adalat-e-Nabavi ke Faislay—Abdullah-Al-Qirtabi, Adabistan, Lahore, 1956.

Ahkam-al-Sultaniyah: Mawardi, Translated by Mufti Intazamullah Shahabi, Printed and Published by Muhammad Sa'eed and Sons, Quran Mahal, Karachi.

Akhlaq aur Falsfah-e-Akhlaq: Maulana Hifz-ur-Rehman Sehvarvi, Nadwat-ul-Musannifin, Delhi, 1964, with reference to Ahya-al-Uloom.

Al Farooq: Shibli No'mani, Madinah Publishing Company, Karachi, 1970.

Al-Hidayah Marghinani, Kalam Company, Karachi.

Al-Muwafiqat : Shatibi, Tijaryah-al-Kubra, Cairo, Egypt.

Insani Duniya par Musalmanon ke Uruj-o-Zawal ka Athar: Maulana Syed Abul Hasan Ali Nadvi, Majlis-e-Tahqeeqat-o-Nashriyat-e-Islam, Nadwat-al-Ulema, Lucknow, 1967.

Intikhab-e-Hadith: Maulana Abdul Ghaffar Hasan, Islamic Publications Limited, Lahore.

Islam men Adl-e-Ijtema' Syed Qutub Shaheed, translated by Dr. Muhammd Nijatullah Siddiqui, Islamic Publication Limited, Lahore, 1971.

Islam ke-Ma'ashi Nazariya: Dr. Muhammad Yusufuddin, Matba'-e-Ibrahimiyah, Hyderabad Dakan, 1950.

Islam ka Nazariyah-e-Milkiyat: Dr. Muhammad Najatullah Siddiqui, Islamic Publications, Ltd. 1968.

Islam ka Nizam-e-Taqseem-e-Daulat: Maulana Mufti Muhammad Shafi, Maktabah Dar-al-Uloom, Karachi.

Islam Ka Nizam-e-Hukumat: Hamid-al-Ansari Ghazi, Published by Nadwah-al-Musnnafin, Delhi, 1956.

Islami Jamhooriyat: Syed Ra'is Ahmad Jafri, Idarah-e-Saqafat-e-Islamiya Lahore

Islami Masawat: Muhammad Hafeezullah Phulwarwi Idarah-e-Tahqiq-o-Tasnif, Karachi, 1971.

Islami Riyasat: Amin Ahsan Islahi, with reference to Al-Iste-ab, Ibn-e-al-Bar.

Islami Riyasat: Maulana Maududi.

Jadah-o-Manzil: Syed Qutub Shaheed, Islamic Publications Limited, Lahore, 1972.

Islami Tahzeeb aur Uske Usul-o-Mabedi, Syed Abdul A'la Maududi, Islamic Publications Limited, Lahore, 1973.

Kitab-al-Khiraj: Qazi Abu Yusuf, translated by Muhammad Nejatullah Siddiqui, Maktabah Chirag-e-Rah, Karachi, 1966.

Ma'arif-al-Hadith: Maulana Muhammad Manzoor No'mani, Maktabah-e-Rashidiyah, Sahiwal.

Ma'alim-al-Quran: Maulana Muhammad Ali Siddiqui, Kandhlavi, Idarah-e-Taleemat-e-Quran, Sialkot, 1974.

Muhsin-e-Insaniyat: Na'eem Siddiqui, Islamic Publication Limited, Lahore, 1972.

Musalmanon ke Siyasi Afkar: Professor Rasheed Ahbad, Idarah-e-Thaqafat-e-Islamiyah, Lahore, 1961.

Musalmanon ka Nizam-e-Mumlakat: Dr. Hasan Ibranum Hasan, translation by Muhammad Ahmullah Siddiqui, Nadwat-al-Musannifin, Delhi, first Impression, 1947.

Rah-e-Amal: Maulana Jaleel Ahsan Nadvi, Islamic Publications Ltd., Lahore, 1972.

Seerat-un-Nabi: Darul Musannifin, Azamgarh 1932.

Siyasat-e-Shariyah: Ibn-e-Taimiyah, translated by Maulana Muhammad Ismail Kalam Company, Karachi.

Siyasi Wathiqhjat: Dr Muhammad Hameedullah, Majlis-e-Taraqqi-e-Adab, Lahore, 1960.

Tafheem-al-Quran: Maulana Syed Abul A]la Maudoodi, Idrah-e-Tarju-manool-Quran, Lahore, 1974.

Tarikh-e-Da'wat-o-Azeemat: Syed Abul Hasan Ali Nadvi, Majlis-e-Tahqeeqat-o-Nashriyat-e-Islam, Lucknow, 1967.

'Umar bin-Khattab: Tantawi, Translation by Abdul Samad Sarin, Albayan, Lahore, 1971.

'Umar Farooq-e-A'zam: Muhammad Husain Haikal, Matabah Jadeed, Lahore.

Reference-II

Article I(I) of the Declaration on the Right to Development. UN General Assembly Resolution 41/128 of 4th December, 1986.

Dogra, Bharat "*Developmefttal Refuges: Displaced Forever*", Frontier, August 31, 1991.

Elementary and Secondary Education, Act, Public Law No. 93-389, 512, 88 Stat. 464, 571 Aug. 21, 1974, as amended by Public Law No. 93-568, *see.* 2, 88 Stat 1855 Dec. 31, 1974.

Gahrana, Kanan "*Human Rights: A Conceptual Perspective*", Indian journal of International Law, July-Dec. 1989.

Myron Weiner, "Rejected Peoples and Unwanted Migrants in South Asia", Economic and Political Weekly.

— Sons of the Soil: Migration and Ethnic Conflict in India, (Prineton, New Jersy: Princeton University Press, 1978).

Nayar, Kuldip "No Decision Yet on Lanka Tamils", the Statesman, 6th October, 1992.

Report of Amnesty International—"*Bangladesh*", *Uniawful Killings and Tortures in the Chittagong Hill Tracts*", September, 1986.

Singh, Amrik "*Human Rights and the Rule of Law*", *Mainstream*, No. 22.

Singh M.P., Position of Aliems in Indian Law, Heidelberg Colloquim "*The Legal Position of Alliens in Nation and international Late*", September 1985.

Sonwalkar, Prasun Exodus of Bangladeshis to India, The Times of India. 6 December, 1991.

Universal Declaration of Human Rights, 1948; International Covenant on Economic Social and Cultural Rights, 1966; and International Covenant on Civil and Polidcal Rights, 1966.

Bibliography

Aiyer, Sir Sivaswamy *Evolution of Hindu Moral Ideals,* (Calcutta University Press, 1935).

Amulya Ganguli, "*Bangladeshi Lebnsraum*", Times of India, 13 July 1992.

Antonio Cassese, *'The Self-Determination of Peoples'*, in Louis Henkin (ed.), The International Bill of Rights (New York, Columbia University Press, 1981).

Amery L.S. Thoughts on constitution, Oxford, 1956.

Antony G.N. Flew, *'Wants or Needs; Choices or Commands', in Fitzgerald, Human Needs and Politics.*

Asborn Eide, *"Human Rights in World Society"*, Oslo. 1977.

Aurobindo, Sri *The Foundations of Indian Culture,* (New York: Sri Aurobindo Library, 1953).

Baral, Lok Raj *"Regional Migrations, Ethnkity and Security"*, The South Asian case, (1990).

Basu, Dr. Durga Das, *Human Rights in Constitutional Law,* Practice Hall of India, Private Ltd. New Delhi, 1994.

Basu, M. Introduction to the Indian Constitution (New Delhi: Rekhi Publishing House, 1960).

Bell Whitaker, *The Biharis in Bangladesh* (London: Minority Rights Group, 1982).

Bhagwati, P.N. *Human Rights in the Criminal Justice System* Indian Bar Review, 1985.

Carter, J. L. Inaugural Address, 1977, quoted in, David P. Forsythe, *"Human Rights and Worid Politics"*. University of Nebraska Press, 1983.

Chimni B.S. "*The Legal Conditions of Refugees in India*" journal of Refugee Studies.

Dagmar Hellmann-Rajanayagam, *Tile Tamil Tigers: **Armed.** Struggle for Identity*, (Stuttgart: Franz Steiner, 1994).

Dhagamwar, Vasudha *Law, Power and Justice: **Protection of Persona! Rights under the Indian Penal Code*** (Bombay: N. M. Tripathi, 1974).

Dorothy Pickles, Democracy, London, 1960.

Dorothy Pickles, "Democracy", Mathuen and Company, London, 1970, p. 101.

Douglas, William O. Bunyadi Insani Huquq Ka Mas'lah (Urdu translation) Lahore, 1965.

Fennessy R.R., .Burke, Paine and the rights of Man, Martiness Nijhaoff Hague, 1965.

Gaur K.D., *"Poor Victims of Uses and Abuses of Criminal Law and Process in India"*, Journal of the Indian Law Institute (JILI) (New Delhi), (1993).

Government of India, Ministry of External Affairs, *Bangladesh Documents* (New Delhi 1972); Richard Sisson and Leo F. of accessions to these instruments, see Human Rights International Instruments: Signatures, Ratifications, etc.

Government of India, Ministry of Labour and Rehabilitation, Branch Secretariat, Administrative Instructions for Transit Relief Camps for Refugees from Bast Bengal, Calcutta, (1971).

Hanson, D.W. From Kingdom to Common-Wealth, Princeton, London, 1970.

Henderson J.J. Craik, Parliament—A Survey, George Allen and Unwin London, 1965.

Jennings, Sir Ivor, Approach to Self-Government, Oxford, London.

Jois, M.R., *Human Rights and Indian Value* (National Council of Teacher Education), Revised Edition, New Delhi, 1998.

Kernig C.D. Marxism Communism and Western Society, New York 1972.

Kernig C.D. Marxism, Communism and Western Society?

Manfred Woelilcke, *Environmental Refugees, Aussenpolitik,* No. *Mr* 1992.

Mathew Thomas *Political Economy of Etimic Conflict in Bhutan,* School of International Studies, Jawaharlal Nehru University, New Delhi.

Mcllwain, Charles Howard, Constitutionalism, Great Seal Books, New York, 1947.

Mcllwain Charles Howard, Constitutionalism.

Montgomery Watt W. The Majesty that was Īslam, Sidwick and Jackson, London, 1974.

Mool Chand Sharma, Judicial Creativity and the Due Process Indian Bar Review, 1985.

Mukherji, Partha Nath *"The Great Migration of 1971"*.

Muni, S.D. and Kalim Bahadur (eds.) *Domestic Conflicts in South Asia* (New Delhi: South Asia Publishers, 1986).

Murthy, T.S. *Assam: The Difficult Years,* New Delhi: Himalayan Books, 1983).

Narayanswamy M. R., *Tigers of Lanka: Front Boys to Guerrillas* (New Delhi: Konark Publishers, 1995).

Phadmis, Urmila *Ethnicity and Nation-Building in South Asia* (New Delhi: Sage 1990).

Phillips O. Hood, Reform of the Constitution.

Phillips, O. Hood, Reform of the Constitution, London, 1970.

Ratanlal R. and Thakore D. K., *Law of Crimes* (Bombay: N. M. Tripathi & Co. and Bombay Law Reporter, 1971).

Ray, Samirendra *Judicial Review and Fundamantal Rights* (Calcutta: Eastern Law House, 1974).

Rose, *War and Secession: Pakistan, India and the Creation of Bangladesh* (Berkeley University of California Press, 1990)

Sandy Gordon, *Resources and Instability in South Asia* Survival. Summer, 1993.

Saxena J.N., *Legal Status of Refugees: Indian Position,* Indian Journal of Int. Law, 1986.

Saxena, K.P. ed. *Human Rights: Perspective and Challenges in 1990s and Beyond* (New Delhi: Lancers Books, 1994).

Scarman, Sir, Leslie, English Law—The New Dimensions, Stevens and Sons, London, 1974.

Seervai H., *Constitutional Law of India* (Bombay: N.M. Tripathi & Co., 1967).

Sharma Sastri R., *Kautilya's Arthasastra* (Mysore: Raghuveér Press, 1951).

Singh, Nagendar Human Rights and International Cooperation (New Delhi: S. Chand & Co., 1969).

Stern, S.M., "Fatimid Decrees" Faber and Faber, London, 1964.

Trikamial R. Desai, *The Indian Easements Act*, lith ed. (Ahmedabad: C. C. Vora, 1956).

Willoughby W., Principles of the Constitutional Law of the United States, Baker Voorthis and company, New York, 1938.

Index